Unreason on Autopilot

Prafull Verma

Santanu Kar

ISBN # 979-8-9884340-2-3

Preface

In common parlance 'Unreason' is understood as the rejection of logic, evidence, and rational thought in favor of blind faith, emotion, or dogma. Hitherto the rise of unreason was happening because of both natural and unnatural phenomena. The consequence is the rise of chaos, decay and harm caused by destruction. Yes, we do not have much control over natural phenomena except to learn to deal with it. However, we can attempt to realize the unnatural phenomenon that may be causing the unreason and thereby at least start thinking about the feasible resources to manage and control some parts of it. The 'Mayday' call is not just about the unreason that humanity is encountering. Rather, the distress signal is multifold in modern days. Hitherto the rise of unreason was happening more or less at a natural pace (explained in the book 'Business of Technology and Wisdom of Nature' by Prafull Verma); but with the technological advancement in Artificial Intelligence (AI) it is now tremendously accelerated. AI, a powerful new tool, is used more unreasonably to accelerate the rise of unreason. This tremendous acceleration is the critical shift and that is why now 'Unreason is on Steroid'! That's not the sole concern. The SOS call is that "unreason is rather on Auto Pilot.'

Unreason on Auto Pilot in the AI era: We are aware of the trending buzzwords 'AI Autopilot' tools that promise end-to-end automation for all kinds of business processes, with promise of little human oversight. This is more an umbrella term that refers to automation of entire workflows or processes without constant human intervention. In effect, the promise is - Instead of having to explicitly direct every action, these AI systems take full ownership of these tasks by making data-driven decisions. But would you board a plane if told there were no pilots in the cockpit? You may keep your answer to yourself to be safe! And just as no one feels safe on a plane without pilots, no company should feel safe relying on technology without professionals who understand it — and take ownership when it matters most.

One may conservatively argue that AI is not a fully self-governing system yet, emphasizing the need for human-in-the-loop involvement for safety and alignment with human values. In other words, AI is evolving from a 'Copilot' (assistant) to 'Autopilot' (autonomous AI agent). But look at the rate of this evolution! This shift is profoundly radical. Such autopilot agentic AI systems have already started managing entire processes, making decisions, and executing multi-step tasks without constant human prompting!

Now even from a usage in daily life perspective as they say – 'AI is already all around us. You just don't see it because it runs on autopilot'! Users are prompted with background recommendation engines without needing conscious thought. From Netflix or Spotify that suggest content you would enjoy to banks' monitoring of transactions for suspicious activity in real-time - are all pervasive and mostly invisible operations running continuously. AI encompasses a spectrum of applications, from background processes to highly interactive, user-facing tools. The news and media narratives are available at your palmtop with all combinations and opinion articles with yes/no, left/right, good/bad, true/fake flavors. One may not have a need to wear one's thinking that at all about what makes the most common sense; but just get dragged on with these autopilot interactions. There is less and less room for reasoning.

At the same time, the industry is moving towards 'AI-powered autonomy.' The first phase is projected as where humans transition from doing the work to managing the AI that does the work, with the goal of collaboration and obvious replacement of human labor as well. This is what we are experiencing now. But the next phase is already on. And the characteristics of that phase sounds a bit awkward at the least. This isn't just about automation; it is a move from simple, programmed tasks to systems that can understand, reason, and act independently, forming closed-loop systems that fix problems without possible human input. It is not just speculation that there is radical, unprecedented and sometimes uncontrolled growth in AI. Some theorize this as an artificial 'intelligence explosion' that may not need human control or rather intentionally could surpass that with its speculative decision making. Yes, the industry is scrutinizing as it faces challenges in proving consistent profitability or managing significant debt. On the other hand, big tech companies are investing heavily in AI to secure a competitive advantage, unlock massive economic growth and revenue streams.

The obvious question is - will AI's growth stop? The fact of the matter is - this is not just another technological trend alone. There is an angle of strategic necessity. There is monumental geopolitical competition among countries for tech dominance. There are also national security imperatives (AI for defense/cyber), economic advantages (productivity, wealth), and massive private investment driven by state interests, creating a self-reinforcing cycle where governments encourage funding and companies race to build infrastructure.

What is the call to action for humanity then? The rise of AI presents an opportunity for humanity to become more, not less, human by focusing on the qualities that define our essence and using AI as a tool to amplify our potential. As the AI industry is rapidly embracing automation and the trajectory of copilot and 'autopilot,' the call to action for humanity is to embrace and elevate its unique human skills and values, such as creativity, emotional intelligence, critical thinking, and ethical judgment. This shift will allow us to focus on areas where the human touch and nuanced understanding remain irreplaceable. Let's no longer delegate our own reasoning to run on autopilot. Don't we want to be more human?

The root cause of unreason is inability or willingness to think. There is more. Even after realizing mistakes from previous errors, humanity unfortunately, instead of controlling, are doing just the opposite by traversing in the opposite direction. Individuals, society, and nations are not developing the ability and habit of thinking and developing the very meaningful 'wisdom.' In fact, the term 'wisdom' is mostly misunderstood ignorantly, conveniently or on purpose. Broken democracies worldwide are becoming unthinking systems by themselves. Wisdom with its true meaning is the only weapon to combat this challenge and not the mere reliance on knowledge. Does that sound a bit perplexing? Not at all. We would like to emphasize that knowledge is often incomplete like history itself, which is mostly distorted, guided and even incomplete. Knowledge is more a kind of data rather than a kind of intellect or wisdom. That is why AI can never be wise because it is learning from incomplete and biased knowledge.

Yes, in detailing the unfortunate scenario of modern days on 'unreason on steroids' we have brought in a Vedantic perspective especially in the chapters on AI and the hard problem of consciousness. The obvious question is - why are we bringing in Vedantic aspects in the domain of science and technology? That is because while the Western world is reckoning this very aspect of consciousness as something new and novel; in reality this core concept has been discovered by the Indian Rishis thousands of years ago. As a reference, it is so fascinating to specify the explanation in the book 'Autobiography of a Yogi' which has been admired by none other than the very technologist Steve Jobs. There Yogi says "*Twentieth Century science is thus sounding like a page from the hoary Vedas. From science, then, if it must be so, let man learn the philosophical truth that there is no material universe; its warps and woofs is Maya, appearance.*"

After more than 50 years of this writing, the philosophical truth Yoganand Paramhans is referring to, has become more persuasive than ever before. Nick Herbert in his book 'Elemental Mind: Human Consciousness and the New Physics' (Penguin Book 1993), says- "*What the math seems to say is that, between observations, the world exists not as a solid actuality but only as the shimmering waves of possibilities. Whenever someone chooses to look at the atom, it ceases its fuzzy dance and seems to freeze into a tiny object with definite attributes, only to dissolve once more into a quivering pool of possibilities as soon as the observer withdraws his attention from it. This apparent observer-induced change in an atom's mode of existence is called the collapse of wave function.*" Yet another astounding example is by John von Neumann (a Hungarian American mathematician, physicist, computer scientist and engineer) as he described the entire physical world as possibilities and suggested that the process that turns some of these wave functions into actual facts cannot be a physical process. He (reluctantly) concluded that the only known entity that can do this is consciousness.

The fundamental disparity is - Western world has relied more on intellect while the Eastern world has relied more on intuition, and it is the time for West to learn from East as Steve Jobs said that intuition is more powerful than intellect. This is the very aspect that is missing in AI. Yes, we must welcome the transformative knowledge impact that AI can bring to medical and material science. At the same time, it is a wasteful debate to even ponder whether the radical technological development in AI will ever facilitate humanity with any meaningful wisdom. The simple solution is to acknowledge the infinite wisdom embedded in every cosmic creation and is the cause of evolution of more and more complex life. After acknowledging this truth, learn to "tap" in this source of wisdom and live in harmony by using continuous supply of this wisdom.

Acknowledgement

Ever since we published the book 'Illustrated Vedant' (Authors: Prafull Verma, Santanu Kar & Kalyan Kumar), we were deeply engrossed in a deliberation among us. We all were sure that there are immediate offshoots of some very significant pointers that need more exploration. This is where we sincerely acknowledge the active contribution of Kalyan Kumar. He played a vital role in engaging in crucial discussions not only from his expert technology and industry viewpoint but also from his pragmatic reasoning as well as philosophical takeaways. That is how the very topic of this book evolved which is focused around 'Unreason,' an addiction of humanity which is not only on steroids but conveniently in an autopilot mode. More so, as humanity is embraced with and rather overwhelmed by the abundance of Artificial Intelligence. Hence, even though Kalyan is not technically a co-author for this work of ours, we would still gladly and humbly regard him no less than that. That is why wherever we cited references from our earlier book 'Illustrated Vedant,' we intentionally used the term 'by the same authors.'

Our special thanks also to Satya Misra who helped us to maintain the flow of our thought process and for his contribution to editorial overview.

Prafull Verma | Santanu Kar

Foreword

I have had the utmost privilege of being in a journey with the Authors over last 3 decades. I have started my career under one of their oversights, have worked with them over decades and also had the opportunity to co-author over 8 books with Prafull I had many sessions of conversations and debates which has become the cornerstone of this book the Author has conceived. When I read the book, I recollect the past 20+ Years of interactions and reasoning captured quite well. I remember the three quotes which was the first reason for unreason

-"If the only tool you have is a hammer, every problem looks like a nail" &

-"A fool with the tool is still a fool"

-"The More I know, I realize How much I don't know"

We have discussed the third point as paradox of knowledge in our book "Illustrated Vedant" where I was also a co-author.

Are you feeling apprehensive about the accelerated rise of unreason that humanity is encountering now with continued rejection of logic and rational thought? Are you overwhelmed by the radical advancement of AI with hallucinated intelligence and confused narratives? Are you feeling puzzled how come humanity is delegating such chaotic state to run on an autopilot mode?

This provocative question is at the core of the distinctive book "*Unreason on Autopilot*".' The book fathoms out that the root cause is the inability to think. That is how individuals, society, and nations are distracted from realizing the true meaning of 'wisdom.' The book strives with figurative illustrations to reiterate that '*wisdom*' is mostly misunderstood ignorantly, conveniently or on purpose more so in the AI world today that is sprinting on steroid.

In this book, the authors explain what leads to the rise of unreason with real world manifestations in society impacted further by propaganda of false narratives. It emphasizes that knowledge can be learnt but wisdom is only earned while accentuating that we have not learnt from '*history*' which by itself is unfortunately distorted and incomplete knowledge. The book decodes with contemporary and historical use cases to establish that knowledge is more a kind of data rather than wisdom. The book explains the myth and reality of AI and suggests that responsible AI is not good enough and we need wise AI. But is it possible to make AI wise? The authors brought in a Vedantic perspective especially to elaborate the fundamental disparity of the Western world relying more on intellect while the Eastern world banking on intuition. So, in an accelerated AI world of unreason if you are excited to introspect that intelligence without wisdom is blind, then this book is for you.

The path the authors lay out with illustrations and examples is simple, focused and relevant; And in doing so, it automatically demolishes the false narratives that surround you in every aspect of life in today's AI world!

Again, in our earlier book "Illustrated Vedant," we explained about the consciousness- the absolute and fundamental reality. That is the point of "*Aham Brahmanasmi* , *Tat Savm Asi*" is one of the deepest quotes in ancient texts of Vedanta. But to be able to really understand that one needs to be on the quest to even be a fraction of what a "*Bodhisattava*" state is? AI will never know because of absence of consciousness within itself. All we need is to be wise and learn from truthful history.

Enjoy the Journey.

Kalyan Kumar

Chief Product Officer | HCL Software

Table of Content

Table of Figures

1 Rise of Unreason

"The whole problem with the world is that fools and fanatics are always so certain of themselves, and wiser people so full of doubts."

-Bertrand Russell

1.1 Is thinking declining in business enterprises and society?

We are witnessing a decline of reason and the insurgence of unreason in our society in general and its proliferation into the business world. It has enormous implications on resolutions of any problem. This trend has not emerged abruptly but developed slowly over a period of time. One of the primary catalysts for the rise of unreason is people's appetite for junk opinion (just like junk food). Unfortunately, technology has fueled it by making it easy to quickly propagate bad information to a very large audience and very easy for users to consume. You can propagate an opinion from anywhere to anyone at any time; thanks to mobility and a connected world (Facebook, Twitter, WhatsApp etc.).

In the past, especially during the pre-web era, opinions were formed with depth and thoroughness of the facts and largely established through books and periodicals including newspapers' opinion columns. Corresponding to that we had IT magazines that would establish an opinion based on details. There was enough time for the opinion to get matured during the forming time itself and correction and maturity was embedded in the process of forming and propagating the opinion. With the proliferation of the web, books and white papers were diluted by blogs and in the past few years it is further diluted by tweets. Depth is a rare thing of the past.

We are now firmly in an era of immature opinions where substance is not the logic, reason and thinking behind the opinion, but the weightage that is acquired by rallying around the opinion tweets. Twitter has oversimplified the trending of opinions where depth is hidden or even non-existent. Substance is the numbers game. You are fed with the news items or tweets that match with your references and biases based on past searches or sites that you browsed, so you see only what you would have liked to see. This is great and it saves your time, but it also deprives you of counterviews and other related peripheral information that is so important for an all-round, holistic viewpoint to develop. This is evident with the increasingly polarized world as everyone gets fed with what one is looking for and towards what one is biased. AI and Machine Learning engines lurking in the background do all the work specific to a consumer (you) in feeding "convenient" information at the "convenient" time. It could be good for many things to simplify life, like telling you your flight is going to be late without you enquiring or pushing you some products that a frequent flier would need. But telling you only views abhorring one political/religious party could make you very myopic and thus heavily polarized.

Even the educated people who have acquired diplomas and degrees in various faculties are also not adequately investing time in 'thinking.' What is missing in such education? Maybe they are thinking but when it comes to actual decision points based on righteous thinking, their decision is eclipsed by compulsive behavior driven by their liking and disliking. This is explained as *Raga/Dwesha* in Indian scriptures. If we track back and refer to the ancient ways of Vedic education system, we may find an answer. The Vedic education system addresses the control of *raaga* (compulsive attachment/desire) and *dvesha* (compulsive aversion/hatred). This leads to the subsequent improvement of thinking power (intellect or *buddhi*) through a holistic approach centered on *dharma*, self-control apart from spiritual knowledge (*jnana*). When the mind is not constantly pulled by the compulsive forces of extreme liking and disliking, an individual gains the objectivity and perspective for an unbiased view. The mind is more conducive to thinking with clear and enhanced cognitive function. These specific philosophical and spiritual components are not explicit aims of most modern, secular education systems. Yes, modern education empowers one in scientific knowledge, technology, and skill acquisition for professional careers. Even if we pause for a moment not to debate on the aspect of compromising the moral and ethical development, are we not skeptical that this is focusing on rote learning, standardized testing, and materialistic goals? The diminished 'thinking' prowess by even the educated lot in today's society is not a mere perception, but an unfortunate offshoot of the modern education system.

This trend is reflected in the IT industry as well (why we are mentioning IT industry because now the IT is embedded in every aspect of business and all the strength and weaknesses of IT are automatically in every business) in the form of immature software products where the substance or value is not in the product as such, but in the weightage, it acquires by getting customers rallying around it. Making a good product is not as important as developing a strong logic or algorithm, but rather a matter of building a customer base, regardless of the quality or value. It can be argued that a customer can be rallied on the basis of merit of the product but that is not necessary. It can be done by alternate marketing skills or even buying the customer base with vested interests.

This phenomenon resonates with the phenomenon of artificial stupidity we mentioned in the book – "Process Excellence for IT Operations," (ISBN 13: 9780615877525 February 2014 Edition). The current trend is - instead of educating people on how to create an informed opinion, we teach people what opinion to make.

A very common concern among CIOs in almost every enterprise IT across the globe is the issue of cost cutting/cost control on IT spend. Authors have decades of working experience with enterprise IT since the old generation MIS department of all big businesses got transformed into the modern Enterprise IT Organization and the CIO title was invented. There was never a time when the exceeding and often "out of control "costs of running enterprise IT was not a problem and there will never be a time in future when this problem will not be there simply because there is no visible sign of willingness to do financial management of IT services. This reminds us a well-known verse from Bhagavat Gita on the eternity of soul when the Lord Krishna explains Arjuna

न त्वेवाहं जातु नासं न त्वं नेमे जनाधिपाः | न चैव न भविष्यामः सर्वे वयमतः परम् || Bhagwad Gita 2:12||

Never was there a time when I did not exist, nor you, nor all these kings; nor in the future shall any of us cease to be.

Almost all CIO organizations are obsessed with technology and confined to technology management only. Somehow it has become a matter of their *Raga/Dwesha* (to do things they like to do and avoid the things they do not like). Is the focus on ***technology has become the opium for CIOs?*** Even C-suite IT leaders become fixated on implementing the latest "shiny object" technologies, such as AI or the cloud, due to excitement or a fear of missing out (FOMO). A distracted obsession on technology is hindering CIOs not even getting into the introspection and analysis of ROI imperative that would demonstrate realistic value.

Problems around the cost of running IT will evaporate if CIO focuses on the value produced by IT. Then automatically it will become a positive business proposition. In our earlier publication we have stated that mere technology management does not provide an advantage to CIO, Service Management provides the differentiating advantage and value management provides the leadership advantage.

1.2 What Leads to Unreason

The illustration portrays what leads to unreason, what are the general impacts and what are the potential harms caused by such Unreason.

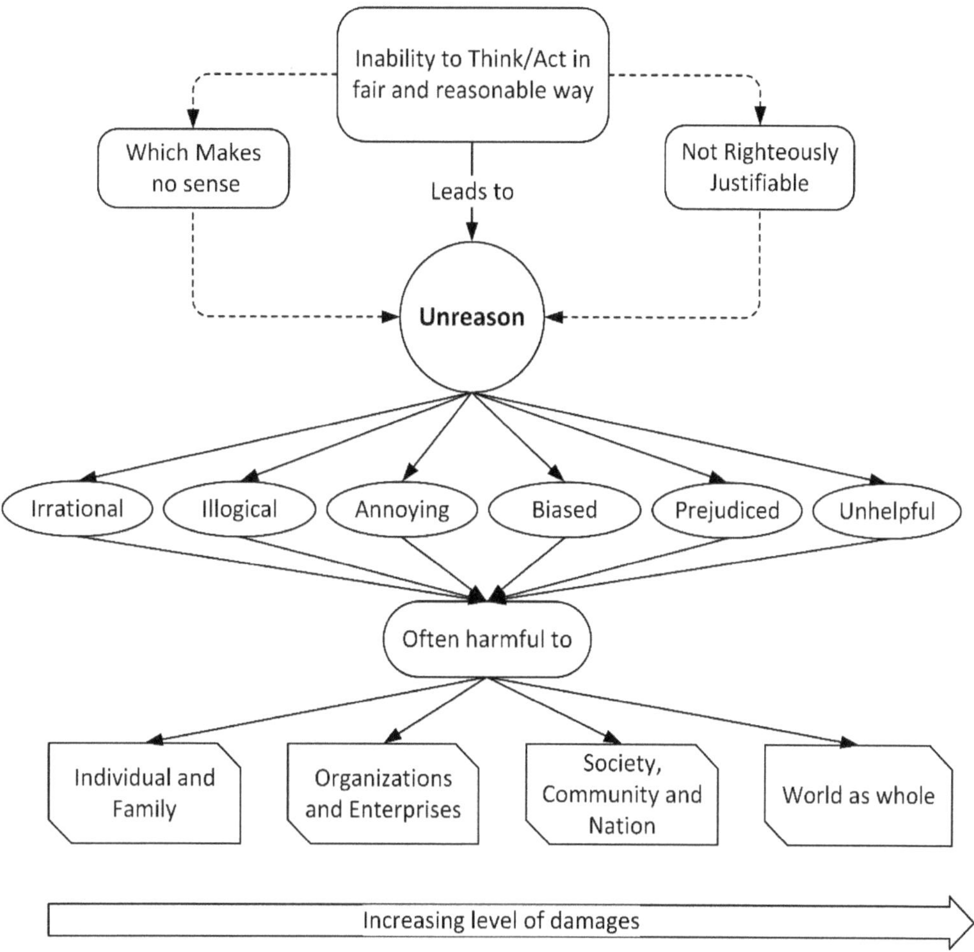

Figure 1: What leads to unreason

The inability to think or act in a reasonable way leads to every form of Unreason

Such Unreason can be making No Sense at all if a minimum logical sensibility is applied or more dangerously it could be Righteously or reasonably Unjustifiable. It is no wonder that Unreason can be Irrational, Illogical, Annoying, Biased, Prejudiced and Unhelpful

Unreason is always manifested in the form of problems or so to say, because of unreason, there generates a consequential problem. Unreason defies common sense. Unreason can also be detected from the hypocrisy of people with unreason.

Unfortunately, the resultant of such Unreason causes an increasing level of damage as it impacts an individual and grows up to affect the whole society. Unreason is hence harmful as it creates a problem as well to Individual and family, Organizations including educational institutions and enterprises, Society, community and nation and World as a whole.

Symptoms of Unreason are primarily:

- Lack of wisdom - Unreason can stem from a fundamental lack of understanding or knowledge necessary to make sound judgments and decisions.
- Increase of Hypocrisy- A consistent increase in hypocrisy, driven by cognitive dissonance, motivated reasoning, or a lack of self-awareness, can be strongly associated with irrational or unreasonable patterns of thought and behavior.
- Anti-commonsense - One acts or believes in ways that go against the grain of what is considered common sense, indicating that one's reasoning process is flawed, illogical, or irrational that exhibits unreason
- Pervasive trend in everything, everywhere- Lots of packaging but no substance inside. This reflects a common societal concern in fields like consumerism, media, social interactions or politics about the increasing emphasis on outward appearances and superficiality at the expense of genuine value and meaning.

Being unreasonable eventually becomes an attitude and becomes difficult to resolve.

Forming the Attitude of Happiness, Unhappiness and attitude of 'I am always Right'

Attitude is basically a habit of thought and can be good or bad. The diagram xx explains how one can develop an attitude of being happy or unhappy, given that happiness is a state of mind and within an individual's control.

Similarly, an attitude of absolute certainty—that one is right, and others are wrong can also be developed. This is a human tendency that appears within any political, scientific, or philosophical views.

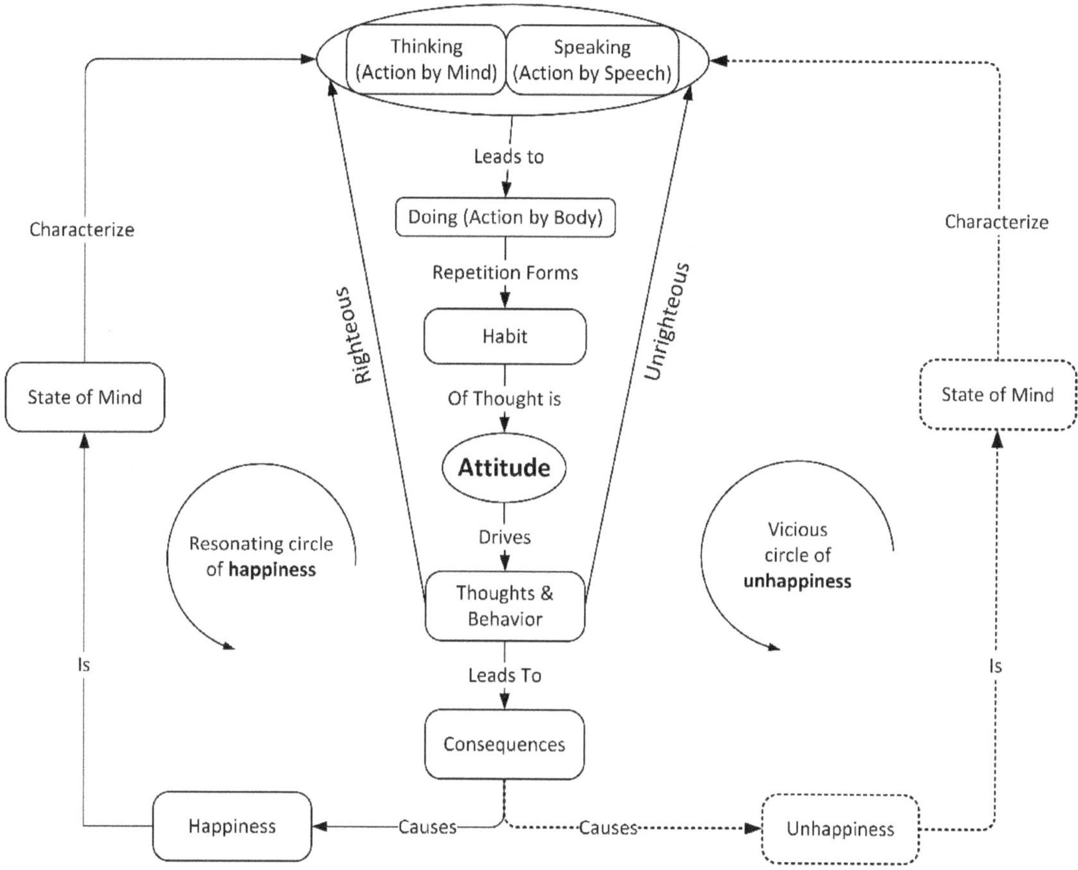

Figure 2: Attitude drives self-happiness or unhappiness

For example, who regularly attend the church, learn that a believer who accepts Jesus Christ as their Lord and Savior, will achieve salvation. A pagan, on the other hand, is someone who follows a religion outside of Christianity, will not. The right and wrong here is tied to mere a kind of belief. Similarly, In Islam, a believer (Mu'min) is someone who submits to the will of God and accepts the message of Islam, including belief in the Quran and the prophethood of Muhammad. However, a kafir (plural kuffar) is someone who does not believe in Islam and will not go to heaven. So the right and wrong is tied to belief. Repetitive teaching can develop the sense of "I am right" and can reflect in all aspects of life outside the religious practices.

So Again these examples are not meant as religious explanations. Such interpretation happens only because there is always a challenge of fundamentalism and dogmatism in religion which are sometimes deep rooted and thereby unfortunately such wrongful development of attitude is institutionalized. This in turn promotes the 'I am right and you are wrong' attitude in an absolutely disastrous manner that creates a disharmony in present day society beyond the world of simple reasoning.

Such an attitude prompts one's thinking in a limited way. Then that thinking leads to speaking and subsequent actions. Unfortunately, no one is willing to accept that. This is the submission to the habit of an attitude that wrongfully makes one feel right all the time and disproves anyone who confronts without any reasoning.

Unreason is not just a Natural Phenomenon but it is rather Compounded Now!

Everything will eventually decay and decay has a natural pace. Intervention can retard or accelerate decay. So, by natural logic, there can be an attrition expected of a true reasonable behavior thereby causing an increased level of unreason by default. However, there is another significant factor that impacts this so-called natural decay of reasoning and accelerates unreason.

Let us take an extension of the very 'Law of Conservation of Problem.' By the way we described in detail the law of conservation of problem (in the book 'Illustrated Vedant' by Prafull Verma, Santanu Kar & Kalyan Kumar) as – "*A real problem cannot be solved. It can only be transformed into another problem by changing its attribute or transformed into a predicament while retaining the attributes.*" The issue is when combined with acceleration of unreason, problems can not only remain unsolved but grow in their severity. In essence, unreason is not just caused by a natural agent of decay but on a path of artificial acceleration now. To elaborate this further, enlisted below are some examples of unreason that are affecting us as an individual or impacting humanity as a whole.

1.2.1 Hot and Visible Examples of Unreason that are Trendy Headlines

It is unfortunately our very nature most of the time either not to collect the whole truth or be satisfied with one sided truth about any information that eclipse even the basic logical reasoning. Here are some examples.

The Global Warming: Debates and Actions

Everyone is discussing global warming in the context of the greenhouse effect and fossil fuel consumption. But the root cause which everyone is avoiding deliberately is affluent consumption of natural resources beyond the capacity to get it replenished. Simply put this means - spending more than earning by which just basic common sense is getting defied.

The correct measurement for global warming per say is determined by ecological balance of natural resources as described by the global footprint network - https://www.footprintnetwork.org/. The fundamental scientific issue is that consumption of ecological resources has far exceeded what the Earth can regenerate in a given year. As a reference, in 2024, Earth Overshoot Day fell on August 1. Earth Overshoot Day marks the date when humanity has exhausted nature's budget for the year. But no one is ready to come out of any instant gratification of opportunistic and political benefits to bully specific countries to limit carbon emission. It is absolutely an unreasonable behavior even from global leadership.

Now, besides the discussion on global carbon footprint or so, let us also introspect the very simple fact about what we are not even trying to notice in our individual day to day life. For example, we use dry cell batteries in everyday life extensively in clocks, remotes, computer accessories, phones, thermostat, toys and what not. Americans buy nearly 3 billion dry-cell batteries a year, according to the U.S. Environmental Protection Agency, these are dumped in the trash bins after usage (disposal - who cares?). The carbon footprint of dry cell batteries, such as AA alkaline batteries, is estimated to be around 0.107 kg of CO2 per battery, considering material, manufacturing, and transportation. Each year, Americans throw away more than 3 billion batteries, totaling 180,000 tons of hazardous waste. This is a horrific pollutant to our mother nature. There are a plethora of such examples of uncontrolled consumption which are never highlighted to safeguard selfish economic profiteering. It is so commonplace now to upgrade mobile phones and laptop computers even within a couple of years. We hear the term 'Fast fashion' which has a significant environmental impact. According to the UN Environment Program, the industry is the second-biggest consumer of water and is responsible for about 10% of global carbon emissions - more than all international flights and maritime shipping combined. Unfortunately, the industry's problems are often overlooked by consumers. There is a seriously concerning trend of shrinking lifecycle of usage and product while there is monumental increase in consumption, thereby impacting carbon footprint. This goes back to the point that we are dangerously living on risky credit as human consumption has been far exceeding the earth's regenerative capacity.

To be specific from a country point of view, it is logical to define measurement as per carbon footprint per capita basis and not nationwide. Western countries are often seen as unfairly criticizing China and India for carbon emissions by focusing on total emissions rather than per capita emissions. This is because while China and India have large populations and high overall emissions, their per capita emissions are significantly lower than those of many Western nations. It is a well-known fact that the service sector contributes a very high percentage to the GDP of both the United States and Europe (70-80%). Hence it is not surprising to have targeted narrative by such western countries against not-so-developed countries where primary contribution will be from core sectors like manufacturing and elsewhere on this issue as well.

Such narratives are an utter demonstration of wickedness to humanity. Every behavior and storyline that is going around in the name of global warming is unreasonable and can be described by a simple word - hypocrisy!

The State of Democracies All Around the World

Democratic systems all around the world are demonstrating unreasonableness. We believe it can be addressed if democratic leaders want to address it seriously by amending the fundamental architecture of democracy. The current system is designed on the principle of stability of a three-point plane.

In Euclidean geometry, any three non-collinear points determine a unique plane. This means that if three points are not all on the same line, there's exactly one plane that contains all three of them. A three-legged structure is inherently more stable than a four-legged one, especially on uneven surfaces. Three legs always form a plane, ensuring a stable base in static position regardless of leg length or terrain, while four legs can wobble if they don't all make contact with a point in the same plane. However, in motion on rough terrain, the equation is quite different where a four-wheel platform would be more stable.

- Geometry: Three points define a plane, so three legs will always rest flat on any surface. Four points do not necessarily define a plane, so a four-legged object may wobble.
- Uneven Surfaces: A three-legged object will always distribute weight evenly across its three points, regardless of the surface's unevenness. A four-legged object might wobble if the legs
- Tip-over Resistance: While three legs are inherently stable on uneven surfaces, they can be easier to tip over than four-legged structures if a large force is applied at a point between two legs.

The derived fact is that - In rough terrain four wheelers are safe and secure. Now let us transpose this to the context of the state of democracy in the world.

1.3 Old Architecture of Democracy is Broken in Modern Era

There are flaws in democracy. Socrates the prominent Greek philosopher explained that flaw with Commonsense logic. Also, by scientific logic, democracy is mathematically impossible.

(Refer https://youtu.be/qf7ws2DF-zk?si=p1ktf_dpjqrFTmCN). It is a system where unequal things are considered equal and where ignorance of a person is just as good as another person's knowledge. But we do not intend to go in that direction as there are flaws in every system. We intend to discuss the problem of outdated architecture of democracy.

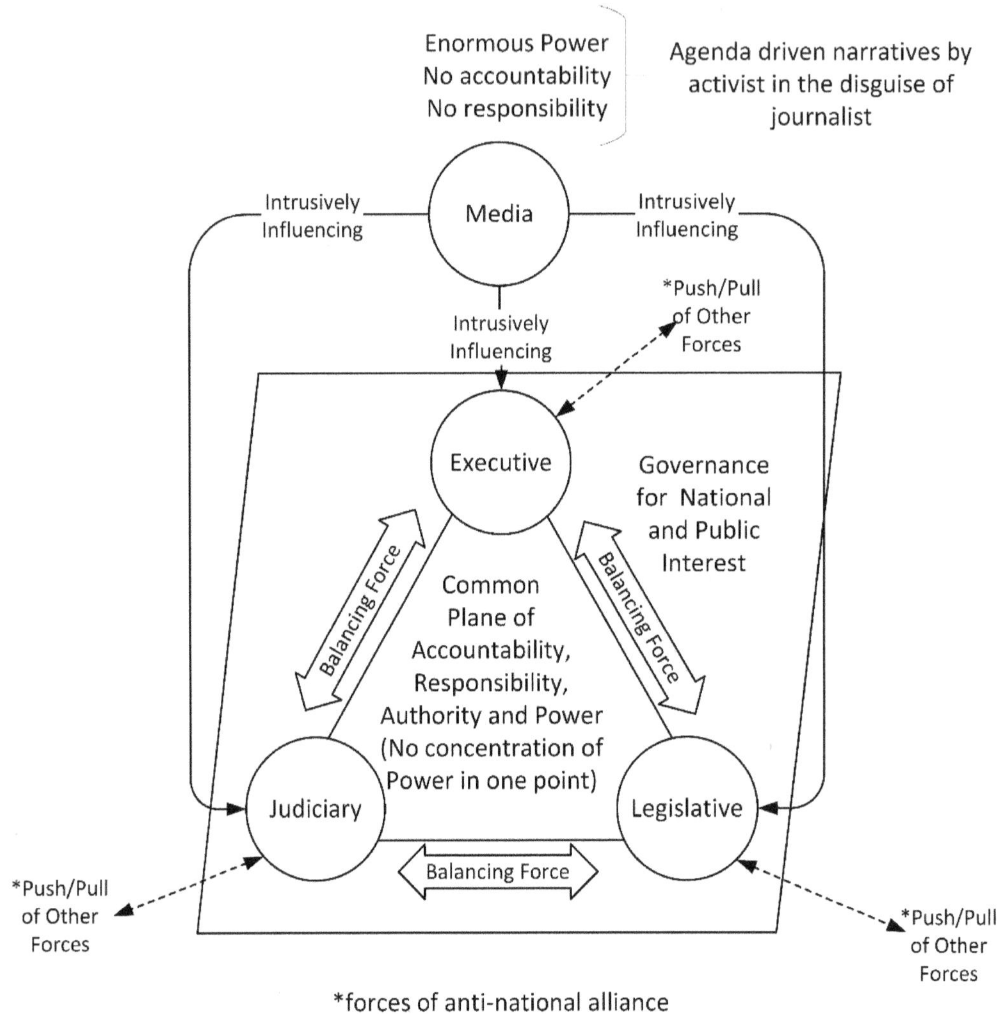

Figure 3: Broken Architecture of Democracy

The illustration depicts that the three pillars of democracy namely the Executive, Judiciary and Legislation are in a common plane of accountability, responsibility, authority and power. There is no concentration of power in any single point and there is check and balance among each other. The media, which is stated as the fourth pillar, may not necessarily be in the same plane while it intrusively influences all the other three pillars of democracy with enormous power and no accountability or responsibility as such. This gets more complex as the media often exhibits agenda driven narratives by activists disguised as journalists.

Now it is commonplace that whether it is Executive, Judiciary or Legislative, all three are influenced by external influencing factors as 'other forces.' The interlink of the balancing forces among them are not sufficient to deal with a damaging multitude of effects due to falsified Media Influence and 'Other forces.' These so-called 'other forces' are the damaging influence of anti-national alliances (This is detailed in the book 'Illustrated Vedant' by the same authors). The assumption or principle itself is broken that each pillar will have power, responsibility and accountability. What if a pillar has power but no accountability and the other two pillars do not have "checks and balancing" recourse? Well, in modern times the judiciary system is like that. It has created its own shield.

We are now at a corner of civilization where the general impression of attaining justice from the judiciary is itself in question as the judiciary is not immune from corruption in many parts of the world it is already corrupt. Another factor is 'judicial activism' which is often maligned by judges that makes it more dangerous. This fumes into incidents like what we observe in the USA about the FBI arresting a Milwaukee judge accused of helping a man evade immigration authorities, escalating a clash between the administration and the judiciary.

In some of the democracies we find limitations of the two pillars of Executive and Legislative who do not possess the power of checks and balances over the third pillar of judiciary. In India, there is the collegium system where incumbent judges of the Supreme Court appoint judges to the Judiciary of India. It originated from three Supreme Court judgments, collectively known as the Three Judges Cases. The system is known for being nepotic. On top of that the executive and legislative realistically do not have any control, thereby the judiciary almost behaves like an unauthorized supreme power raising doubts about incidents on judges charged with corruption but with no visible corrective action. There is a bizarre occurrence where a bench of Justices challenges the state Governor's delay in clearing bills. This resulted in the President, in a rare move, seeking the opinion of the Supreme Court, on whether the court can "impose" timelines and prescribe the manner of conduct of Governors and the President while dealing with State Bills sent to them for assent or reserved for consideration.

Despite such confused state of affairs, it is laudable that the Indian government rightfully meandering the rightful path withstanding the obstacles by raising public opinion and honoring the democratic means of doing things even though such damages are continuous. The point we would like to make is that - there is no room for faulty assumption that judiciary cannot be corrupt or judiciary will not encroach executive authority since the fundamentals of checks and balance is missing.

Power without Accountability

One conversation between a journalist and Elon Musk speaks it all:

Journalist to Elon Musk:

Let us start with this: You're the richest man in the world, you own a media platform, you are influencing space, AI, energy and now even politics. Do you think it's healthy or even democratic for one unelected billionaire to have this much power over public discourse and global infrastructure

Elon Musk Answers:

Power? I build things people choose to use. No one elected me and no one's forced to buy a Tesla or launch a satellite with SpaceX. That's called the free market. The real problem is when unelected journalists push narratives without accountability, shaping minds with zero innovation, zero risk and zero skin in the game. So, if you're worried about power with no checks maybe look in the mirror.

So, who is running your government? The phrase "government of the people, by the people, for the people" is widely recognized as a powerful description of democracy, primarily associated with U.S. President Abraham Lincoln's Gettysburg Address in 1863. In this regard we would like to bring attention to a book named "Who Is Raising Your Children?" by Rajiv Malhotra that explores the influence of Western education models and ideologies on child development, particularly in India. The author argues that some imported frameworks are pushing agendas like global citizenship, comprehensive sexuality education, and social justice, which can potentially undermine traditional values and prioritize ideological indoctrination over academic rigor. In essence, the book examines the impact of global education trends on child upbringing, emphasizing the importance of conscious parenting and critical evaluation of external influences.

In a comparable way, though the masses may think that they are voting and selecting the government, the reality of execution may be different. The point to ponder is still intriguing as to who is actually running the government and thereby raises questions towards the fundamentals of democracy itself. There is fundamental question about its proper functioning itself and quite naturally ***democracy cannot solve radical problem***.

By the way, we would like to clarify here that we are not comparing democracy with autocracy or monarchy or any other system. The purpose here is to focus on the challenges and perils of a broken democracy which is nowhere comparable to an ideal world of working democracy.

1.3.1 What could be a Possible Recourse?

If things do not change with time, they will become irrelevant like UNO today and potentially current democracies are also on the same path. Nonetheless we have hope and opportunity to change and remain relevant.

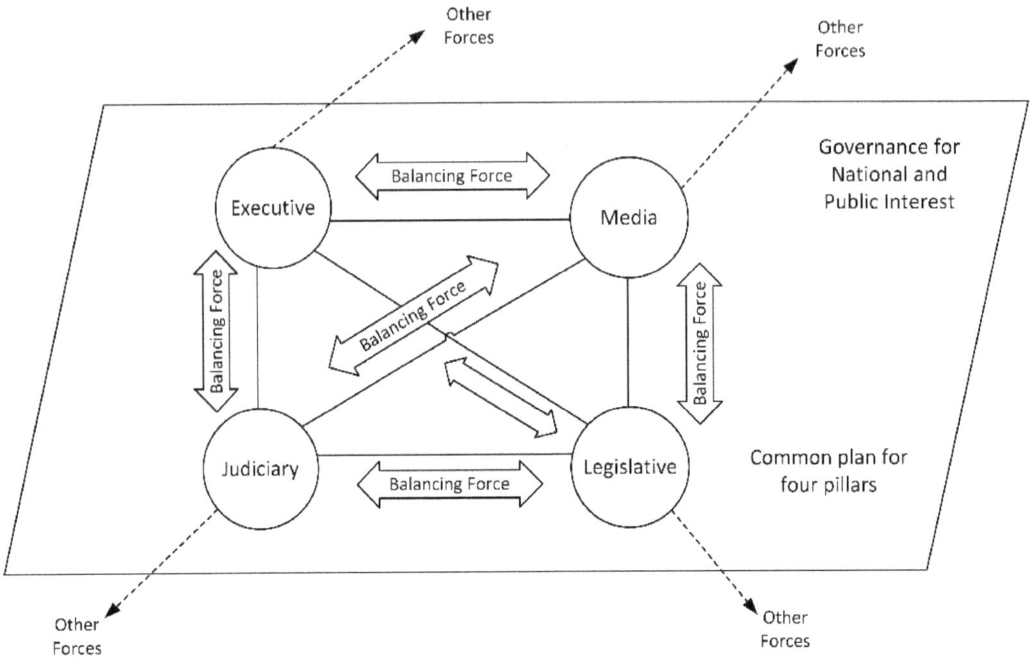

Figure 4: New architecture of democracy required now

The illustration portrays a proposal for a new architecture of interplay of the four pillars of democracy for a better functioning. Media as the fourth pillar has to be necessarily pulled into the same plane with the other three pillars of democracy and not dangling away as it is currently. By that the architecture will be tremendously strengthened by six balancing forces among the four pillars that will not only create harmony of checks and balances but also will extensively mitigate the damaging influence of the 'other forces.'

One may recall the Model T from Ford (introduced in 1908) that became a symbol of the "democratization of the automobile" and had a profound impact on American society and the global automotive industry. Now we are in a different EV world. It is quite obvious that the ideal old school definition of democracy has lost its relevance and needs a new architecture. It is illogical to claim that democracy is a great system now unless rearchitected.

1.4 Propaganda is now the mainstream media's business

Everyone is now busy making money. Propaganda is a lucrative business hence the mainstream media has chosen to pursue this. Business model is very similar to any other product business and the illustration depicts the analogy

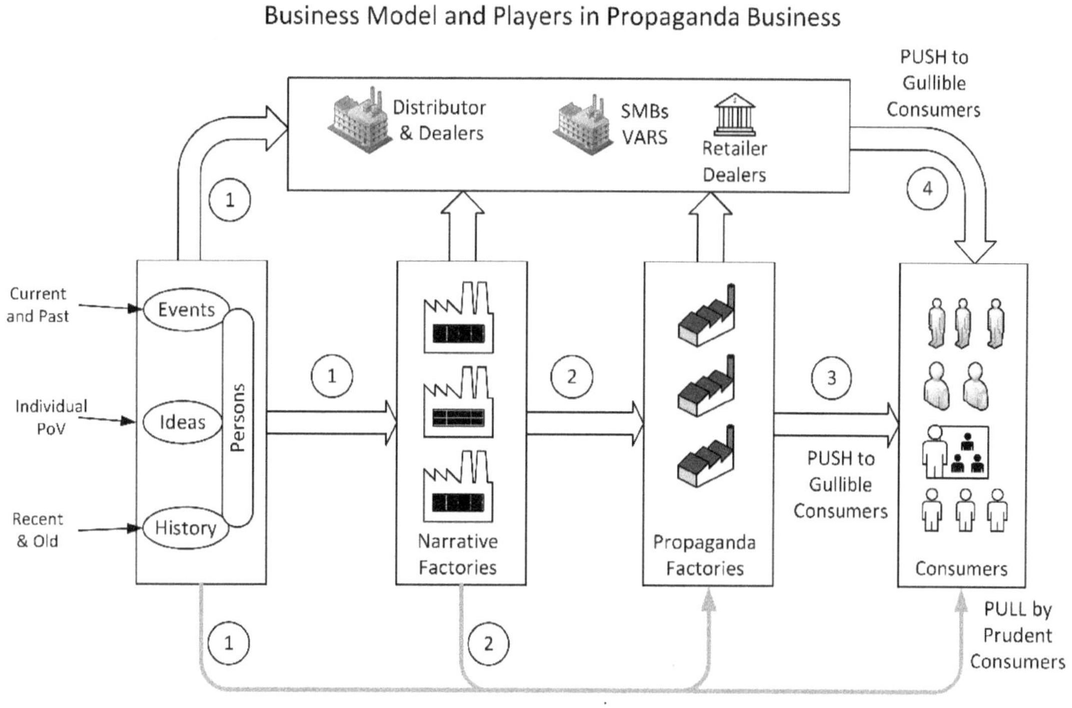

Business Model and Players in Propaganda Business

Figure 5: Business Model of Propaganda

The illustration thrives on key notes as

- Business thrives on Gullible customers and even educated people are gullible
- There are Gullible consumers and Prudent Consumers

In a product business, the raw material flows through the channels of Distributors and Dealers to the SMBs (Small and Medium Business) and VARs (Value Added Resellers) and then through the Retailers to reach the end consumers. In the media industry the raw materials are the Events (Current and Past), Ideas (Point of Views by individuals) and History as such (Recent and old) which are often linked to specified personas which are processed in the Narrative Factories. These are further fine-tuned to meet certain objectives to create specified propaganda in the Propaganda Factories and pushed to the consumers. In the modern digital day, consumers are also open to connect directly to the interim stages of media online i.e., can connect to the raw events or while this is in the narrative stage or further down the road. There is obviously further erosion of the nature of the raw event as it flows across the path anyway.

Basics of Narrative

A narrative is a story, a story constructed for three major purposes # 1 to channel people's attention and emotion in a specific direction #2 to get the public's approval on a specific matter and most important, #3 to give people a sense of progression.

A sense of progression is very important because it tells people that we are working towards something meaningful (or rather creating the illusion that we are working on something meaningful for them). Of course, we are very busy with something important for you.

But the thing with narratives is that they are just stories, which means they never materialize, nothing ever comes of it. That is why the people who have pushed that narrative will now instead allow it to fade into the background gradually and slowly without you even noticing by simply stopping talking about it. That is how it works. But at a certain point in the near future they will bring it back again to give you that sense of progression to create an illusion that we are changing something or something that we are monitoring is changing. Nothing ever changes though.

Narratives could be rather simple facts like a news reporter reporting from onsite about something live which may have lesser chance of harmful deviation of fact except any personal bias of the reporting style. However, when the same message is passed on the media studio, the so called editing and further processing is mostly agenda driven to promote specific interest i.e., a blatant propaganda is pushed to consumers.

Yes, consumers need not ideally wait for the evident push and can pull events from a previous stage for better transparency. However, pulling needs not only individual effort but also is a difficult and unsure proposition. Such an attempt is more complex and may not yield desired results as one is never sure about what you are consuming - is it actually clean or has been already polluted!

And off course, Propaganda is a lucrative business that thrives on how gullible the consumer is

- While 'Narrative' has more scope, 'Propaganda' is a tool used strictly to convince a population of a certain idea or action. Narrative is anything associated with the expression of any idea. So, for instance, science has a narrative, and hopefully no propaganda. History has a narrative and hopefully without propaganda. Narrative includes propaganda, but propaganda doesn't include all narrative.
- Propaganda is always conscious of itself as propaganda, with a precise goal of persuasion. Narrative is both conscious and unconscious. You produce narrative whether you are intentionally aware of it or not. Propaganda, by definition, is always conscious of itself as propaganda. All propaganda is narrative, but only some narrative is propaganda.
- In the absence of real Information, propaganda can step in and become that information. Because of social media it is in check. However the propaganda is combined with a heavy dose of marketing with vested funding, it makes a significant impact.

One of the strong propaganda techniques is - calling someone for an interview on one side of an issue and posing loaded, "gotcha" trap questions, often used to create a negative impression or manipulate the audience. This technique can be used in various contexts, including political debates, media coverage, and even everyday conversations, to sway public opinion. For example, in a political debate, a candidate might be cornered by loaded questions about their past actions or policy positions, creating the impression that they are dishonest or incompetent.

Here lies the significant difference between a Prudent and Gullible consumer. A prudent consumer will pull information from reasonable sources and attempt to validate with application of reasonable jurisprudence. This may sound like a complex initiative but not so much if one is at least keen to absolve in utilization of fundamental common sense. However, people are in general gullible and such gullible consumers are characterized by someone

- Who do not think and reason
- Who do not want to think and reason
- Who have no interest in learning the truth

They will use dirty water that is flowing towards them but not fetch clean water because of laziness, stupidity, sheer ignorance or even a 'don't care' attitude. But there is no reason to sympathize with such gullible consumers. One cannot shy away just being a helpless gullible one, If one is gullible, then it is only that one who is at fault at the very core.

In this context, it is interesting to point out that there is no exact word for propaganda in Sanskrit based Indian languages. In the Dictionary you often find "*Prachar*" and sometimes used as "*Protsahan*". This is because there is no concept of propaganda. Now with the need of this word in modern times it is made with the conjunction of Dush and thus "*Dush-Prachar*" becomes the true equivalent of propaganda. If there is true Sanatan Dharma, there will not be any propaganda. This is like the word 'Divorce' in Indian Language that we discussed in an earlier publication. There was no concept of divorce in India. Now this word is made by the conjunction of two different words "*Vivah-Vichchhed*" (Separation from marriage).

In Vedant, *Maya* is the veil that covers our real nature and the real nature of the world around us. It is the power of *Maya* with *Aavaran(cover)* that covers the truth and in turn projects the unreal by *Vikshep*. This could be referenced as an interesting analogy to modern day on propaganda that puts a veil on the truth and manufactures a false narrative.

The media business is largely a monopoly dominated by few major houses worldwide quite similar to the airlines industry. The entire global media landscape is thus turned into selective propaganda manufacturing factories. Another aspect is that - ***technology produces garbage and then another technology to clean that garbage.*** There are medicines promoted left and right that result in severe side effects. One basic health problem leads to another side issue and then there is the vicious cycle of a series of side medications to counter each. In the software industry, a prominent example of this cycle is the development of the Pegasus spyware and the subsequent technologies created to defend against it. The Pegasus example illustrates a continuous cycle in cybersecurity with exploitation, detection, countermeasure (new security tools or patches) and adaptation (to wait for another attack).

An unsettling example is the forced exit of BBC top executives (Nov, 2025) over the alleged criticism that its flagship TV news program spliced together sections of a speech of Donald Trump made on Jan. 6, 2021. Whether such a situation is an existential crisis for the BBC or not is a separate topic. However, this is not a one-off case and there were examples before with other media agencies. These cases highlight how editing, while essential to news production, can lead to serious ethical issues when it mischaracterizes statements or alters meaning by juxtaposing separate clips or presents crafted context edits. The immediate question is how gullible are we with media narratives? The fact is – the burden lies with us if you call that a burden or rather an accountability. We as the public tend to forget past media controversies until another high profile one crops up. This can be due to a combination of cognitive biases, the overwhelming volume of information, and the rapid nature of the news cycle. Yes, but can we ignore our own accountability? The adoption of AI is taking this to a new scale. AI technology is used rampantly to produce fake news including voice cloning to generate robocalls, deepfake videos to spread disinformation, and AI image generators to create fabricated photos that go viral. To counter such garbage, now there is another AI business for detecting and countering fake news. It is a multi-modal AI system that attempts to analyze and cross-reference an article's text, images, and user engagement patterns to assess its credibility. What level of trap the society is succumbing to in this vicious bad business! It is no longer a surprise as you may commonly hear 'I don't believe mainstream media; they are 100% biased. I trust them only to refer to a cricket scorecard where there is no chance of manipulation!"

So, the feasible alternative trickles down to ...yes, you got it right - the independent YouTube channels. There is more abundance of transparency there. By the way, we do not want to demean the topic with fake news and disinformation that flows every day in the WhatsApp university. As an individual, you have a much better opportunity to connect a verifiable resource right there on the internet specifically by the efforts of many of the independent channels. It is much more worthwhile to pursue that identification research. There is absolutely no rationale left any longer to remain overwhelmed with biased and vested mainstream opinions.

Media Trial in a Democratic System

Every organized legal system has a judiciary (courts) to hear cases and determine guilt or innocence for accused individuals, especially after a formal accusation like a charge sheet or indictment is filed, ensuring the rule of law and rights like a fair trial. The judicial system is made to administer justice independent of any discrimination and biases and it is strictly governed by the legal framework where every accused goes through a just trial.

In today's broken democratic system, the media goes beyond that. It runs the trial in public ahead of a judiciary trial based on a vested agenda. Biased narratives in news and other media compounded by social media coverage shape public opinion and create a presumption of guilt or innocence before even a legal verdict is reached in a court of law.

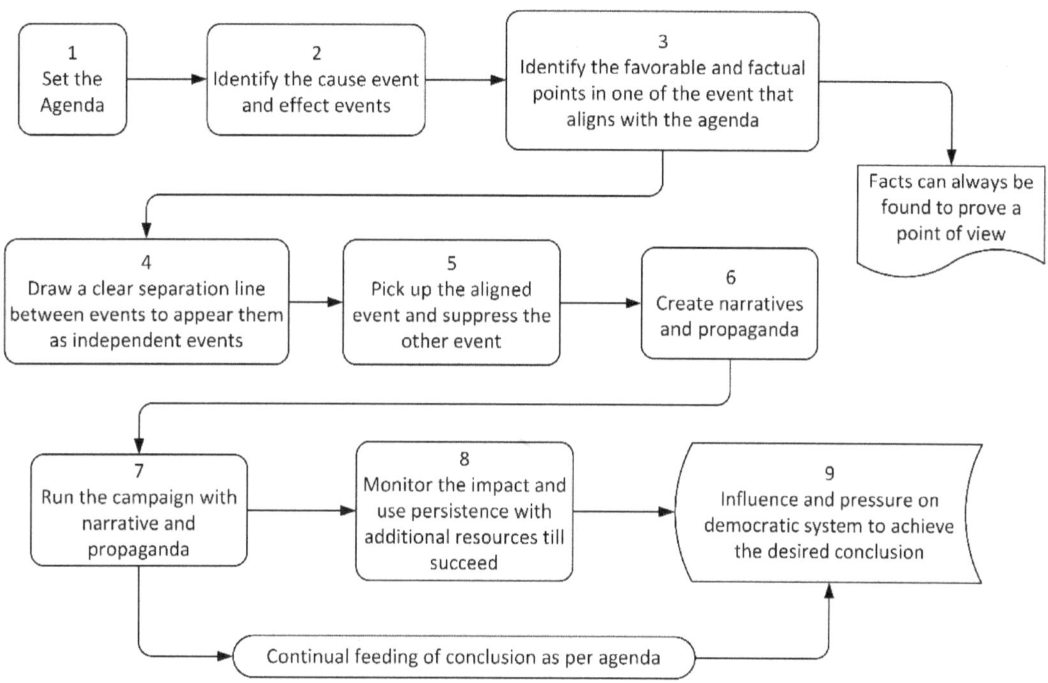

Figure 6: Framework for Media Trial in Democratic System

The framework for media trials is depicted in the above illustration. The interesting point to note is how a particular factual point is picked up carefully only with an intention to align the same with a favorable narrative. 'Facts can always be found to support a viewpoint' which could be intentionally away from truth. These are adept usage of selectively chosen fact-points (cherry-picking) or interpretation of pseudo-evidence through biased 'stories' to support a specific agenda, leading to different perspectives even with the same data. Then the business runs the campaign and propaganda meticulously thrusting the same vested narrative again and again till it succeeds to create the influencing impact.

The cause-and-effect timeframe and their relationships presented in media trials can vary significantly in their nature and timeframe.

- Variation in timeframe: Arguments can focus on short-term, medium-term, or long-term effects. As in standard legal arguments, a defense highlights immediate positive outcomes, while the prosecution emphasizes potential long-term harm that has not yet fully materialized. A planned media coverage influences the perceived truth depending on the time scale applied by pre-trial publicity, framing a story with bias and subtle impact on jurors.

- Instantaneous impacts: Some media coverages are focused on a single or series of dramatic instantaneous events (a visible confrontation often cooked up and scripted). This is done with an intention to overshadow the details and cover-up the underlying causes or consequences.

- Effect on visibility: Effects can be visible (like portrayal of a protest). But some effects like a slow shift in public opinion, hidden financial transactions or long-term health risks could be invisible. Either way, powerful rhetorical tools and framing are utilized by the media to persuade, influence, and mobilize audiences.

Let us explore that with an example.

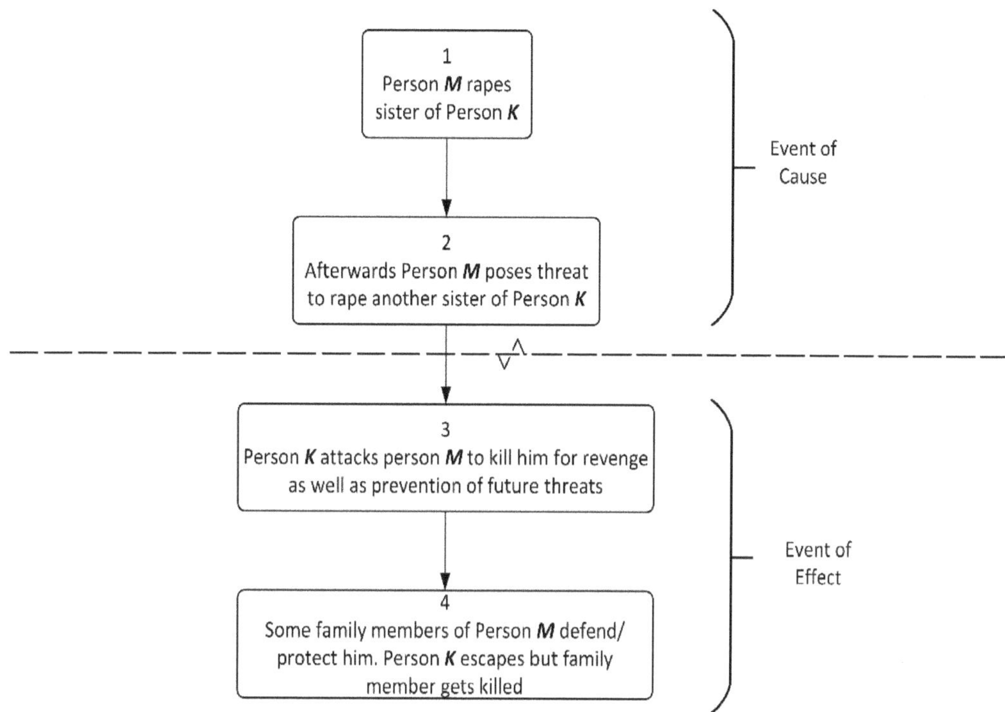

Figure 7: A hypothetical case for illustration of media trial framework

As the above illustration depicts the 'event of cause' and the 'event of effect' is clearly demarcated on purpose to create chaos and confusion around factual points blurring the vision about where to focus. Let us examine this above incident further and we would realize how the origin of the 'event of cause' is subtly manipulated to relegate focus from the sinful person M towards the apparent victim K.

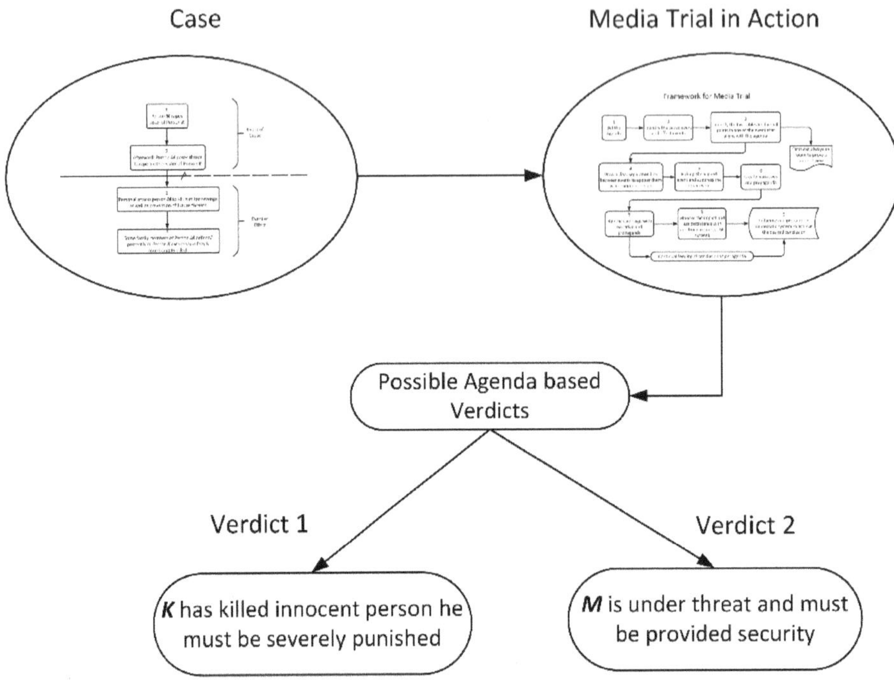

Figure 8: Conclusion to align agenda in a media trail- An illustration

Here is the shocking realization of how the original case is convoluted by a media trial in action. There is no longer any talk or mention about the sin of person M at all. No media coverage talks about the hostage still under torture. All is covered that person K killed an innocent victim. Media is focused on the agenda-based conclusions are with vested narratives absolutely against person K. On top of that there is also a parallel agenda on how person M should be provided with security by administration. What a media manipulated trial that cuts from both ways!

It is no longer a surprise that we encounter such media trials whether Israel or Russia as a nation or Jews and Hindus as a community.

Censorship in Democracy

In our attempt to search for the truth of various prevailing problems in the world, especially the wars and terrorism, we get the signs of press/media censorship, not only in the non-democratic countries but also in democratic countries.

The difference is that in autocratic countries it is enforced by the government and in democratic countries it is "self-imposed" by the mainstream media as it promotes the business of propaganda. On top of that, the mainstream ***media implicitly terrorizes the truth-tellers while the government just watches silently, helplessly or even deliberately***. This is exacerbated by the rise of anti-national elements across all democracies in the world today that aggravates further (Please refer to details on this aspect in the book 'Illustrated Vedant' by the same authors in the figure; The rise of antinationalism).

Propaganda of Characterizing Democracy

There is an uproar sometimes that characterizes democracy as authoritarian. This is despite the fact that the democratic government is formed by winning a majority in an electoral mandate i.e., the fundamentals of the formation of the government rests solely on its majoritarian principles.

Now a coalition government, where multiple parties collaborate to form a government, is indeed not majoritarian. Numerous European nations regularly operate with coalition governments, including Austria, Belgium, Croatia, Czech Republic, Denmark, Estonia, Finland, France, Germany, Greece, Iceland, Ireland, Italy, Liechtenstein, Luxembourg, Netherlands, Portugal, Romania, Spain, Switzerland, and the United Kingdom (although less frequently). The prevalence of multi-party systems and proportional representation in Europe means that coalition governments are the norm rather than the exception. Such a strong tradition of coalition governments eventually faces the challenge of being majoritarian.

A democracy based on majority electoral verdict does not face such an obvious challenge. And if such a government pushes an agenda for rightful implementation that serves the majority, then it is a good thing. Of course, democracies must guard against authoritarianism by codifying unwritten norms, modernizing legislative procedural safeguards, and establishing institutional checks against manufactured electoral majorities. We deliberated already on various challenges and aspects of broken democracy per say with the old and new architecture. At the same time, before blindly characterizing a democracy as authoritarian or so, one has to also realize that democracy is not just a mere political system. It is a shared endeavor and there is action for the citizens as well for a common will to safeguard its majoritarian principles.

Vedic Wisdom and Democracy

Traditionally India was not a democracy. The social and governing system was based in Vedic wisdom where the citizens had a bottom-up responsibility, not rights but responsibilities towards their own *Varna* and towards the nation (*Rashtra*). and the *Varna (jati)* looked after citizens. A *jati* optimized the well-being and the King optimized the well-being, so it was not a democracy-oriented thing but the responsibilities of people more than the rights of people and the collective So there's a dynamic between the individual and the collective individual has responsibilities towards the collective and the collective has responsibilities to look after the individuals. Now this is different system than a democracy system which is based on individualism Also in a democracy everyone has the same vote Whether you are a brilliant person who knows who has a lot of subject matter expertise or whether you are a duffer or somebody who not even educated and who has a lot of opinions who may be corrupt everybody has the same but you know if you look at a distribution of intelligence and a distribution of competence it's generally not evenly distributed in a society and we don't have cricket teams or sports teams run by democracy We don't have businesses making decisions based on democracy having all the workers with equal rights to vote for every decision We don't have militaries that run on democracy of every soldier will be equal in making a decision So it it's strange that the largest democracy India has inherited this democracy because that was the system the British left

In 1961 when John F Kenndy made his famous statement in his inaugural speech "ask not what your country can do for you--ask what you can do for your country" – he was actually giving the Vedic wisdom of governing a prosperous and progressive society/nation.

1.5 Examples: Manifestation of Unreason

The Debate on Gun Control amidst incidents of Mass Shootings

Today, many proponents of gun rights would refer to a 'high-capacity magazine' that does not exceed 10 shots as average, when using guns for self-defense or so for common usage. But what really does it mean for 'arms to be in common use'? Does it have to be used in self-defense incidents only? If so, then how to demarcate that?

With every shocking incident, the debate emerges again starting with the frivolous question - what should be the baseline of an assault weapon? It is shockingly annoying indeed to only get restricted with prejudiced viewpoints of various lobbyists while the core issue stays hidden under the carpet.

Increase in Destructive War amid Desire of Peace

We read news articles and view series of social media vlogs but yet not get our basic fact right that the defense industry utilizes the threat of war and self-fulfilling prophecies to promote military engagements even though we have been seeing this for more than two decades in several countries.

We do experience bizarre situations where a previously listed terrorist is favored and invested for a regime change in Syria. It is illogical to accept the unreason in the name of geopolitics which is harmful not only to a specific country but the world as a whole.

The Pretention around Terrorism

Money begets Power and Power begets Money. And the uncontrollable spiraling greed has generated big money and immense power acting on an ever-increasing massive scale in modern day. Unlike publicized corporate business, there is billion-dollar business growth in huge business empresses which are not publicized as corporate entities and rather masked as clandestine business invisible to the society. There is the huge play of money and power in the business of war, in the business of terrorism and in the business of fake war on terrorism.

These are promoted by a global alliance of anti-nationalist forces that is hurting humanity as the sole victim.

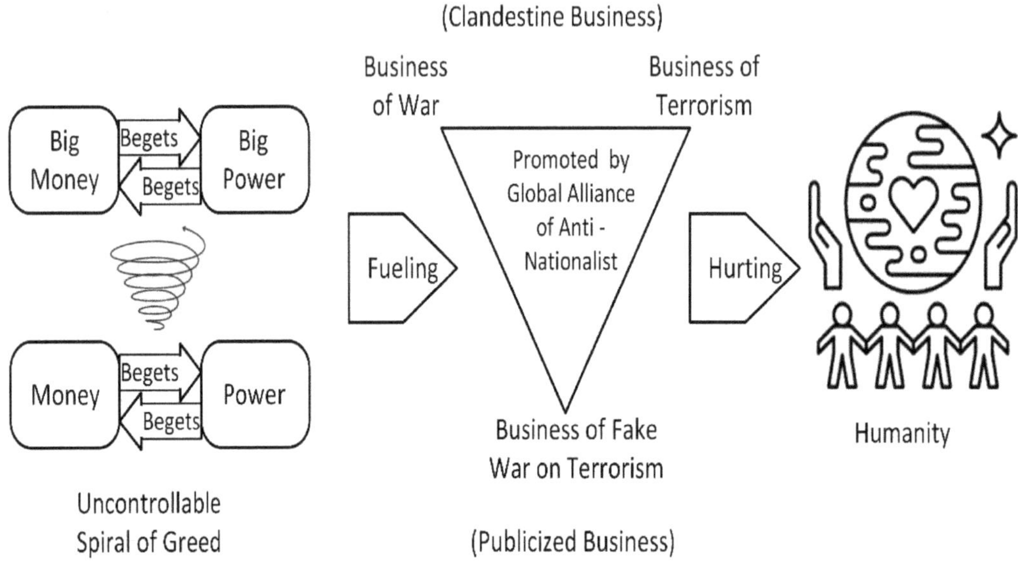

Figure 9: Business of Terrorism

Western Europe and America are condemning terrorism and yet continue to support countries harboring terrorism. We're living in a very unusual world where suddenly people who professed hatred of the West and in particular designated as 'terrorist' to the United States are now being accepted as potential allies and partners as head of state. This is not just an isolated event in Syria. We see Pakistan's defense minister openly admitting to supporting terrorist groups for the US during the Soviet Afghan war and post-9/11 and just calling it a mistake or dirty work. At the same time USA designates North Korea as a state sponsor of terrorism. This is indeed an unusual subject of convenience making terrorism as a matter of what suits me and what does not suit me. In this context, one may refer the book 'Confessions of an Economic Hit Man' by John Perkins where he described 'his primary role at Chas T. Main was to convince leaders of underdeveloped countries to accept substantial development loans for large construction and engineering projects, thus trapping them in a system of

American influence and control.' Yes, there is outcry to dispute this as a false claim, but that sounds too obvious, doesn't it?

It is frustrating and annoying but it is a fact that terrorism has also fallen into the trap of a lucrative business. In this context, let us not avoid to mention that the dominating business in the world today are

- Business of War – why is there a constant cry about the USA being the global Leader in this business?
- Business Of Terrorism – while one of the most common projections has always been that Pakistan is the Global Leader of terrorism, why to ignore the angle that USA's support is sustaining that business?
- Business of Fake War on Terrorism – why are there a plethora of debates around the narrative of the USA to gather the support on the above two businesses?

Like any other business the market condition and business partners also keep on changing. For example, in 2013 USA designated Al-Sharaa (formerly known as Abu Mohammad al-Julani) as a Specially Designated Global Terrorist, and a $10 million bounty was placed on his head. In 2024 this designation was removed and then he visited White House in November 2025. Similarly, sometimes military dictatorship is installed and supported in various countries to eliminate democracy and support state sponsored terrorism because there is big money in it. So, when after about 77 years again USA rebrand the erstwhile Department of Defense (DOD) to 'Department of War', it is not a surprise. Instead of a passive connotation of defense, possibly this is rather a disrobed representation!

Debate about 'Rouge State'

Who decides which is a rogue state in the world? If we apply common sense and righteousness, then it is easy to find the correct answer. If a nation is acting as the bully of the world, destroy other nations on false accusation, promote and support terrorism to use for its own benefit, promotes war to fuel the business of weapon is a rogue nation or a nation who does not trust the bullying nation and take all the actions to protect themselves is a rouge nation?

The Deception of Healthy Food

Following the 90s the era came for health food for cornflakes followed by quinoa, oats, smoothies, kale, seeds that cluttered our everyday meal plates. This glamorized syndrome slowly replaced our traditional home cooked meals. Entering 2020 with the virus pandemic and eventually 'healthy' alone was not marketable enough. 'Immunity' became the latest sales pitch and all of a sudden, we were prompted to absorb that milkshakes and ice cream promise immunity!

Are we not being fooled in the name of health and wellness? It is no wonder that a simple search in Instagram on just the search word 'healthy' generates about 160 million posts. That is the level of obsession. And who is teaching such flawed ideas? That is Instagram University on the subject of 'health.' Let us make a note that the global health and wellness market was valued at $6.3 trillion in 2023 and is projected to reach $9 trillion by 2028, according to the Global Wellness Institute. This represents a 7.3% annual growth rate between 2023 and 2028. The market is growing due to increased consumer awareness and spending on health and wellness products and services. But are the consumers being pushed to be aware? Just to drill down, the global market for green tea, the highest selling wellness product, is about 16 billion and is projected to reach $ 32 billion by 2032. You know that product promises so many good things and even mentions to cure cancer. Well, green tea improves metabolism; but is that not true for any other tea which does not look green? Moreover, does it automatically entrust you to believe the side note that it can cure cancer just like that? Consider another fad - 'Gluten free'! Science says gluten is a mixture of protein found in carbohydrates like wheat, barley and rye. Are any of those bad for our health? They are not. So, by simple logic there may not be any need for us to buy gluten free products unless someone is having 'Celiac disease' which is an autoimmune disorder triggered by gluten sensitivity. The fact is that such Celiac disease affects roughly about only 1% of the population of the USA while at least 20% of America is trying to eat gluten-free. This is despite the fact that an average gluten-free product is about 240% more expensive. By 2032, this global gluten free market is expected to reach $15 billion. Again, Instagram teaches us alternatives like almond milk and soya milk saying cow milk makes us fat. No wonder since the global almond milk and soya milk market is stated to reach $17 billion and $7 billion by 2030, respectively. Composition wise there is no proof that they are of healthier choice compared to cow milk. There is pragmatic analysis that plant-based drinks are not real alternatives to milk in terms of nutrient composition (https://pmc.ncbi.nlm.nih.gov/articles/PMC9650290/). Take the 'protein powder' which at best can be just a supplement but why the need even for any supplement when basic protein is very much achievable in a normal diet? You are just lavishly contributing to its global market that is projected to reach $47 billion by 2032.

The buzzwords like low-cal, baked-not-fried, air-fried, cholesterol-free, fat-free actually do not matter, the fundamental ingredients do. Then there is masking of common names of the ingredients with technical cryptic numbers. For example, in Europe it is hard to find MSG Monosodium Glutamate) in the ingredient list while that is hidden in the name of E-621. Carrageenan is masked as E 407. Many ready-made yogurts have as much sugar as a candy bar, protein bars have all kinds of unhealthy ingredients, vegetable chips can be as bad as potato chips. False advertising has reached an unprecedented level. Vitamin water claims to be healthier than soda; but a closer look reveals that a bottle of Vitamin water in the US may harbor the same amount of fructose as a bottle of regular Coke. Advertising, packaging and advice – they can all be purchased. Studies too are for sale. For example, in 2020, Annals of Internal Medicine issued a correction about researcher's undisclosed conflict of interest linking chief researcher to the meat industry. The original published article explained there is no need to reduce red or processed meat consumption for good health. But it failed as it did not disclose ties with AgriLife Research, an arm of Texas A&M University that is partially funded by the beef industry. All you get is 'Orthorexia' which is a term that describes an obsession with eating healthy food.

The Narrative on Secularism

In the largest democracy in the world, which is in India, its interpretation of secularism is misleading and that has caused great harm and injustice in the society. It is a separate subject to talk about the hypocrisy of all the major media houses in the world including TOI, BBC, CNN, Al Jazeera (you can include many names worldwide); but the point is that false narratives are promoted for vested interests. The foundation of narratives and propaganda by western media is built upon a wrong understanding of Sanatan Dharma and translating the word Dharma as religion. We have explained that Dharma is not equal to religion in the book Illustrated Vedant (ISBN 979-8-9884340-1-6). So, learning from these news channels on Dharma is like taking guidance from a blind man.

The Woke Culture

Are we not seeing that religious radicalism and vested political ideology are constantly twisting the facts 'sometimes for' and 'sometimes against' the motion; but either way for fulfilling vested interest in the name of human rights? The vested intent is playing the game affecting both sides of the coin causing a cancerous humanity as if awaiting a termite-struck house to be collapsed.

The Marketing of Bug-free Software

Somehow, a wrong concept is institutionalized that it is not possible to produce bug free software. This is how the software producers are shying away from accountability. In fact, the acceptance of bugs is institutionalized to serve the industry's business purpose. Sounds as if there is an imposed bias for sale!

The Rise of Incompetent Scientific Publications

There is significant pressure on scientists, particularly in academia, to publish research papers that leads to less valuable or even useless research. The pressure can be due to university prestige, funding or even artificially staged competition. But the focus on quantity over quality is producing enough junk publications.

The Confusion of Open System in Information Technology

Sometimes we argue that the so-called 'Open systems' are relatively open which possibly hints that some interfaces and functionalities are more open than others. But does 'open system' necessarily imply full and total openness? We are aware that the mobile app ecosystem like iOS is not truly open in the sense that it lacks the complete freedom to control and modify the core operating system or access all hardware features without Apple's permission.

The Challenge of Agile Methodology

The perceived unreason of 'Agile' stems from its potential for being misused and its difficulty in being fully embraced across an entire organization. Agile can become a bureaucratic exercise, failing to deliver real value when its principles are not genuinely adopted.

Also think of a real-life customer order which forces start of work based on a trusted letter of intent (LOI) activating the agile project scrum in anticipation of magical quick implementation. However, in reality even the formal customer purchase order gets delayed for months due to several corporate and legal issues.

The Claim of Customer Service Satisfaction

Customer service satisfaction often is manipulated in numerous ways. This can involve practices by companies with deceptive marketing SLAs, Artificial Intelligence (AI) and chatbots or even dishonest ratings.

On the other hand, even customers may try to exploit service guarantees with opportunistic behavior for refunds or false claims.

The Outcry of Health Insurance Premiums

On this topic, the less said the better. The rates are increasing every year while there is constant outcry on coverage. We can somewhat guess that the issue of health insurance prices and coverage stems from several factors, including market concentration among insurance companies, lack of transparency in rate and factors like administrative costs and insurer profits. Of course, this contributes to premiums that outpace inflation and wage growth.

It is important to take note of such research articles that inherently possess a pre-decided outcome to promote vested intent.

The Delusion of Psychic Healing

Spiritual peace is not a commodity that can be purchased for a few thousand dollars. Psychic healing in the hands of fake Godmen is not Sanatana teaching. For example, 'renunciation' in the Hindu doctrines, does not mean running away from routine life because one is incompetent to manage it. True renunciation involves sacrificing all materialistic pleasures.

Similarly, as stated in Bhagwat Gita, 'Karma yoga' advocates that one should always be engaged in work but should not be attached to the fruits of the deeds. This does not mean at all that one abstains from performing basic duties and escapes from accountability. These are fraud interpretations that in turn promote false narratives in defying Sanatana by a section of Westerners.

The Argument of Conspiracy Theorists

Yes, conspiracy theories are the result of a complex interplay of psychological, personality, and social factors that can make individuals more susceptible to believing in them. But that sounds like a lame excuse. Are we not prone to get excited about finding a conspiracy theory out of anything?

We know it but intentionally refuse to accept that we are drawn to such theories due to a need for control or a desire to feel superior, or sometimes for a feeling of being marginalized.

Theft is also a Business!

(https://youtu.be/gFYfOpES8dE?si=xRgJylP8LF4oGVvh)

A US federal court has fined the tech giant Google and has been told to pay $425 million. The reason, something most of us fear, but cannot always prove, is violation of privacy. It all started in 2020. A lawsuit was filed against Google, a class action lawsuit. It covered more than 98 million users and 174 million devices. The charge, Google secretly collected third-party data even after users asked it not to.

You know those apps where you sign in using your Google account, Uber, Amazon, Instagram and countless other apps. The moment you log in using say your Gmail credentials, Google does not just stop at authentication. It starts talking to those apps. It starts tracking you. Your rides, your shopping, your messages, your scrolling patterns, all of them are tracked by Google. Of course, there are checks in place. So yes, Google asks for your consent. And yes, you can toggle privacy settings. But here's the core of the lawsuit. Even after users opted out, even after they told Google to stop tracking them, Google kept collecting data behind the scenes. And it wasn't just storing this data; it was also selling it. At least that's what users claim that the company was selling their data.

Now about 5 years later, a US court has passed the verdict and it has found Google guilty. It says Google breached user privacy, which is why the company has been slapped with a massive fine.

Earlier this year in the month of May, Google agreed to pay $1.4 billion. This was in a separate case involving people's facial features, voice prints, and their location. All allegedly tracked even when users opted out.

And you may remember what happened last year. Google was told to destroy billions of user records. Apparently, it tracked people even though they were browsing privately on the incognito mode.

What's worse, this is not just about one company. Zoom out and you'll see a pattern. It is the same problem with most companies, especially tech giants.

Look at the reports between 2019 and 2022. Tesla employees shared invasive video recorded by their customers' cars. In 2023, Amazon was fined $30 million. Its AI assistant Alexa and Ring doorbell camera unlawfully collected voice recordings and kept them for years. This year, Meta agreed to settle a lawsuit for $8 billion. It was sued after data of millions of users was leaked. So pick any industry, tech, auto, social media, and you will see the same problem. Thus, ***in the world of unreason, this kind of robbery is also institutionalized!***

The False Narrative of 'Developed Country' served by Western Capitalism

Let us start off by exploring a dictionary interpretation. Oxford dictionary says that a 'developing country' is a <u>*poor agricultural country*</u> that is seeking to become more advanced <u>*economically and socially*</u>. Let us discuss this definition breaking into parts.

- 'poor agricultural country' : Just note how the words' poor' and 'agricultural' are used side by side. The point to note is even though agriculture accounts for a small fraction of its GDP and employment, the USA is the world's largest agricultural exporter. Historically, all currently so-called developed nations started as agricultural economies and later transitioned to industrial and service-based economies. But that does not mean that an agricultural country is necessarily barred from becoming a developed country. The dictionary definition itself is a bit tilted.
- 'Economically and socially': Now let us discuss how these specific wordings are used for this definition. Again, Oxford says 'economically' means - in a way that involves careful use of money or resources i.e., in a way that uses no more of something than is necessary. In an analogous way 'socially' means - in a way that relates to society or its organization. How come one can be assured that an agricultural country is not utilizing its resources frugally or in a way that does not relate to society?

What is the Bias in the Existing Categorization that Brands a Country as Developed?

From dictionary meaning let us delve into institutional definition by none other than the United Nations. The UN uses criteria like the Human Development Index (HDI) and Gross National Income (GNI) per capita to classify nations, particularly through the Least Developed Countries (LDCs) category.

Categorization	UN Criteria	Obvious Characteristics
Developed Country	Countries with high scores on the Human Development Index (HDI), which considers life expectancy, education, and income.	High-income, industrialized nations with a strong economy, high standards of living, robust infrastructure, and advanced technology.
Developing Country	Intended for low-income countries; UN also uses other metrics for specific classifications, such as the HDI.	Low-income countries with lower living standards, less

		industrialization, and weaker economies.
Under-Developed Countries (Least Developed Countries - LDCs)	The UN specifically identifies Least Developed Countries (LDCs) based on three main criteria: • Per capita income: Low Gross National Income (GNI) per capita. • Human assets: Low levels in health and education, such as nutrition, school enrollment, and literacy. • Vulnerability: High susceptibility to economic and environmental shocks and a small, remote geographic location.	Characterized by widespread poverty, lack of access to basic necessities like healthcare and education, and very poor living conditions.

The categorization is stressed towards demarcating the 'Underdeveloped countries' (essentially the same as LDCs) which are low-income countries with high vulnerability to shocks and possess low human development. It is clear that 'Developed countries' have high living standards, advanced economies, and robust infrastructure, while 'Developing countries' have lower living standards, less industrialization, and weaker economies. However, specifically for developed and underdeveloped countries ***does that definition not rely on questionable benchmarking metrics? Is it not creating a misleading dichotomy, leading to a false hierarchy among nations?***

The problem starts with the LDC classification itself. Yes, it is a useful tool for signaling development needs and securing international support. The countries in this LDC list are reviewed every three years by the Committee for Development Policy (CDP). But the chance of a country to graduate to an upper grade is rather bleak as the classification process has several features that make it inherently slow and deliberate, rather than dynamic. It is important to take note of the Issues with such Classification:

- Oversimplification: The criteria (income, human assets, and economic and environmental vulnerability) are meant to capture longer-term progress but does not necessarily reflect short-term changes or the complexities of modern challenges.
- False Hierarchy & Stigma: The use of terms like 'developed' and 'underdeveloped' creates a misleading hierarchy, promoting a sense of paternalism and patronization rather than focusing on mutual development and support.
- Limited Scope: The criteria does not capture crucial aspects like inequality, the severity of debt burdens, or the disproportionate impacts of climate change, which are critical for a complete understanding of a country's development situation.

But is Infinite Growth on a Finite Planet Possible?

We live in a world of finite resources. Humanity cannot continue to grow GDP at high exponential rates over the long-term, because key resources are finite. On top of that we have already significantly and permanently damaged our fragile biosphere. It is no longer just a coffee table debate about how Carbon dioxide (CO_2), emissions from fossil fuel usage, unsustainable farming practices or water and land degradation are dangerously contributing to the destruction of our planet. Humanity is using nature 1.7 times faster than our planet's biocapacity can regenerate. That's equivalent to using the resources of 1.7 Earths. The Ecological Footprint for the United States is 8.1 gha per person (in 2018) and global biocapacity is 1.6 gha per person (in 2018). Therefore, we would need (8.1/ 1.6) = 5.1 Earths if everyone lived like people living in the United States (https://overshoot.footprintnetwork.org/how-many-earths-or-countries-do-we-need/). Simply put, if all ***developing countries consumed resources at the rate of today's highest-income countries, it would require far more than seven times the Earth's available resources.***

What is the Feasible Recourse to Address this Bias?

It is evident that the benchmarking criteria for developed countries itself is biased. That is because the UN's criteria are just focused on materialistic consumption. The Human Development Index (HDI) does not actually move beyond purely economic metrics and does not comprehensively account for unsustainable consumption or its environmental and social consequences. The Gross National Income (GNI) per capita can be exhibited as increasing while it is actually driven by the country's exploitation of resources or military spending. How come that reflects the nation's overall well-being?

Again, high-income countries have a disproportionately high material footprint per capita compared to low-income countries. The defined so-called developed or rich countries use six times more resources and generate 10 times the climate impacts than low-income ones

(https://www.unep.org/news-and-stories/press-release/rich-countries-use-six-times-more-resources-generate-10-times)

So, the recourse is to fundamentally redesign the benchmarking parameters of branding a country developed or developing, so to say. We propose the following approach:

Approach 1: Sustainable growth that properly accounts for environmental and social factors

It would be a superior parameter for a country's development compared to traditional metrics. Such an approach will be more holistic and will provide a better measure of long-term prosperity and human well-being. This will have a strong alignment to both the environment and society.

- Environmental benefits: Long-term resource security (it is important to decouple economic growth from resource depletion), Reduced environmental impact and Enhanced resilience against climate change and biodiversity loss

- Social benefits: Greater social equity (benefits of progress are shared more inclusively across society) and Improved quality of life (the well-being factor)

Approach 2: A True Happiness Index for Country's Wellbeing will be a better measurement.

The approach 1 described above brings again the point that we must be conscious to preserve, nurture and respect our mother earth and nature. We must not exploit (*soshan*) nature and must be conscious of nurturing (*poshan*) the same. This is nicely depicted in Hindu Scripture 'Rigveda' as "*Vasudhaiva Kutumbakam*" which translates to 'The world is one family.' This ancient Indian saying conveys the idea that the entire world is interconnected, and all people including the natural creations of sentient and insentient beings are part of a single global family. This in turn is deeply connected to happiness through the promotion of collective well-being, empathy, and spiritual fulfillment. We feel the manifestation of happiness is more significant for true development of a country.

In this context it would be important to refer to a pragmatic implementation as well. We are talking about Bhutan's unique approach to national well-being which is measured by the Gross National Happiness (GNH) Index, which assesses various aspects of life beyond traditional economic indicators. This aspect is discussed in detail in a separate chapter in this book.

It will not be much out of context to portray that all the institutional measurements like development index and even international awards sponsored by the west are actually a political tool to build narrative and propaganda. Even the Nobel peace prize is a candidate in this category. Anyone who is willing to analyze the circumstances and the winner will not have much difficulty discovering the truth of the Noble Peace Prize. The West has repeatedly utilized the discourse of democracy, human rights and freedom not as universal values but as tools to justify its geopolitical interests. It is so evident that there is no need to provide examples. A genuine Nobel Peace Prize should be granted to those who sacrifice personal comfort and life itself for humanity. But alas, it has become a political theatre!

Measuring countries on faulty development ideas is nothing but a vested propaganda tool of Western institutions. Another common example is the measurement of corruption by the criteria which are again set by the same Western institutions. There is something called "institutionalized" corrupt practices that are not counted in such measurement to manipulate scores. This is indeed a point that can be elaborated in much more detail. However, we leave this point for some other publication in future.

Reference Information Sources to Check Out

"To argue with a man who has renounced the use and authority of reason, is like administering medicine to the dead.

— Thomas Paine, The American Crisis

To start with, do stop believing in information messages rampant in WhatsApp university. It is rather unfortunate that we tend to forward such messages to others without simple checks. You are not only misusing your common sense but also compounding it to greater complexity by involving your WhatsApp connections. Yes, that is exactly the trap of propaganda for which it is intended! The funniest part is - even a 2 minutes glance on the internet will reveal falsified claims in most of those messages. The baseline is to process information as an enabler to think or act in a reasonable way

Here below are some sources that we leave for our esteemed readers to judiciously refer to.

- Earth Overshoot Day marks the date when humanity's demand for ecological resources and services in a given year exceeds what Earth can regenerate in that year https://www.footprintnetwork.org/our-work/earth-overshoot-day/
- YouTube channel of Sebastian Saas on his geopolitical analysis on various topics including the Russia – Ukraine war – https://www.youtube.com/watch?v=BVNZrpmgiAU
- Another example is about an article which was published by Bloomberg talking about the return of western companies to Russia. Here they begin

with propaganda, and then they spend the rest of the article dismantling their own propaganda point by point. This is an example of practicing unreason. Why not just remove the lie communicating headline? Because the rest of the article, for the most part, is factually correct.
https://youtu.be/zTrThzEzLXg?si=RxU-z4dClpWGiiXC

- The book 'The Murder of History' by Khursheed Kamal Aziz that explains the various errors, misquotations, misinterpretations and misleading statements found in various curriculum textbooks taught in Pakistan. These are alleged to deliberately teach distorted history and this trend continues today (May also refer to the address of their army chief who runs an apparent puppet government) despite visible consequences. We will discuss more in the chapter on 'Paradox of History.'
- UAE's Foreign Minister shares WILD foresight regarding Europe's Woke Culture
  https://youtube.com/shorts/0jOYl_AxvFk?si=99iQou7vzA3_-6km
- The country Bangladesh today glorifies the nation who raped and murdered millions of their women at the time of their formation and adopt hostility to the nation who came out as their savior.
- The book 'Illustrated Vedant' by Prafull Verma, Santanu Kar and Kalyan Kumar where details of problem examples due to unreason are described.
- You Tube channel (Regional) of Dr, Rizwan Ahmed with his freelance journalism & news analysis -
  https://www.youtube.com/@RizwanAhmedAdv

2 Why Rise of Unreason

Unreason is born from the absence of thinking or some kind of hindrance or problem at the thinking stage itself in the "thinking and reasoning" process. This problem at the first stage may further be expanded as shown in the diagram xx.

1.1 Inability to Think & Reason:

The inability to think and reason can be described in many ways. There are some who apparently lack the basic concern or awareness. For example, a farmer in a remote village may have good understanding about his way of conducting agriculture, but he may not possess the so-called methodical understanding about other geopolitical matters. This may affect his thinking umbrella and such people are generally prone to be deceived by or swayed into some direction that eventually may not seem just for themselves or for the overall society.

However, we have a bigger issue in hand. In general, people have a tendency not to think. It is commonplace that people do not have time to think and a quick-fix solution is more welcome. Whether you brand them as simply ***intellectually lazy*** or ***passive***, the very fact remains that such individuals stay far away from the indulgence of thinking a bit, prefer to rely on others for thinking and are mostly addicted to instant gratification.

Now, there are individuals who ***apply thinking but are self-corrupt*** because they do not verify the source of the knowledge.

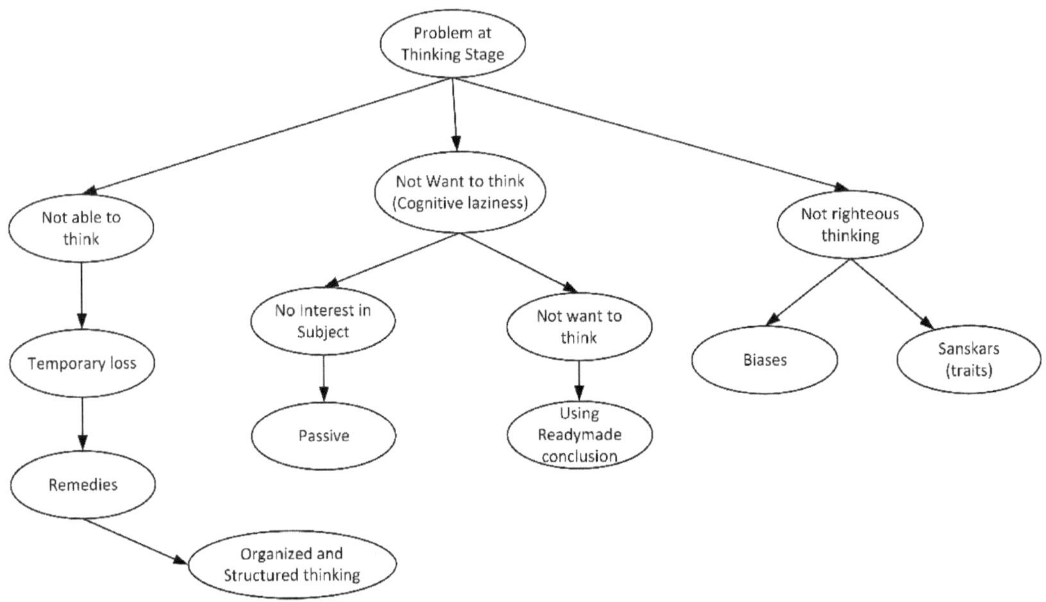

Figure 10: Reason of unreason

The dictionary meaning of 'Unreason' says 'inability to think and act reasonably.' The essential pointers that we would like deliberate here are:

- A person can never stop thinking at any moment or so to say 'just manage without thinking'
- Our mind is not lazy or passive but actually is always active even while sleeping and dreaming
- Our thoughts are random in nature which may not be meaningful as they are not structured as such. (For advanced detail, please refer to the illustration of samadhi in the 'Illustrated Vedant' by the same authors).
- When someone stops thinking, it is actually a "*Samadhi*" state as per Advaita Vedanta. *Samadhi* is a state where the mind is still and there is no discursive thought, but not necessarily the absence of all consciousness. It's a state of deep absorption and unity with the Self, where the mind is not actively engaged in thinking or mental processes, but there is still a state of awareness.
- It is only for someone who earnestly seeks liberation through the path of knowledge (*Jnana*) can potentially achieve *Samadhi*. The key lies in

dispelling ignorance (*Avidya*) and realizing the true nature of reality (*Brahman*), which is understood to be one's own self. Achieving the *Samadhi* state isn't a matter of universal inability, but rather a matter of a deep commitment and specific actions.

- There may be temporary "seemingly loss of thinking" because of some accident or event or being overwhelmed by emotion (For an advanced detail, please refer to the illustration Slippery slope in the book 'Illustrated Vedant' by the same authors).
- So it is not that one is just not thinking or having an inability to think. It is a matter of thinking in an organized and structured manner.
- Also, It is not the thinking problem but a cognition problem
- In essence, If you are passive your action may contribute to unreason

1.2 Inability to Validate Data and Knowledge

People are more inclined to absorb an available ready-made conclusion rather than thinking or analyzing the merit of the foregone conclusion. This is actually buying bad knowledge as such knowledge is often agenda-driven or biased.

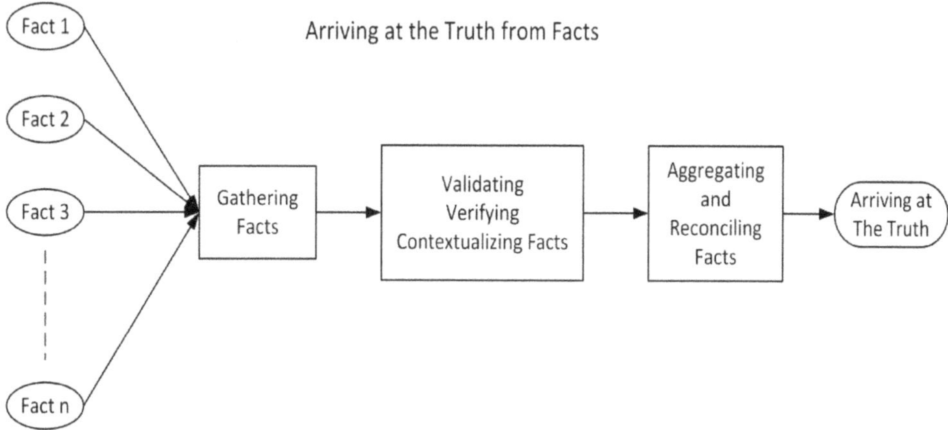

Figure 11: Search of the truth

The illustration above from the book 'Illustrated Vedant' by the same authors depict that It not only takes time to arrive at the truth that may contain many facts and more importantly one must have a condition-free mind.

In this context, it is no-brainer that social media manipulation of public opinion has become an enormous growing threat. But is that all? ***May we just blame the media and get off? Are we not responsible to think and decipher what is being told to us?***

Hurdles of Righteousness (Right way of Thinking)

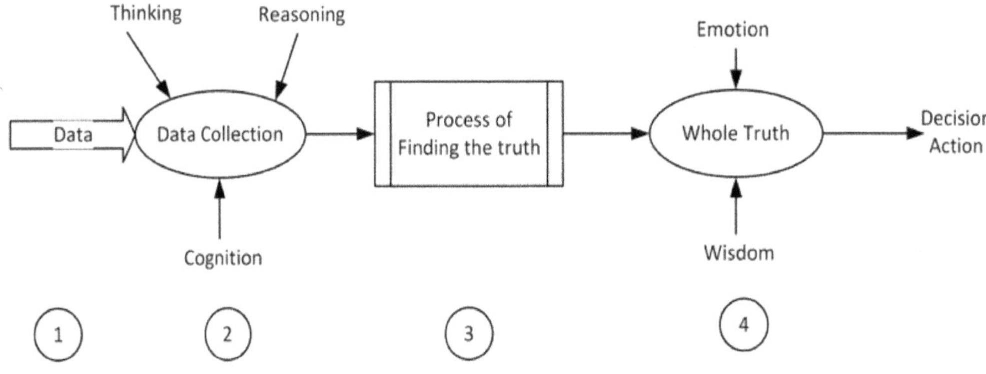

Figure 12: Hurdles in various stages of finding the truth

As depicted in the illustration above, the power to reason is affected or rather gets eclipsed at every stage from left to right

Stage1 – This is due to relying on improper data

Stage 2 – This is due to non-validation of collected data (absence of partial presence of analytical reasoning of unverified date or suspicious source of knowledge which are often specific agenda-driven and falsified propaganda. This also comes from an individual's preconceived bias which is again related to improper verification of knowledge.

Stage 3 – This is due ignorance and non-adherence of Process of finding the truth (For advanced detail, please refer the chapter 'Searching for Truth' in the book 'Illustrated Vedant by the same authors)

Stage 4 – This is due to the gap in realizing the whole truth and recognizing only partial truth where the decision is influenced by an individual's emotion and wisdom. A common example is a wise decision to quit smoking from tomorrow; however, mind or emotion delays the decision just on the next day and possibly the decision never gets implemented.

1.3 Natural Decline of Righteousness

Perspective from Sanatan Scriptures

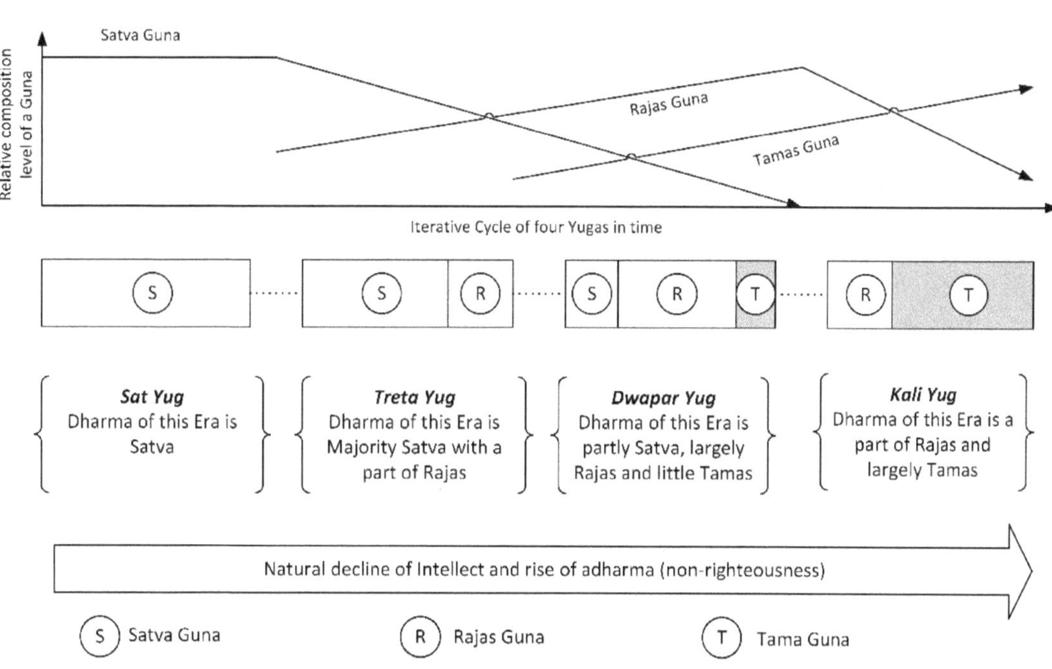

Figure 13: Natural decline in Vedic context

It is interesting to note a simple statement on the second law of thermodynamics which is that - heat always flows spontaneously from hotter to colder regions of matter (or 'downhill' in terms of the temperature gradient). In a similar way, the illustration depicts how there is a natural decline of intellect and rise of *Adharma* (Non-righteousness) in the four *Yugas* (which are world ages or eras that divide time into iterative cycles). In the *Yugas*, there is a remarkable transition of the

Three *Gunas* or *triguna* which are the three qualities that are always present in all things (*Padartha* or matter) and beings (*Jeeva*) in the world.

Sat Yug : *Dharma* of this era is *Satva* (qualities are driven by wisdom and desire for knowledge i.e., expansion, intelligence, purity, harmony, light, wisdom, good/elevating mood)

Treta Yug : *Dharma* of this era is majorly *Satva* but also partly with *Rajas*)qualities are driven by action and desire for material things i.e., activity, passion, motion, energy, desire, struggle, activating mode).

Dwapar Yug : *Dharma* of this era is partly *Satva* but majorly *Rajas* along with a small part of *Tamas* (qualities are driven by lack of knowledge or inaction i.e., obstruction, mass, ignorance, inertia, inaction, darkness, destruction, evil mode).

Kali Yug : *Dharma* for this era is partially *Rajas* but largely *Tamas*. By the way, this is the era humanity is currently living in.

In essence, from the earlier era of *Sat Yug* as humanity progresses to the currently living *Kali Yug*, there is a decline from *Satva* quality to *Rajas* that negatively impacts mankind's intellect towards non-righteousness (*Adharma*).

It is interesting to note that

- There is no contradiction in Nature but the above portrayal is only in human design. Our mother nature is ever abundant with its precious patience to succumb to mankind's selfish consumption. Off course, dominance over the nature is a faulty concept, harmonical existence with nature is the righteous way
- Today often the so-called "Scientific minds" (embraced with *Tamas* Intellect (Buddhi) believe that all existence has to be obliged to human logic.

Nonetheless, the above is a limited approach of a few imposed upon the whole of humanity and a reasonable individual should not get fooled by this. The whole existence cannot fit into these heads, rather their head fits into the whole.

Human capability in different Yuga (from Material to Spiritual Realm)

In Kaliyuga the intellect capacity of men is confined to the gross material nature of the world. He is completely servile to the boundaries imposed by power of the natural forces, though the attempts are continuous to win over the natural phenomenon. Men derive energy from matter and do so in increasingly efficient manner but only from the "naturally" designed type of matter. Any matter cannot be converted into energy other than "fuel" type of matter including nuclear energy fuel. Even though we know matter = energy by Einstein's equation $E=mC^2$ it is not a reversible equation - you cannot convert energy into mass. (We can call it "Material Age)

In Dvapara Yuga man gains comprehension and use of electrical and atomic constituents of matter and realizes the nature of every kind of matter as energy itself. (we can call it Energy Age)

It goes further in Treta Yuga man acquires knowledge and mastery of the structure below the atomic level that are fundamental forces of nature and can develop seemingly supernatural powers (*Siddhi*).

Finally, in Sata Yuga, he works at the level of Unified force from which every form of matter and energy has evolved. We can call it the age of spirituality.

Many Yogis have ascended to the levels of divine powers by attaining mastery over the forces of creation. Eight *Siddhis* have been defined as follow

1. *Anima*: Ability to shrink body as small as desired
2. *Mahima*: Ability to enlarge body as large as desired
3. *Laghima*: Ability to be as much lightweight as desired
4. *Garima*: Ability to make body as much heavyweight as desired
5. *Prapti*: Ability to obtain anything desired
6. *Vashitva*: Ability to bring anything under own control
7. *Prakmya*: Ability to satisfy all desires by force of own will
8. *Ishatva*: Ability to become lord over everything

1.4 Rise of Artificial Intelligence: Eclipse of Natural Intelligence

There is an interesting video published that sums up 7 Deep Reasons Why society's brightest minds are vanishing

- (https://youtu.be/lHp10QJ86zA?si=TXQvKHTP3QDMDR7d)

- The points discussed in this video are:
- Intelligent people leaving social circles - There is a hollow depth of social norms. Social interaction has become just a mere script. In conversations, people talk without listening and interactions just fill time but waste life.
- Why smart people feel isolated – People abandon their individuality for the comfort of the crowd. Again in team conversations, the crowd does not engage with your idea; rather it tries to correct your thinking.
- The psychology of high intelligence - People define themselves by their purchases, identity reduces to brands. The system creates insecurity, sells the solution to deliver temporary satisfaction and then creates new insecurity that repeats forever.
- Modern society vs intellectual minds – An intelligent mind sees the emptiness of digital connection which is connected but is alone. There are more ways to connect than ever before and yet we have never been more isolated. We fail to recognize the difference between connection and contact, between communication and conversation, between networking and relationship. Digital platforms promise community but deliver crowds. People mistake viral content for wisdom. Such shallow engagement transforms human interaction into mere data points.
- Social withdrawal patterns – A sharp mind needs time to process, to integrate, to understand, to connect dots that others cannot even see. But modern life is designed to prevent thinking with constant stimulation, endless distractions and perpetual motion.
- Intelligence and loneliness connection - Modern systems reward the wrong behaviors. Politics rewards manipulation over truth; business rewards exploitation over value creation; media rewards sensationalism over accuracy; education rewards conformity over creativity.

- Deep thinkers in a shallow world - Intelligent people are withdrawing themselves, thereby society is not only losing more than just their contributions; it loses its conscience. 'They are becoming invisible, silent, irrelevant and the world becomes a little bit dumb, a little bit less aware of its own problems.'

This is also appropriate for the root cause of unreason- why thinkers and intelligent people are withdrawing. Since intelligence and wisdom is not a prerequisite to make money and wise thinkers are withdrawing, we see idiots and mediocre running the world.

Punishing Righteous People

It is ironic that a bunch of idiots can form a group and punish the righteous. This can be illustrated by the well-known story about a group of kids playing on a railway track. A group of say 12 kids decided to play on a railway track. Two of the kids were smart to point out the fact that the track is operational and therefore dangerous. They suggested playing on another abandoned track that was a little away. But the kids would not agree, so these two decided to go to the other track and play there. And then comes the train. The controller saw at the last moment, and he had only a choice to divert the train to the nonoperation track at the interchange. So basically, it is an ethical or moral dilemma to take the decision. In real life, a similar situation occurs where a bigger group of idiots can create a situation to punish righteous individuals.

Crowd cannot think but Individuals can Think

This is an extension of the example mentioned above. Let us recall about Socrates who provided a metaphor in asking who would rather be controlling a distressed ship in the sea, opinion of the collective random passengers, or the experienced captain? He logically argued for the captain as the obvious choice and extended his distrust with the broken democracy. Yet another aspect of broken democracy is that it often becomes the government of a small group in disguise. It is pragmatic that an individual can at least attempt to think but a crowd cannot.

This is the aspect that is utilized by the *Paid Media to influence public opinion* by control over narrative, targeted advertising that can have an adverse potential for manipulation and impact on an individual's perception and reasoning. As an extension, here is a point to ponder *whether democracy itself can ever be wise at all!* This is also to be noted that radical problems require radical solutions. A broken (defective) democracy cannot solve radical problems.

Individuals' behavior and thinking is conditioned by the prevailing conditions in the environment/society

We cannot resist referring to an Indian folklore which was also noted in another book by one of the authors of this book previously. The story begins with a great king who had a prosperous, well-governed and happy kingdom. But the king had no offspring as successor and he relinquished all his responsibility to the ministers and started living in other activities like hunting and listening to music etc. One night the king had a strange dream that ferocious wolves and foxes are roaming all over his kingdom. Next morning he called his advisers to know what the meaning of such a dream could be. No one could explain. So the agitated king issued an emergency order and also announced a reward for anyone to come by who can explain.

Now here the story goes with a simple farmer sitting by a lake who suddenly encounters a big snake. The snake told the farmer that it could explain the king's dream if it could get half of the reward. The farmer agreed and the snake whispered the meaning into his ears. The farmer went to the courtyard and informed the king the meaning of his dream. The interpretation was that the kingdom is full of treachery and corruption and no-one is to be trusted like a den of foxes. The king was convinced, rewarded the farmer and took control of his kingdom. The farmer set off for home, but he succumbed to greed and kept all the reward for himself.

Time passed and then one night the king had another weird dream that a sword was hanging from the ceiling above his head. This time the king straightway ordered his minister to get the farmer for explanation and also announced double the reward. The farmer was horrified but he knew that only the snake could save him with an interpretation. So he went back to the snake, promising to compensate him for the previous and upcoming reward. The snake agreed and whispered the meaning into his ears. Accordingly, the farmer put forward to the king the meaning as an immediate caution for the king that his enemies are preparing for revenge and warfare. The king was convinced as obviously because of his taking control again, there is possible resurgence of conspirators. He rewarded the farmer and started preparing to identify the conspirators and take appropriate reform action for peaceful governance again. Now the farmer once again could not control his greed. Rather while meeting the snake, he attacked with a knife. The snake ran away.

And time passed. Then one night the king dreamed a third dream about a vast green field with a lot of white cows roaming and grazing in nice sunny weather. So, again the king ordered the farmer to be brought and tripled the reward. The farmer had no choice other than swallowing his misdeed. He went back to the lake, requested the snake for its forgiveness and again promised to compensate and cover up by sharing a reward. The snake again agreed and told him the meaning of the dream. The farmer accordingly explained the interpretation to the king was – the kingdom is now back with its peace and prosperity and the people are all happy. The king was relieved and rewarded the farmer. This time the farmer went back to the snake. With tears in his eyes, he said that he is very ashamed about how he mistreated the snake and put across all the rewards.

But the snake did not take any reward and rather said that the farmer did not do anything wrong. The snake explained that the farmer was governed by the environment. When the kingdom had corruption and treachery, the farmer acted cunning and treacherous. Next time when the kingdom got revenge with a sword, the farmer also attacked with the knife. And now as the kingdom is back with peace and prosperity, the farmer too is suddenly filled with kindness. But this is meaningless for the wise snake.

The striking morale of the story is - Individuals' behavior and thinking is conditioned by the prevailing conditions in the environment or society. One may recall that there is a *theory on Reciprocal Determinism* that was proposed by psychologist Albert Bandura suggesting that a person's behavior is influenced by and influences individual factors and the environment. The question to ask ourselves is – while there is no room for reason here, who is not affected by that fear of isolation?

While the prevailing conditions in society heavily influence individuals' behaviors and thinking, this does not mean it is immutable or that individuals have no agency to question or change these conditions. Yes, the environmental conditioning is a powerful force for most people; but that does not justify to get trapped in. It must not be the sole determinant of behavior highlights the value placed on individual freedom, moral accountability, and the potential for progress in human societies.

People Who Live More Near to Nature Tend to Do Less Sinful Acts

Yes, the concept of "sin" is subjective and varies across cultures and religions. The context here is that the proximity and kinship to our mother nature instils a desirable moral framework in an individual's mind to act reasonably and responsibly.

'People who feel more connected to the natural world are more likely to support reconciliation.

- Study by University of Manitoba

https://news.umanitoba.ca/people-who-feel-more-connected-to-the-natural-world-are-more-likely-to-support-reconciliation/

This also connects to Vedantic concept about the embodied self (*Atman*) is forced to act according to the body it is into. While the *Atman* (true self) is essentially pure and unchanging, the sense of its embodied form (*jeeva*), gets limited by the body's needs, desires, and experiences.

People living closer to nature tend to engage in fewer unreasonable acts due to increased moral concern, appreciation for nature's value and influence on pro-environmental behaviors. There is also an impact on happiness and well-being being connected to nature (Refer a study published by the National Institutes of Health (NIH)

- https://pmc.ncbi.nlm.nih.gov/articles/PMC7054437/).

Nature's creations possess inherent reason and purpose across logical, physical, and ideal levels. On the contrary it is only in the man-made or human creations, there is this very lack of reason as such. Human creations are unnatural, temporary, lacks systematic unity and often driven by short-term, selfish, or artificial goals.

Are We More Afraid to Reason Now?

The answer to this question may simply boil down to not feeling safe to act on something even after thinking about it. The fear is for potential consequences. We're often afraid of the backlash, punishment, or negative outcomes that may follow. One may feel singled out that prohibits a reasonable act. We still have examples of individuals who stood against all perils to act on reason.

Edward Joseph Snowden, an American former NSA intelligence contractor and whistleblower leaked classified documents revealing the existence of global surveillance programs.

Chelsea Manning, while working as an intelligence analyst for the U.S. Army (in 2010), released the largest set of classified documents in U.S. history.

However, in general the fear is about self-delusion, the fear of being labelled as an outcast. We cry about democracy. But even in democracy, there is an uproar on debates that political rights and civil liberties around the world deteriorated to their lowest point in the last decade. The so-called democracy is characterized by a handful of emboldened autocrats severely affecting the global struggle for human freedom. There is *'unreasonable activism' within the judiciary* where judicial decisions appear to be driven by personal preferences or political agendas rather than the strict application of law. There is also increased *media activism* that gives disadvantaged groups the ability to have their own voices heard and organize in bigger groups allowing for more autonomized activism to enact social change.

That is why you experience unreason at a far higher level in democracies all around the world because all democracies are the government of the crowd. The leader represents the crowd and once again, the crowd cannot be wise.

Do Our Reasoning get Impacted by Poor and Blind Belief?

The important aspect is – our poor and blind belief may play an influencing factor to demarcate between reasonable or unreasonable thinking and subsequent action. In simpler terms, if one buys a stock on face value without basic information or analysis, then that could be an unreasonable act. However, what we are pointing out is something beyond one's general bias of pre-conceived notion. In life, there are actions which are driven by belief towards the sense of loyalty or commitment a person shows towards his promise, oath, or an organization. There is no choice between believing in reasonable things versus belief in unreasonable things. This is all about whether you believe something, or do not believe that. By default, this transcends into something which is often a blind belief.

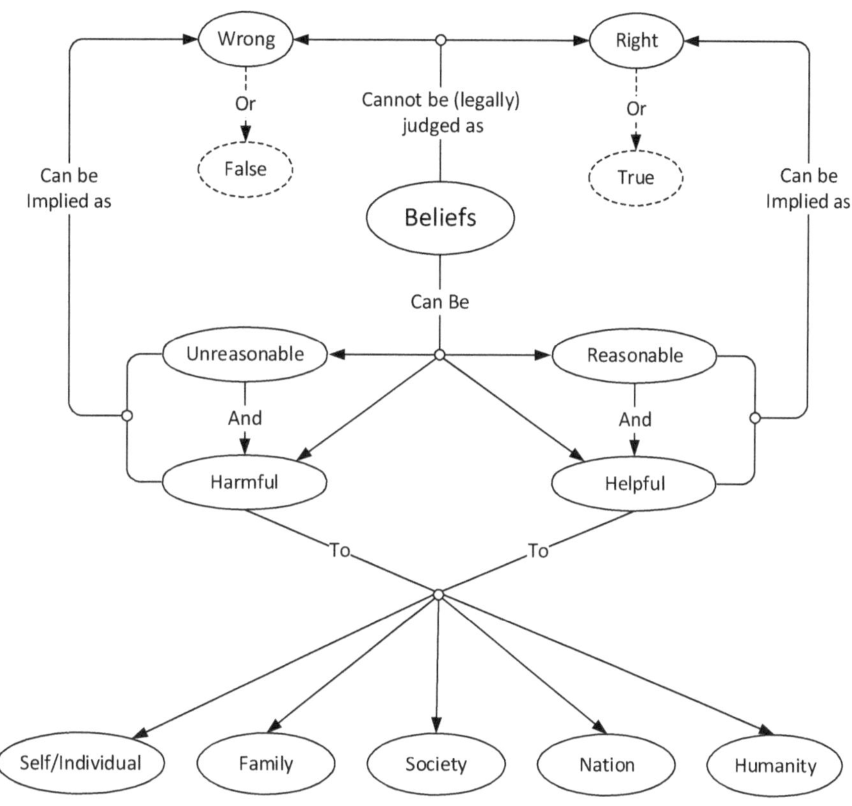

Figure 14: Can belief be judged?

Is there an Accelerated Rise of Unreason?

There is an accelerated rise of unreason in modern society, fueled by numerous factors some of which are described above. There is one common factor cutting across all of those factors is the explosion of data and technology that we are experiencing in modern day. The digital age, with its technologies like the internet, smartphones, and social media, has created a surge in data generation that dwarfs anything in the past. Recent analysis indicate that approximately 90% of the world's data has been generated within the past two years (https://www.information-age.com/data-forecast-grow-10-fold-2025-5199/). The data explosion, or the rapid increase in the amount of data generated and stored, are already contributing to a sense of information overload and anxiety. The more the data, the more the vested opportunity of data manipulation potentially leading to increased unreasonable behavior.

If we talk about technological advancement, we also have to account for the very fact that weapons are generally more advanced and capable of inflicting greater lethality and damage compared to the past. We now have autonomous weapon systems, such as swarms of drones or autonomous vehicles equipped with facial recognition for targeting humans. Also, we have hypersonic weapons, which can travel at speeds many times faster than sound, which can be configured as guided ballistic missiles, tremendously lethal due to their speed and maneuverability. Such technological advancement in weapons can kill more and kill quicker.

In a comparable way, this has been impacting 'Unreason' which is accelerated. More and more data means to process more and more facts and thus more and more effort of thinking and analyzing. So instead of getting overwhelmed person is choosing to take shortcuts at the cost of adding unreason. It is more in abundance and much quicker. We will be discussing this aspect more in later chapters.

1.5 So What Minimum Can We Do?

The rise of unreason eventually creates a problem which in turn is the root cause of a trouble or undesirable deviation from the standard and normal state of any system. We explained the 'law of conservation of problem' in our book 'Illustrated Vedant' that states that – "A real problem cannot be solved. It can only be transformed into another problem by changing its attribute or transformed into a predicament while retaining the attributes." In other words, people are not ready to resolve any problem.

That does not mean there is no oasis in the desert. There are good people and there is good reasoning despite all the problems as humanity possesses a tremendous capacity to survive and sustain hope. While people are certainly affected by the things they experience in their environment, they also have the power to exert a change on their situation and circumstances through their own choices and behaviors. Yes, 'Thinking is a high value work.' A thoughtful, analytical, and strategic thinking is crucial for achieving goals and contributing effectively to work or any endeavor.

"Individuals are neither powerless objects controlled by environmental forces nor entirely free agents who can do whatever they choose."

— Albert Bandura, psychologist

It is up to an individual to "earn" wisdom and contribute to society rather than moving in "*Bhed Chaal*" i.e., just sheep walking or running with the crowd. It is important to lean into what our gut and irritation is telling us and face up the fears we dread to act if we value taking action in life. Yes, the truth is - there is a lot of unreason in the world connecting individuals and nations to climate change, poverty, divisive politics, racism, consumerism, mental health struggles, access to health care, natural disasters, malnutrition, gun violence, and more. But for each of this unreason, it is the same ordinary individual that always steps up to do something, to create change, to make a difference.

"The reasonable man adapts himself to the world: the unreasonable one persists in trying to adapt the world to himself. Therefore, all progress depends on the unreasonable man."

-George Bernard Shaw

The kick start is to begin with just one which is yourself. You can control yourself as an individual so that the world is good for you. You yourself have to drive to introspect and not get influenced by external factors. You can train your mind to be under your own control. You must not fall into the trap of your mind getting under control by others or outside influences and be happy with your reasoning.

So, the minimum that we can do is to develop 'Wisdom' and use 'Wisdom' *and to do that-*

- We must nurture *vivek*
- Refrain from 'Not thinking'
- Develop intellect into wisdom

- Use wisdom for anything that you think. And then practice 'Speaking and doing.'

3 Knowledge is learned while wisdom is earned

At the outset, let us explore how a dictionary defines the meaning of wisdom in several ways.

- the quality of having experience, knowledge, and good judgment; the quality of being wise: *listen to his words of wisdom.*
- the soundness of an action or decision with regard to the application of experience, knowledge, and good judgment: *some questioned the wisdom of building the dam so close to an active volcano.*
- the body of knowledge and principles that develops within a specified society or period: *the traditional farming wisdom of India.*

In our view the meaning is much deeper because of the spiritual angle. In the biblical aspect wisdom is a didactic book included in the Roman Catholic canon of the Old Testament and corresponding to the Wisdom of Solomon in the Protestant Apocrypha. From Vedantic point of view it is nearer to the power of knowing, especially knowing the truth, the absolute reality. We take the help of a diagram to explain the wisdom and associated vocabulary.

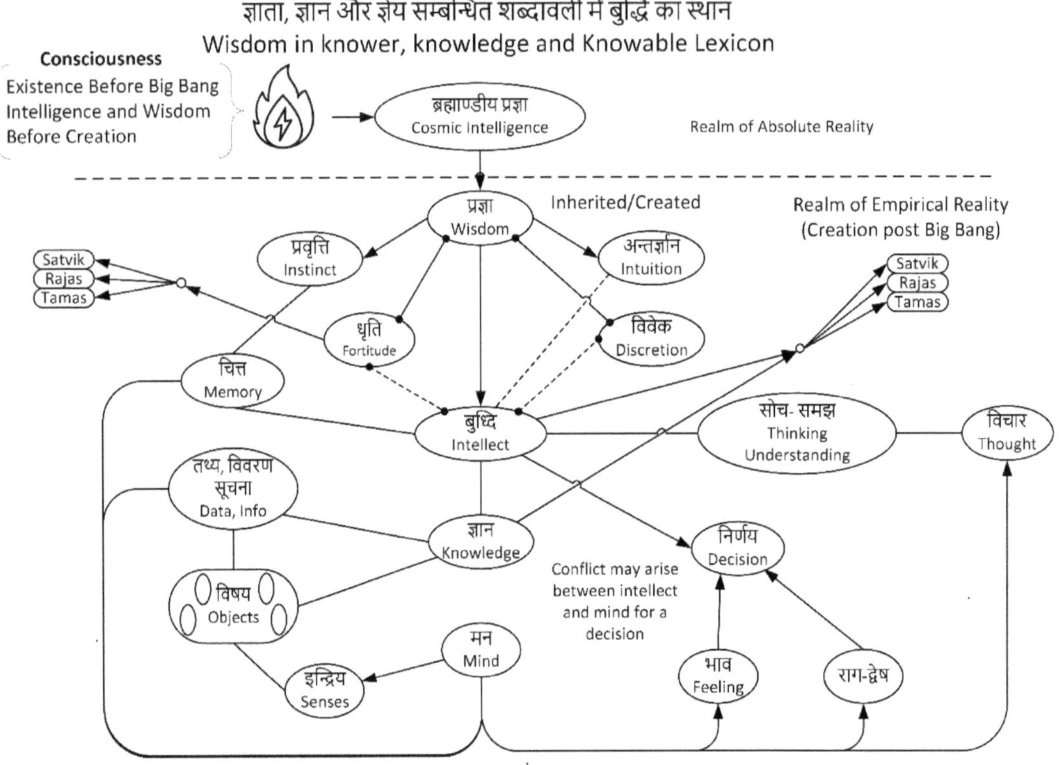

Figure 15: Wisdom in knowledge and knower lexicon

3.1 Quest for Knower, Knowable and Knowledge

To explore a true meaning of wisdom, it is important to evaluate the quest for knower, knowable and knowledge as depicted in the illustration. We would like to explain the two separate segments separated by dotted lines in the diagram above i.e., the Realm of Absolute Reality and the Realm of Empirical Reality.

Realm of Absolute Reality

Our universe sprang into existence about 13.8 billion years ago. Before that the so-called Time, Space, Material and Energy were all condensed into a Singularity that came into creation or existent form with the Big Bang explosion. The iron in our blood, the calcium in our bones, the oxygen we breathe - all were born or created in this epic cosmic process and sustained thereafter as we live today. The point to note here is that – before our universe came into existence, every aspect of this fundamental super intelligence was condensed into a Singularity. With the Big Bang, this got manifested or created in our empirical world.

This supreme wisdom that was condensed in the Singularity before the creation of universe is what we term as "Cosmic Intelligence" (*Brahmandiaya Prajna*) That is the realm of absolute reality where the forever existent Cosmic Intelligence was there albeit in unmanifested form before any creation triggered by Big Bang. The Big Bang invites contemplation just not on the origins of the universe but also on the role of Consciousness. That stimulates philosophical inquiry into the complexities of existence. We will be discussing further about 'Consciousness' after walking through the next segment i.e., the realm of empirical reality.

Wisdom existed before creation.........Using that wisdom universe was created......and the same wisdom is embedded in the creation itself

Realm of Empirical Reality

Let us now expand our discussion to the segment below the dotted line i.e., to the realm of Empirical Reality.

The concept of Time and Space or Matter and Energy – all came into its creation or manifested form after the Big Bang. All or a set of the logic of creation and sustenance from the supreme 'Cosmic Intelligence' got embedded in this empirical world that we live today in our nature, in its all living and non-living creatures. Living beings possess intellect to varying degrees while non-living beings do not. It is astonishing to realize the "super wisdom" that we perceive in our mother nature that maintains and sustains its dynamic ecological equilibrium or in the human brain cells that possess the DNA history of genomic evolution. This leads to our explanation of the very usage of the term Prajna (Wisdom).

3.1.1 *Prajna* (Wisdom) and its Functions

As articulated above, this very aspect of the intelligence post Big Bang that was inherited and embedded in the entire creation of the empirical world is what we term in our parlance as *Prajna* (Wisdom). *Prajna* possesses four important associated qualities : Instinct, Intuition, Discretion and Fortitude. In this context the solid and dotted lines in the above illustration represent direct and indirect cause or effect of the constituent elements.

Instinct (*Pravritti*) - In simple terms, this a natural tendency of any human being to react and respond to a situation. This is how a newborn apparently with no worldly knowledge so to say, responds to being fed milk by his/her mother. As we live along, this instinct develops towards worldly matters like name, fame and wealth that enriches our attachment to "I and mine.

- Intuition (*Antarjnyana*) - That refers to inward or secret knowledge that inculcates Intuition. This is a striking feature of instinctive knowing (without the use of rational processes)
- Discretion (*Viveka*) – This signifies the demarcation between what is wrong versus what is right.
- Fortitude (*Dhriti*) – Along with Discretion (*Viveka*) it is also important to stand firm and not vacillate in decision making prowess and this is where Resolute (Dhriti) plays its significance.

It is important to reiterate that whenever we talk about *Prajna* (Wisdom) all four of these the significant characteristics are attached by default namely Instinct, Intuition, Discretion and Fortitude. By the way, the depiction of the diagram should not necessarily portray any ordering sequence of Wisdom to Intellect to Knowledge as such and that we would explain now further starting with Knowledge first.

Knowledge (*Gnyan*) and the Role of Mind

As we coin the word 'knowledge,' quite naturally there is someone (ज्ञाता or the knower) who is trying to acquire the various specific areas of knowledge (*Gnyan*). These areas of knowledge are based on specific data and information (*Tathya, Bibaran* or *Suchana*) on specific objects of knowledge.

Let us view this from the angle of Mind (*Mana*) of the knower. The Mind acquires the data and information about objects of knowledge areas through sense organs (Indriya) like reading and comprehending by utilization of eyes, ears, touch etc. In this context it is to be understood that there are obviously some objective areas of knowledge which are not necessarily acquired by physical senses (*Indriya*) but may be by additional evaluations. For example, we may not look at the Sun directly because they contain harmful ultraviolet (UV) and infrared (IR) rays. The safe way to is through specifically designed solar filters, using solar eclipse glasses for direct viewing and solar filters for telescopes and binoculars. Another example is about dogs that detect sounds with frequencies ranging from about 40 Hz to 60,000 Hz (60 kHz); nearly three times higher than the highest frequency humans can hear. This is where the information is analyzed through high frequency noise detectors like Sound Level Meters, Sound Level Meters, Sound Level Meters, Sound Level Meters etc. Our Mind (*Mana*) will still consider such data and information to be acceptable even though these are not acquired by direct physical Sense (*Indriya*) but logically through extended Sense with facilitation of scientific instruments.

The specific virtue of Mind is that – it is affected by its own emotions or feelings (*Bhav*) and its strong likes and dislikes. These are more profound with the nature of mind for its compulsive Affinity (*Raaga*) for something that the mind desires very much and also the reverse i.e., the compulsive Aversion (*Dvesha*) of something that the mind does not approve at all and rejects by default. This inherent mind behavior significantly impacts its way of decision making (*Nirnay*). In turn this fundamental process of acquiring knowledge affects the Intellect that we would discuss now.

Intellect (*Buddhi*) and its Challenges that deviates itself from *Prajna* (Wisdom)

Such acquisition of knowledge is utilized by Intellect (*Buddhi*) to derive Decision (*Nirnay*). We have already described that such decision-making prowess of Intellect gets impacted by the characteristic of Mind which has inherent Feeling and also strong affinity or aversion. In a similar way, this also impacts the Thinking and Understanding (*Soch, Samajh*) for any Thought (*Vichaar*) that Intellect encounters.

It is interesting to decipher the effect of the four fundamental characteristics on Intellect (*Buddhi*) as well which are Instinct, Intuition, Discretion and Fortitude.

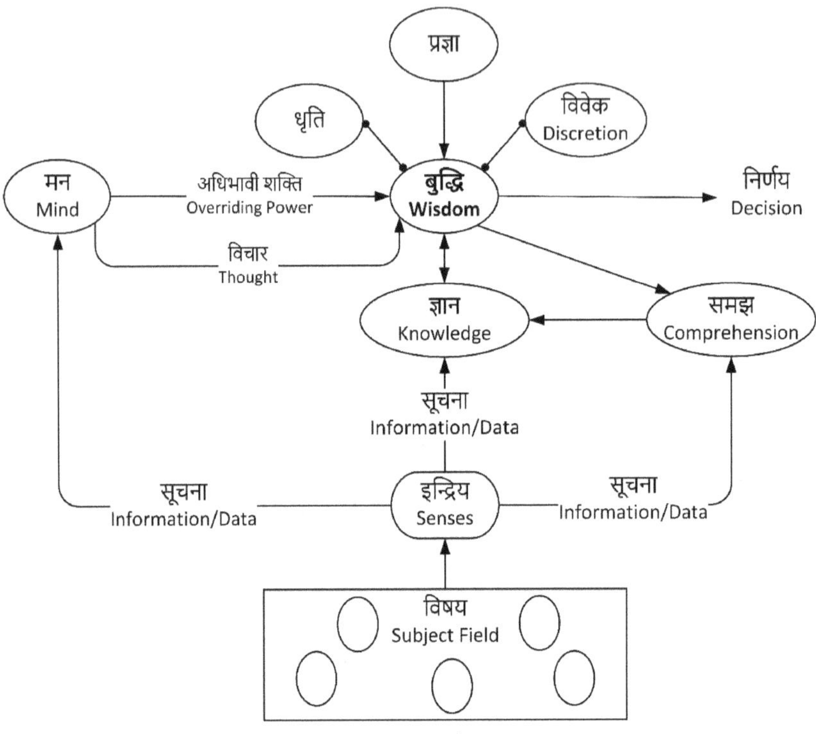

Figure 16: Gap between Prajna and Wisdom

How The Role Play of Intuition impacts Intellect? The Intuition (Pravritti) is somewhat natural with Intellect preserved in Memory (Chit). Now from a human consideration it may sound that the power of memory is limited or up to an extent. In our daily habits we utilize the phone book in our palmtop which in this context can be considered as an additional storehouse of memory as our inherent Memory (Chit) can utilize that as appropriate.

- How The Role Play of Intuition, Discretion and Fortitude Impact Intellect? : Of course, all these three parameters affect Intellect to derive decisions (*Nirnay*). Along with just Intuition (*Antarjnyana*) the level of intellect is definitively affected by the influencing factors like Discretion (*Viveka*) and Fortitude (*Dhriti*) to not only distinguish between the evil versus good but also to stay firm and accomplished in that decision making. Here lies the catch. While these are mandatory factors in Wisdom (*Prajna*), that precondition does not apply for Intellect (*Buddhi*). That is why you may specifically notice that the connection lines are dotted from Intuition, Discretion and Fortitude towards Intellect. This means that Intellect may operate in absence of either or all of such crucial important influence factors. Yes, this is tricky indeed!

- What is The Challenge of Intellect (*Buddhi*) in Decision making in absence of Intuition, Discretion and Fortitude? As we see, though ideally speaking it is expected that these influencing factors will be utilized by Buddhi for proper decision making, but there is no guarantee of that. This is where Intellect (*Buddhi*) faces a serious challenge. What happens if there is an absence of discretion? This means that the fundamental ethical conduct will be missing. Consequently, this will no longer allow Buddhi (Intellect) alone to distinguish between righteous and unrighteous actions. Now, even if the discretion is working within acceptable limits, it is to be ensured to stay firm and steady on a correct decision that is already taken and legitimately sustain that. If that Fortitude is absent, then once again Intellect will fall short of the resolution of a correct decision to fortify for. Either way, the challenge gets compounded at various phases.
- What is The Challenge of Intellect (*Buddhi*) due to conflict with Mind? : On top of that, as articulated before, the mind plays a different ball game influencing the decision making by a completely unique path through its natural emotions and strong affinity and aversions. Such conflict is very natural as we all are humane. Hence the rise of conflict between the bias of mind and intellect for decision making is very obvious.

The Influencing *Gunas* that demarcates Intellect from Wisdom (*Prajna*)

Let us consider the dotted line at the top of half of the diagram again that differentiates the realms of absolute and empirical reality. This time let us reckon that you are looking through a glass window (the dotted line) eyeing downwards to the bottom half of the diagram i.e., looking towards the realm of empirical reality. There are some interesting observations accordingly.

How Intellect is Affected by a Generic Loss due to Distortion and Attenuation? : As you look through the glass window, your view will be affected by the dirt or transparency of the glass window. This causes either a distortion and attenuation effect or both similar to a transmission signal. In a similar way Intellect (*Buddhi*) in general loses some degree of Discretion (Viveka) and Fortitude (*Dhriti*) with this decreased or distorted effect. As we embarked on the challenge of Intellect before, there is no precondition that Intellect (*Buddhi*) must operate with either of Intuition, Discretion and Fortitude which are mandatory for Wisdom (Prajna). Now here is another somewhat downsized impact on Intellect due to distortion and attenuation.

What is the Challenge due to the influence of *Gunas* (Attributes) on intellect and Knowledge? The level of tint of the glass window of reference can be varied like transparent, opaque or in-between. In accordance the object viewed could look absolutely clear, completely black or semi-transparent, something similar to our RGB color code where White, Black and all in between colors can be created with three primary codes. Let us transpose this RGB color code idea to Vedanta as it describes the three gunas or three qualities that are always present in all things (*Padarth* or matter) and beings (*Jeeva*) in the world. They are *Sataguna, Rajoguna* and *Tamoguna.*

The utilization of Fortitude (*Dhriti*) on Intellect may not be considered at their face value to be ideally solid all the time. Rather, the demarcation of *Dhriti* is of three types:

- *Satvik Dhriti* (Refer as Clear as color code White) - This represents positivity that upholds the mind to stay firm on the decision and sustains all the activities of the senses.
- *Tamas or Tamasik Dhriti* (Refer as Opaque as color code Black) - This refers to negative perseverance by which a person completely falters on decision. In our empirical world this also refers to a person who does not give up vanity, anxiety or sorrow.
- *Rajas or Rajasik Dhriti* (Refer as all in between color codes) – In this band, the power to stay firm can be varied with various degrees. In our empirical

world, this is a kind of determination that one keeps in the hope for some reward or material gains.

Similarly, there is a demarcation of Intellect (*Buddhi*) and (*Gnyan*) Knowledge as well for three types:

- *Satvik* Intellect (*Buddhi*) and Satvik Knowledge (*Gnyan*) - Pure intellect and pure knowledge
- *Tamasik* Intellect (*Buddhi*) and *Tamasik* Knowledge (*Gnyan*) - Highly impure Intellect and knowledge
- *Rajasik* Intellect (*Buddhi*) and *Rajasik* Knowledge (*Gnyan*) - Impure intellect or Intellect driven by worldly desires and impure knowledge

Here below are predominant traits that are exhibited by modern-day individuals:

***Buddhi* (Intellect)**	**Key characteristics**	**Contextual example**
Satvik Intellect (*Buddhi*)	• Balanced • Clear-headed • Empathetic • Healthy lifestyle • Purpose-driven	• A dedicated, selfless volunteer in a non-profit organization • A wise teacher or a true spiritual leader
Rajasik Intellect (*Buddhi*)	• Workaholic • Restless in future-focus • Solely desires for validation • Self-centered • Attached to outcomes only	• A power-driven politician who is primarily motivated by a desire to dominate and hold authority.
Tamasik Intellect (*Buddhi*)	• Stagnant & lethargic • Indulgent & addicted • Cynical to be harmful • Self-destructive • Apathetic in self-improvement	• A malicious and destructive leader • An individual with addiction or radicalized view • A cynical and apathetic person

	• Emotionally confused and in a state of delusion	

It is sometimes attractive and more grasping to align the above aspects to leadership qualities as in general we tend to shout out about leaders and their behaviors be it in the corporate, political or societal world. The fundamental motivation and thereby the ethical compass is the most important differentiating factor.

- ***A satvik leader is guided by wisdom and selfless service***
- ***A rajasik leader is driven by ambition and personal gain (me. myself and that's all!)***
- ***A tamasik leader is motivated by apathy, delusion, or destructive tendencies.***

Key Attribute	Tamasik leader	Rajasik leader	Satvik leader
Foremost motivation	Only self-interest, greed, refusal to adapt, in apathy and negativity	Ambition, power, desire for personal gain and rewards.	Serving the common good and achieving a higher purpose, without self-interest or attachment to personal reward.
Ethical perspective	Unethical, deceitful, and malicious	Will bend rules of ethics for benefiting own success.	Highly ethical and transparent
Impact on followers	Generates a toxic environment marked by fear, chaos, and confusion	On paper drives performance through competition and passion, but mostly causes stress, burnout, and rivalry among followers.	Creates an environment of trust and empowerment inspiring followers to become better human being.

In nutshell, it is the intent of a leader that makes him *Tamas, Rajas* or *Satvik*. *Tamas* intent is only or primarily my benefit, *Rajas* intent is consideration of others' benefit without compromising self-benefit and *Satvik* intent is only others benefit matters.

Hence only a combination of *Satvik Buddhi* and *Satvik Dhriti* can be interpreted as an ideal combination with *Satvik Gnyan*. Such a person is a *Satvik* Doer (*Karta*). However, mostly, In the empirical world that we live in, people are a mix of *Tamasik* and *Rajasik* combination with a faltering *Dhriti*, and they mostly get driven towards worldly desires (*Tamasik Buddhi*). This delusion adversely impacts Intellect (*Buddhi*) further in its decision making.

Chintan-Manan and Thinking

In this context of 'thinking' per say, it is important to understand the concept of thinking that is meaningful i.e., the area of *Chintan- Manan*. In Vedanta, *Chintan* and *Manan* are two of the three key steps in the spiritual path to self-realization or attaining *moksha*. These stages, which follow *shravana* (listening), are processes of deep reflection and contemplation on the profound teachings of the scriptures.

- *Chintan* is a supreme mental process by which a person arrives at the solution of a problem. Even though a person is constantly thinking about something or other, but the process of *Chintan* is not evoked till some kind of intellectual or practical problem is not presented.
- Other than humanity, other sentients do not have this capability or have very little of this capability
- Most of the time when we are not engaged in any work, many thoughts evolve in our mind. These thoughts just evolve and dissolve. There is no aim behind it. We cannot consider these as thinking as it does not have any purpose and does not lead to solution of any problem.
- In the *Chintan* process the flow of thought is in a specific direction. *Chintan* has the following association

- ✓ Aiming towards a specific aim , usually an intellectual or practical problem
- ✓ Initiation of an attempt to solve some problem or finding answer to a question
- ✓ Recall of past experience
- ✓ Flow of thoughts in a specific direction
- ✓ Trial and Error process to find the solution/answer
- ✓ Use of past experience in new situation
- ✓ Use of "inner Speech"

- *Manan* is an integral part of the *Chintan* and refers to use of logic and inference during *Chintan*

In simple words a mere 'thought' can be out of random thinking (without specific aim or purpose). Here lies the significance of *chintan-manan* in the pursuit of wisdom.

The Ultimate Source for Cosmic Intelligence and *Prajna* (Wisdom)

The harmony of natural law reveals an Intelligence of such superiority that, compared with it, all the systematic thinking and acting of human beings is an utterly insignificant reflection."

— Albert Einstein

At the outset let us first salute the astonishing level of super intelligence that we may perceive in our mother nature with some amazing examples.

What is that intelligent property of water that sustains marine life? Water exhibits a form of intelligence that surpasses that of artificially intelligent devices. Water exhibits the unique property of contracting upon cooling only until 4 degrees C after which it starts expanding and its density decreases and volume increases. Once you get below water's freezing point (32°F/0°C), the density of water decreases because ice is less dense than water. How beautiful it is to acknowledge such a unique and intelligent property of water by which the entire marine life continues on a frozen lake!

What is that coincidental intelligence that causes total solar eclipse? The Sun's diameter is about 1,000,000 miles, and its distance from Earth is about 100,000,000 miles. Again, the moon's diameter is a bit less than 2,300 miles, and its distance from Earth is a bit more than 230,000 miles. What a coincidental relationship! From our perspective on Earth, in either case, the size/distance ratio is similar (1 to 100). In an astoundingly amazing alignment of the universe, both the moon and Sun are about 100 times farther from Earth than the sizes of their respective diameters. This is how the moon blocks out, or "eclipse," anything behind it that has the same 1-to-100 size/distance ratio. Is it just a "cosmic coincidence" that makes solar eclipses possible?

Another example is our Earth, which is believed to be the only planet in the universe known to have life. There are many reasons why this might be the case like distance from the sun (right distance from the sun to receive optimal heat), atmosphere (that atmosphere insulates the planet and contains oxygen), magnetic field (protects it from harmful solar radiation), water (enough for life to survive), chemical ingredients (right ingredients including water and carbon), gravity etc. It is again so amazing to appreciate the super intelligent laws of nature that made this amazing balance on our mother earth to create and sustain life!

There is no comparison to such a superior level of intelligence. It is astonishing with its resilient beauty in every aspect and stage of all natural systems that have the inherent super-ability to evolve and adapt to change and outside influences. There is indeed a limitation for any language or logic to describe how every "Natural Law" that sustains the Universe is so intelligently designed! The infinite intelligence! Could we grasp the idea of "infinite"? It is not just a mathematical symbol to interpret some observation in a mathematical model but a reality of the real world.

As we deliberated, the trigger of the Big Bang caused the condensed Cosmic Intelligence (*Brahmandiya Prajna*) to manifest by which the profound Wisdom (Prajna) got embedded in the empirical world in its entire creations. This is like a cosmic vibration with its underlying intelligence that guides, organizes, and governs the harmonious functioning of the entire universe. This cosmic intelligence exists within all creation, within every cell of our body, and in every thought and emotion of our mind.

Now, what is the source of this Cosmic Intelligence? In simpler terms, the fundamental of this Cosmic Intelligence is the information or knowledge and the processing of that knowledge. However, where does that illuminating power of knowledge come from that can create such a cosmic intelligent vibration by which the entire universe can be created in its manifested form? Not only in Vedanta, we also find the reference in the Bible for such wisdom before the creation of the universe.

Proverbs 8:22-31 NCV - "I, *wisdom, was with the LORD when he began his work, long before he made anything else. I was created in the very beginning, even before the world began. I was born before there were oceans, or springs overflowing with water, before the hills were there, before the mountains were put in place.*"

From a Vedantic perspective, consciousness is the ultimate source that illuminates the power of every intelligence, every knowledge. By the way, the cosmic intelligent vibration is also referenced by the sound of *Om* (*Aum*), in the realm of Absolute Reality, or Brahman. It is like - *Om* is a sound and the entire universe is its vibration. It is the vibration of the primordial sound associated with the creation of the universe. The cosmic Intelligence can be thought of as a subset of consciousness as consciousness is much more than just the fundamental knowledge, intellect and wisdom as such. This is the essential nature of Brahman, or the ultimate reality and is described as Existence Consciousness Bliss (*Sat Chit Ananda*). From a Vedantic perspective, Consciousness is represented as the purest form where the knower (ज्ञाता) becomes one with the known, and the seer merges with the sight.

Knowledge is learned while wisdom is earned

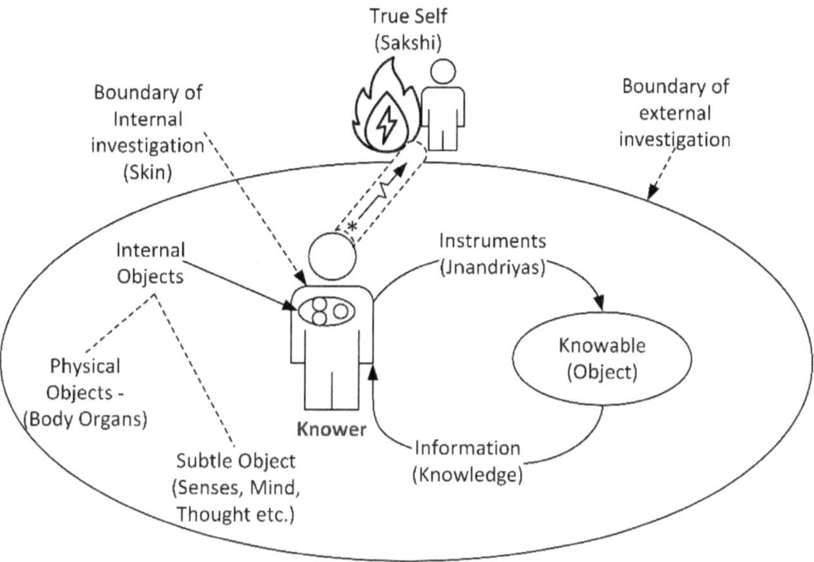

* Merging of Knower, Knowledge and Object by successful internal investigation

Figure 17: Merging of knower, known and knowledge

In this context, the Bhagavad Gita emphasizes the importance of a resolute and single-pointed intellect, known as *Vyavasayatmika Buddhi*, for success in any endeavor, particularly on the path of self-realization or spiritual progress.

व्यवसायात्मिका बुद्धिरेकेह कुरुनन्दन । बहुशाखा ह्यनन्ताश्च बुद्धयोऽव्यवसायिनाम् ॥ Bhagwad Gita 2:41

Translation: "Those who are on this path are resolute in purpose, and their aim is one. O beloved child of the Kurus, the intelligence of those who are irresolute is many-branched."

Vyavasayatmika Buddhi is "*Nischyatmika*" *Buddhi* because it makes "*Nischya*" or unshaken determination with respect to a purpose. It is important to note the term *Vyavasayatmika Buddhi* signifies a firm and unwavering intellect, characterized by a single, clearly defined goal or purpose.

In what Context Wisdom, Knowledge and Intellect used interchangeably?

Bible Ecclesiastes 7:12 ESV – "*For the protection of wisdom is like the protection of money, and the advantage of knowledge is that wisdom preserves the life of him who has it.*"

In many ancient scriptures the words like knowledge and wisdom have been used with similar interpretations. Well, that does not mean that there was something utterly wrong; rather such usage needs to be evaluated on the basis of the very context where they were applied. Again, in various other books that our esteemed readers may come across, it is but natural that you will find the terms like 'Wisdom,' 'Intellect' and 'Knowledge' might have been interchangeably used in various contexts. Here context is the key. Here we would like to provide some examples of some interchangeable usages that you may come across.

Let us explain this illustration starting with the circle in the middle. As we deliberated, Consciousness encompasses all aspects of wisdom, intelligence and intellect. This knower, knowledge and knowable – all collapse and merge into this purest form. An interesting reference is a phrase "It from Bit" coined by John Wheeler, the great physicist of 20th century. According to him, the material universe (It') that we experience, actually comes from 'bit' (binary unit of information as per computer terminology). As articulated before, consciousness is beyond the current realm of scientific and other philosophical postulations. The universe is an appearance in Brahman, pure consciousness. *Nama* (Name), *Rupa* (Form), and *Vyavahara* (Use) are three aspects of imposition upon reality (together referred to as *Maya*) of the universe which is consciousness itself. Now what is this manifest form being referenced here? It is the *Chit* i.e., pure consciousness. Courtesy Swami Sarvapriyananda, Vedanta Society of New York, the coining of the phrase is appropriately extended as an interpretation of Consciousness as – "It from Bit from *Chit*."

Now let us explore some interchangeable terms as depicted in the illustration.

Interchangable use of words in context

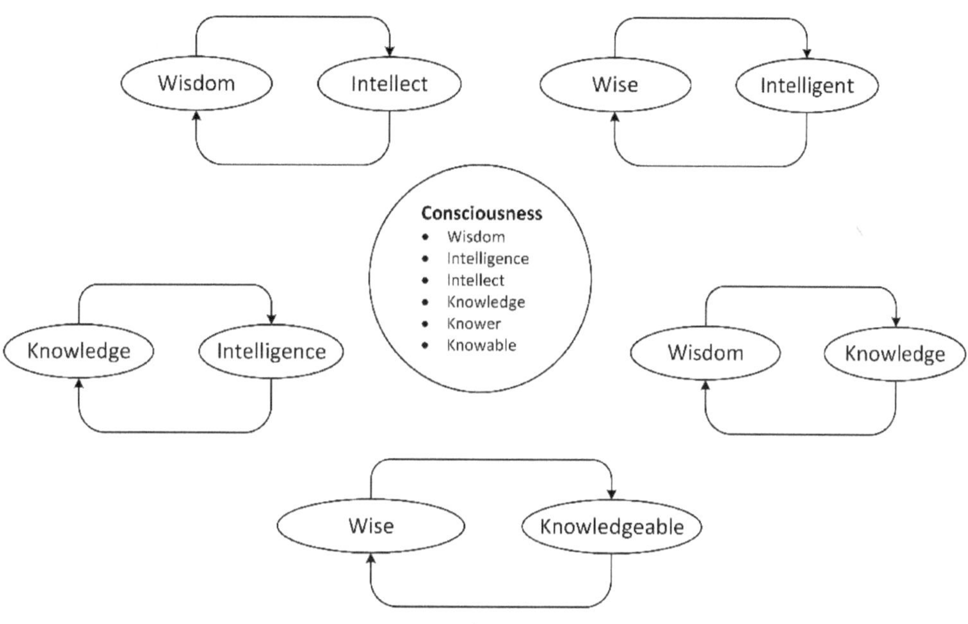

Figure 18: Meaning of wisdom in context

Contextual Usage of 'Wisdom' interchangeable with 'Knowledge'

In ancient times, not everyone was lucky to have privilege and access to education unlike today's world. So, in those times, by the virtue of someone having education and knowledge, it was assumed by default that he is a wise person. Hence it is quite commonplace in ancient scriptures to find references where the wording like knowledge and wisdom have been used interchangeably,

However, may we table the same situation in modern days? Not at all; mostly education is more accessible to common all in modern civilized world with progress of science and technology. One does not need to have any special privilege to have access to knowledge. But that does not mean that knowledge and wisdom can be used as synonyms now. That is the point that we would like to draw attention to. In today's world, there is a fundamental difference in the true meaning of 'wisdom' vis-à-vis 'knowledge' as such.

Contextual Usage of 'Wisdom' interchangeable with 'Intelligence'

Let us take the example of the Central Intelligence Agency (CIA which is a civilian foreign intelligence service of the USA that collects and analyzes specific data and information from around the world. This data and information are utilized for intelligent service for an intended task towards advancing national security. Similarly, Business Intelligence Consulting firms provide analysis of industry intelligence databases that is utilized for say marketing campaign for a specific product or services. These are classic references where you would find the term 'wisdom' may be conveniently used as an interpretation of 'intelligence.'

Contextual Usage of 'Wisdom' interchangeable with 'Intellect'

In the Manhattan project spearheaded by Oppenheimer, it is alleged that nuclear secrets were compromised to the Russians. Irrespective of whether you believe this conspiracy or not, a nuclear scientist may be immensely knowledgeable but his actions could be despicable far from being wise. Knowledge is the base foundation to develop *Buddhi* or Intellect. In this example of the faltered scientist, at the minimum the discretion (*Viveka*) to distinguish between right and wrong is missed out which is otherwise a mandatory precondition for wisdom (*Prajna*).

If we refer back to our discussion on looking through the glass window – it's only when a person is 100% *Satvik*, he/she can be so intellectually excellent as to be wise as well. This a practice and journey to spiritual liberation that facilitates one to see through the illusory nature of life and the world. However, that is not common at all. Hence the point to ponder is - one may have garnered excellent knowledge to exercise intellect, but is he/she 'wise' by default?

From fundamental Knowledge to *Prajna* - the Profound Source of Wisdom

Knowledge has a progressive path of enhancement. In other words, if you desire you can gain knowledge and the level of knowledge increases. This in turn may facilitate intellect (*Buddhi*) to better decision making. Yet Intellect is constantly facing the conflict with mind with its emotions, affinity and aversions that may over-ride making intelligent decisions. On top of that, if the discretion (*Viveka*) and resolute (*Dhriti*) gets missed out, then there is a fundamental issue about the *nirnay* (decision) that intellect erroneously makes.

On the contrary, wisdom cannot be gained by passively accepting what we read or by believing what another person tells us. Wisdom requires a higher level of awareness and a willingness to ask ourselves—and experience firsthand—what is true for each of us. In Vedanta we find the reference word *Prajna* which is actually at a higher level than conventional wisdom. It is better to be acknowledged as the source of wisdom. Apart from the power of discretion (*Viveka*) and resolute (*Dhriti*), this also encompasses instinct (*Pravritti*) and intuition (*Antarjnyana*). it is important to decipher - knowledge can be learnt and applied by intellect to a feasible extent; but wisdom can only be earned.

Knowledge is Learned while wisdom is Earned

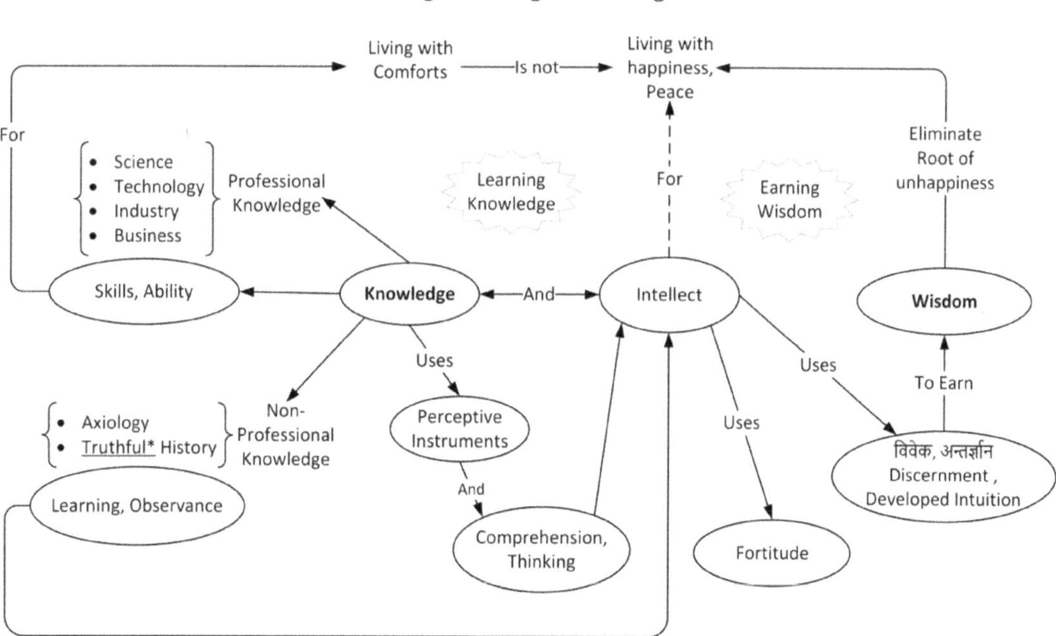

Figure 19: Knowledge is learned while wisdom is earned

The illustration portrays how knowledge per say is learned vis-a-vis how wisdom is rather earned. Some people earn early in life, some late.

Professional knowledge is learned by study of science, technology, industry or business that enables us to acquire specific skills or ability for living with some level of comfort. How such comforts do not translate to living with happiness or peace as such.

The non-professional knowledge is acquired through learning and observation of axiology (i.e., the philosophical study of value, encompassing both the nature of value itself and how we determine what is valuable) or so-called truthful history. A crucial point to note here is that history in reality is full of bias and agenda-driven narratives everywhere in every country. Hence knowledge learnt in this regard has a fundamental problem. Again, it is no longer a secret that mainstream media is a business in the modern era to make money by promoting agenda and narratives rather than publishing news and therefore they do employ news activists rather than news reporters. This aspect of bias and agenda-driven history will be discussed in more detail in upcoming chapters when we discuss areas on history and artificial intelligence. This is important as one measurement of wisdom – how much you have learned from history?

The knowledge learning process uses perceptive instruments and the ability of comprehension and thinking that is enabled by intellect.

Now knowledge, as it is learnt together with intellect, may strive for some level of happiness and peace, however again such is not guaranteed. As articulated before, only when intellect uses fortitude (*Dhriti*), discernment (Viveka) and developed intuition (*Antarjnyana*), is it able to earn wisdom. Such wisdom eliminates the root of unhappiness and thereby attains true happiness and peace.

Wisdom leads to Discovery, Intellect leads to Invention

Intellect represents the capacity for logical reasoning, problem-solving, and acquiring knowledge. Thereby, it is the driving force behind the systematic application of knowledge and skills to create something new, often in response to a perceived need or a desire for improvement. Eventually in this sense, it leads to invention.

Wisdom, however, transcends mere intellect. With the application of fortitude (Dhriti), discernment (*Viveka*) and developed intuition (*Antarjnyana*), wisdom involves a deeper understanding of life, human nature, and moral principles, often developed through experience, reflection, and empathy. Wisdom enables individuals to discern the bigger picture, recognize the underlying truths of existence, and make sound judgments that benefit not only themselves but also the greater good. This deeper understanding can lead to breakthroughs and insights into how the world works, thus fostering discovery.

In this context there are some interesting pointers that we would like touch upon here:

- Intellect provides the tools and methods to create things, while wisdom guides the pursuit of deeper truths and reveals what is truly valuable and meaningful to discover.
- For an individual, it is evident that the path to learn knowledge and intellect is not a cakewalk. It is arduous and not for all and sundry. But it is feasible. The interesting point is - Individuals can think and earn wisdom but the crowd cannot think therefore cannot be wise.
- Another point of caution is - the apparently good-looking democracy is not a government of majority. Rather it is actually controlled by a small group of vested interest in disguise pseudo - majority. In such an environment. an individual can at least attempt to think if at all one is willing to but a crowd cannot. Individuals have learned to an extent but unfortunately humanity as a race did not.

Why are We Using Sanskrit Words in the Diagram

Swami Vivekananda's lectures and writings in the late 19th and early 20th centuries played a key role in popularizing Vedanta, particularly Neo-Vedanta, in the West. The Vedas are composed in Vedic Sanskrit, which is significantly unique in phonetics, grammar, and syntax. Scholars often face challenges in interpreting these texts; a well-interpreted translation for many Sanskrit words are not found in English.

For example, the Cambridge dictionary meaning of wisdom is - the ability to use your knowledge and experience to make good decisions and judgments. This meaning is quite sub-optimal as we explained wisdom from a Vedantic concept where this particular terminology is Prajna. Even with a standard search for its meaning depicts that Prajna (Sanskrit: प्रज्ञा) is the highest and purest form of wisdom, intelligence and understanding. Prajna is the state of wisdom which is higher than the knowledge obtained by reasoning and inference.

Our endeavor in this work is to adhere to proper usage of some of the important terms as we described here that float around rather in a casual interchangeable fashion in various texts, podcasts or even distinguished seminars. They may fit in specific contexts and may not in others.

We deliberated in detail so as to avoid general confusion and focus on clarity in communication. As we explained this lexicon, in this book of ours we will be using the terms 'wisdom,' 'Intellect' or 'Knowledge' with the interpretation explained in this chapter.

3.2 Law of Constancy of Wisdom

Knowledge Increasing but not the wisdom

There is a data explosion as the world is accumulating more and more data and thereby more and more information per say. Naturally just knowing about the increasing level of information enhances the span of more and more knowledge. With the advent of technology, there is more flexibility, extraction and maneuverability of huge amounts of data now as we invented terms like 'big data' as such with sophisticated analytical capability. Large Language Models (LLMs) are generating synthetic data, which are used to augment or even replace real-world datasets. This in turn further is providing an increasing level of intellectual knowledge. Today with gen-AI applications, various creative additions and alteration of input data prompts are generating new data in complex image or video formats and thereby such intellectual knowledge levels are further enhanced.

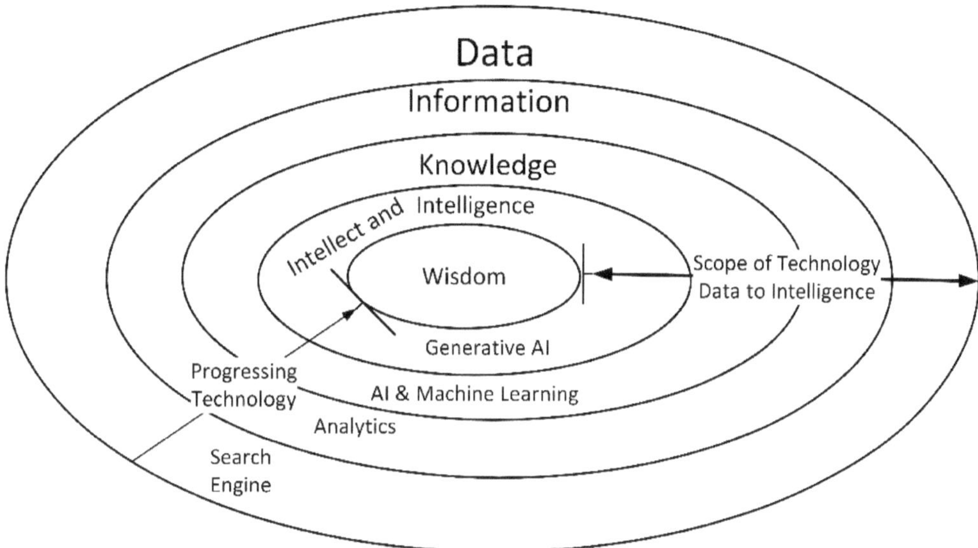

Wisdom is beyond the scope of technology

Figure 20: Technology does not increase wisdom

On the contrary, wisdom as such is a unique ball game. It is interesting to refer to the fundamental concept of entropy. Entropy, in the context of physics and the Second Law of Thermodynamics, generally refers to a measure of disorder or randomness in a closed system. The second law of thermodynamics states that the entropy of an isolated system will increase over time or remain constant in the case of a reversible process. This means that in any natural process, the total disorder or randomness of the universe will either increase or stay the same, never decrease. Note that this is related to the degree of chaos as such. We can take a clue similar to this when we talk about wisdom. In previous chapters, we explained the true meaning of wisdom (*Prajna*). Even in the realm of conventional empirical reality, wisdom (Prajna) possesses four important associated qualities: Instinct, Intuition, Discretion and Fortitude. We deliberated various role plays of these qualities affecting intellect and the Influencing Gunas that demarcates Intellect from Wisdom (*Prajna*).

Let us take this forward to articulate a few interesting points.

Knowledge can be learnt but wisdom is earned: Just to reiterate, wisdom is not passive acceptance of what we study or read or acquisition and formatting of data and information. In Vedanta, wisdom (*Prajna*) is the deep, intuitive understanding of the true nature of reality, particularly the unity of the individual self (*Atman*) with the ultimate reality (*Brahman*). It's not just intellectual knowledge, but a transformative insight that leads to liberation (Moksha). This requires a higher level of awareness and a willingness to ask ourselves and experience firsthand— what is true for each of us? It is better to be acknowledged as the source of wisdom. As we deliberate before, apart from the power of discretion (*Viveka*) and resolute (*Dhriti*), this also encompasses instinct (*Pravritti*) and intuition (*Antarjnyana*). it is important to decipher - knowledge can be learnt and applied by intellect to a feasible extent; but wisdom can only be earned. So, as you learn more, your knowledge traverses through a path of enhancement i.e., knowledge increases. Wisdom on the other hand looks for introspection to your inner self and does not have any free flow path of increment.

To earn wisdom - It is a journey of self-discovery: The process of earning wisdom involves a multi-faceted approach encompassing study, reflection, self-inquiry, and specific practices. This may involve:

- Self-Inquiry (*Vicharana*): To engage in deep reflection and contemplation of your learnings and experiences, questioning assumptions and beliefs to discern truth from illusion.
- Discernment (*Viveka*): To develop the ability to differentiate between the real and the unreal, the eternal and the fleeting.
- Renunciation (*Vairagya*): To cultivate detachment from worldly pleasures and material desires, focusing on inner peace and contentment.

Unlike wealth, wisdom is not inherited - wisdom remains constant: Wisdom is a result of true understanding and learning from those experiences. This is not expected at a younger age. As you earn more life experiences as you age, you have an opportunity to be more towards this path. You get older; at the same time, the passage of time can provide more raw material (experiences) for cultivating wisdom. And if you take this opportunity to actively engage with life's lessons, reflecting on them, and applying that understanding – it will truly lead to greater wisdom. Possibly it takes a whole life for an ordinary person to attain even knocking at the door of such level of wisdom and this goes away along with his death or departure from this material world. Unlike the wealth of a rich businessperson, wisdom is not passed on to the next generation. In other words, wealth can be inherited but there is no room to inherit wisdom. Hence there is natural growth of wealth as such, however the accumulation of wisdom of an individual retains with him and perishes with his life. Thus, wisdom overall has no room of increment and it remains constant.

The average level of wisdom or Wisdom per capita in the world is constant: As we know in general, the global wealth is increasing; but does that mean that the per capita GDP is also rising by default? There are factors like wealth concentration, population growth, and limitations of GDP. In many developing nations, population growth can outpace the increase in overall wealth, leading to a stagnant per capita wealth. Even if global wealth increases, it can be concentrated in the hands of a few, leading to a situation where GDP per capita rises but a large segment of the population experiences no improvement in their living standards. So even if the wealth is increasing, possibly the per capita remains constant. A similar analogy can be applied as – though knowledge is increasing, wisdom remains constant.

How is Wisdom (Intellect) Manifested - by '*Karma*'?

While intellect might refer to the ability to acquire and process information, wisdom involves the capacity to apply that knowledge in meaningful ways, make sound judgments, and navigate the complexities of life effectively. *Karma*, in this context, plays a significant role in how wisdom is manifested and developed.

- The pursuit of wisdom and *Karma*: Our intentions and actions, which form the basis of *karma*, can influence our ability to gain wisdom. Ethical conduct, honest self-reflection, and seeking knowledge contribute to a positive *karmik* foundation, facilitating the cultivation of wisdom.

- Wisdom guiding *karmik* actions: Possessing wisdom can lead to more mindful and ethical choices, resulting in positive *karma*. Wise individuals consider the long-term consequences of their actions and strive for choices that promote well-being and positive outcomes.
- Learning from experience: *Karma* manifests through the consequences of our actions, providing experiences that can lead to growth and wisdom. By reflecting on these experiences, and applying the lessons learned, individuals can develop a deeper understanding of themselves and the world.
- Understanding the nature of action (*karma*): The Gita reveals that all actions are influenced by the three qualities (*Gunas*) of nature) – *satva* (goodness), *rajas* (passion), and *tamas* (ignorance). A wise individual recognizes this influence and strives to act with *satvik* qualities, cultivating pure intentions and aligning their actions with *dharma*.

In Bhagavad Gita chapter 18:30-32, we find description of three types of intellect (*buddhi*), categorized by the three qualities (*gunas*) of nature: *satvik* (goodness), *rajasik* (passion), and *tamasik* (darkness).

Satvik (goodness) intellect: It is characterized by its ability to clearly understand what actions appropriate (pravritti) and what actions are should be avoided (*nivritti*), what is one's duty and what is not, what is to be feared and what is not, and what leads to bondage and what leads to liberation. It can discriminate between right and wrong, good and evil, and make appropriate choices.

प्रवृत्तिंच निवृत्तिं च कार्याकार्ये भयाभये | बन्धं मोक्षं च या वेत्तिबुद्धि: सा पार्थ सात्त्विकी ||

Bhagwad Gita 18: 30||

Rajasik (passion) intellect: It is influenced by personal attachments and desires, leading to a clouded judgment. It may be competent in some areas but make poor decisions in others due to these attachments. It is unable to distinguish between the important and the trivial, the permanent and the transient.

यया धर्ममधर्मं च कार्यं चाकार्यमेव च । अयथावत्प्रजानाति बुद्धिः सा पार्थ राजसी ॥

Bhagwad Gita 18: 31||

Tamasik (darkness) intellect: This intellect is completely deluded, misinterpreting everything due to ignorance. It mistakes the unreal for the real, the impermanent for the permanent, and fails to understand what is truly beneficial or harmful. It is the worst form of bondage, as it leads to self-destruction.

अधर्मं धर्ममिति या मन्यते तमसावृता । सर्वार्थान्विपरीतांश्च बुद्धिः सा पार्थ तामसी ||

Bhagwad Gita 18: 31||

Bhagavad Gita 18:33-35 describes three types of steadfastness (*dhriti*) or determination, each influenced by the three qualities (*gunas*): goodness (*sattva*), passion (*rajas*), and ignorance (*tamas*).

Satvik Dhriti: This is steadfastness rooted in yoga, where one's mind, life-airs (prana), and senses are directed towards righteous action without attachment to the results. This is a balanced and stable state, conducive to spiritual growth.

धृत्या यया धारयते मनःप्राणेन्द्रियक्रियाः । योगेनाव्यभिचारिण्या धृतिः सा पार्थ सात्त्विकी ||

Bhagwad Gita 18: 31||

Rajasik Dhriti: This is the determination driven by desires and attachments. It's a forceful kind of steadfastness, but one that is ultimately bound by the fruits of action and limited by self-interest.

यया तु धर्मकामार्थान्धृत्या धारयतेऽर्जुन | प्रसङ्गेन फलाकाङ् क्षी धृति: सा पार्थ राजसी ||

Bhagwad Gita 18: 31||

Tamasik Dhriti: This is misguided determination, clouded by ignorance and negativity. It's associated with qualities like fear, grief, despair, and conceit, hindering spiritual progress. This type of determination is ultimately self-destructive.

यया स्वप्नं भयं शोकं विषादं मदमेव च | न विमुञ्चति दुर्मेधा धृति: सा पार्थ तामसी ||

Bhagwad Gita 18: 31||

A fascinating point to note is about the interplay between Karma and wisdom.

Wisdom Enables Selfless Action: Wisdom empowers one to realize the nature of karma and the importance of acting without attachment (*Nishkama Karma*).

Selfless Action Cultivates Wisdom: Engaging in selfless action purifies the mind and guides one transcends ego, thereby cultivating wisdom and leading to spiritual growth.

Action in Inaction: A wise person sees inaction in action (when action is performed without attachment) and action in inaction (when one is not performing their duties). This means that the wise person understands that true action is not just physical activity but also the intention and state of mind behind the action.

कर्मण्यकर्म य: पश्येदकर्मणि च कर्म य: | स बुद्धिमान्मनुष्येषु स युक्त: कृत्स्नकर्मकृत् ||

Bhagwad Gita 4:18 ||

Liberation through Wisdom and Selfless Action: Finally, by understanding the principles of *karma* and practicing selfless action, one can gradually purify their consciousness and move towards liberation (*Moksha*).

So, a person can be intelligent but he/she continues to make mistakes and possibly learn from those mistakes to refine intellect further. However, wisdom is above intellect. That is why – a wise person does not make mistakes and intelligent people learn from every mistake.

Notional Measurement by Manifested Factors -*Karmafala*

One's relationship with the fruits of their actions, or *karmafala*, significantly impacts the development and manifestation of wisdom.

Attachment to *Karmafala* hinders wisdom: If you act with an ardent desire for specific outcomes, this attachment can cloud your judgment, lead to ego-driven actions, and cause disappointment when results don't meet expectations. This hinders the development of wisdom.

- Detachment from *Karmafala* facilitates wisdom: *Nishkama Karma* or selfless action is the way to perform your duties without attachment to the results. Focus solely on the action itself, acting with sincerity, dedication. This inner clarity is crucial for cultivating wisdom.
- Wisdom manifests through balanced action: A truly wise person (*Sthita Prajna*), remains steady in both success and failure, happiness and distress. which is the hallmark of wisdom.
- Intention is crucial: The intention behind your actions significantly affects *karmik* reactions. Pure intentions lead to positive *karmik* reactions, while negative intentions lead to suffering. This signifies a wise and detached mindset, focusing on righteous action.

Karmafala Deteriorates as the Yuga Cycle Progresses

This is described with a diagram in the chapter 'Reason for Rise of Unreason.' This concept of fruits or results of one's actions i.e., *karmafala*, is understood within the framework of the *Yuga* cycle, a cyclical progression of four ages: *Satya*, *Treta*, *Dvapara*, and *Kali Yuga*. As indicated, the Yugas are characterized by a gradual decline in dharma (righteousness, virtue, moral values) and, consequently, an intensification of the effects of *karmafala*:

So, in the current *Kali Yuga*, as dharma diminishes, the impact of *karmafala* becomes more pronounced, with individuals facing the fruits of their actions, both positive and negative, in a more intense and accelerated manner.

It's important to remember that *Karma* is not a judgement enforced by a God or other supernatural being, but rather the outcome of a natural process of cause and effect. Even in *Kali Yuga*, by practicing *dharma* through compassion, honesty, selfless service, and mindfulness, individuals can strive for positive *karmik* outcomes and spiritual growth. Here lies the significance of the fruit or results of your actions (*Karmafala*) that impacts the manifestation of wisdom.

Knowing Wisdom vs Being Wise

It is by now almost obvious that there is a distinct difference between 'knowing wisdom' and actually 'being wise.' Knowing wisdom is about possessing information and facts. It is about knowing by reading, understanding, reasoning and getting convinced and then learning by experiences in life. So, one can be knowledgeable about a topic, but that does not guarantee towards 'being wise,' as wisdom involves a deeper understanding of when and how to use the knowledge, often through reflection and learned lessons from both successes and failures.

Being Wise is actually practicing, living by it, while dwelling upon righteousness. It is the right use or application of knowledge with discernment, good judgment, and perspective.

3.3 Can Wisdom be Measured?

This is an interesting debate. A somewhat convenient and diplomatic response can be - while measuring wisdom presents significant challenges, it is not entirely immeasurable. Psychologists have developed methods to assess wisdom, primarily through open-ended problem-solving scenarios and self-report scales. These approaches aim to evaluate aspects of wisdom like knowledge, reflection, and empathy. However, the subjective nature of wisdom and the difficulty in defining it definitively mean that existing measures are still evolving and may not capture the full spectrum of what it means to be wise.

Let us delve through some of the efforts described in some interesting articles here.

Reference	Synopsys
Cambridge University Press: 07 October 2021)- Robert J. Sternberg and Judith Glück - How Is Wisdom Measured	Methods devised by psychologists with two classical types of measures: self-report scales and performance measures. Scales are susceptible to both unintentional and intentional distortions and also influenced by rather theoretical thinking about a problem.
Essential components of wisdom and ways to measure the trait, July, 2023 - Eric Hamilton, University of Florida News	A three-dimensional wisdom model I developed based on earlier research by neuropsychologist Vivian Clayton. The primary idea is - by seeing one's own

	weaknesses, one might become more tolerant of the faults of others. This tolerance reduces ego and therefore makes it more compassionate.
A new scale for assessing wisdom based on common domains and a neurobiological model: The San Diego Wisdom Scale - Journal of Psychiatric Research, 2019	Takes forward the idea that wisdom is relevant to well-being and healthy aging from a neurobiology point of view. It is impacted negatively with emotional distress, but positively with well-being.
Comparing the psychometric properties of two measures of wisdom: predicting forgiveness and psychological well-being with the Self-Assessed Wisdom Scale and the Three-Dimensional Wisdom Scale - Matthew Taylor & others Webster - Comparative Study Exp Aging Res. 2011	Focuses to predict relevant personality (i.e., forgiveness) and life satisfaction (i.e., psychological well-being) variables.
Scientists Made A 7-Question Test To Measure Your Wisdom – Tushar Mehta, Dec 5, 2021	These seven components include acceptance towards other perspectives, decisiveness, emotional regulation, pro-social behaviors (such as altruism, compassion, and empathy), self-reflection, social advising (helping others with rational advice), and spirituality. high wisdom score with happiness, mental well-being and resilience, while loneliness, depression, and anxiety were correlated with lower wisdom
Journal of Gerontology, Oxford Academic - Measuring Wisdom: Existing Approaches, Continuing Challenges, and New Developments Open Access by Judith Glück, 2017	It discusses the specific challenges of both open-ended and self-report approaches with respect to content validity, convergent and divergent validity, concurrent and discriminant validity, and ecological validity.

Now from gerontology perspective, researchers face challenges related to the definition and measurement of wisdom, methodological limitations, and the nuanced relationship between wisdom and aging. Nevertheless, the study of wisdom in gerontology has made significant progress. While a neurobiological approach offers promise in understanding the underlying mechanisms of wisdom, it faces considerable hurdles stemming from the complexity of the trait itself, methodological limitations, and the current state of neuroscientific knowledge. Again, while psychometric measures can offer some insights into specific dimensions related to wisdom, they alone cannot fully capture its complexity and richness. Therefore, attempting to "measure" wisdom in a conventional, quantitative sense, as one might measure academic knowledge, lacks either some direct alignment or creates some more unanswered questions.

Indicator of Wisdom – A Vedantic Approach

Our approach here is to explore Vedanta which emphasizes that ultimate wisdom (Prajna) in a fundamentally unique approach as a profound, transformative insight into the true nature of reality (*Brahman*) and the Self (*Atman*). We have to note again that this wisdom is not merely intellectual knowledge but a direct, intuitive experience that transcends ordinary understanding.

We know that as per Vedanta philosophy, true happiness, also known as Ananda (bliss), is not considered a temporary state of pleasure derived from external sources, but rather the intrinsic nature of the Self (*Atman*). It is not something to be sought externally but realized within oneself.

Now let us take a fundamental pointer about Your Problem versus Your suffering:

You may rightfully say that you cannot avoid problems, but have you attempted to avoid sufferings? A wise man knows how to avoid suffering and that is why they are happy. Vedant clearly distinguishes between problem and suffering. While problems are the trouble, suffering is how you respond to it. Further, Vedant states that your true nature (Atman) is problem-free and the problem of body and mind are not your problems. You suffer because you identify yourself with body and mind rather than identifying with "true self." So, the only problem is the ignorance about your true identity.

True Happiness as an Indicator of Wisdom

Happiness is the manifestation of wisdom. If you are unhappy, then you do not know how to accept the reason for your unhappiness. Here by happiness, we are not talking about a mere fulfillment of a desire which is nothing but a state of mind, but we are referring to the true inner happiness.

- You must not miss to focus your meaningful journey towards realizing '*Sat-Chit-Ananda*. Our true nature is divine and eternal, characterized by existence (*Sat*), consciousness (*Chit*), and bliss (*Ananda*). Wisdom is the realization of this inherent nature, leading to a state of deep, unwavering happiness.
- You need to differentiate between pain and suffering. Being away from the transcending dualities like pleasure and pain, a wise individual cultivates detachment and equanimity, leading to inner peace and a deeper happiness independent of external circumstances. In a materialistic way, the problems get tagged to you since you miss the fundamental notion that those are just transactional impacts. They may cause instantaneous discomfort or pain. But. Once you start training yourself to say that you are just the 'observer,' you will begin to detach yourself from the transactional discomforts and eventually accept those materialistic pains as normal, so to speak. You would no longer react or complain about such problems. This will enable you to develop your attitude not to convert such daily experiences of pain and discomforts succumbing to suffering.
- Happiness is ultimately linked to self-realization and liberation (*Moksha*) from the cycle of suffering. Realizing the Self's true nature leads to infinite bliss, which is a natural outcome of Vedantic wisdom.

That is why true happiness (*Ananda*), which is an inner state independent of external factors, is an indicator of wisdom. It eventually indicates the progress towards spiritual understanding and self-realization. As one gains wisdom, the capacity for this lasting happiness increases. In essence, Vedanta posits that true happiness isn't something to be sought and acquired, but something to be realized and re-recognized as your inherent state once the veil of ignorance is lifted through the wisdom of Self-Knowledge.

Righteousness as an Indicator of Wisdom

Righteousness (*dharma*) is not merely a set of rules but a deeply integrated component of the path to wisdom (*prajna*) and ultimately, liberation (*moksha*). There is a symbiotic relationship between righteousness and wisdom. Righteous living lays the groundwork for acquiring wisdom, and true wisdom naturally expresses itself through virtuous and compassionate actions. This integrated approach emphasizes the practical application of spiritual principles in daily life as a necessary means for self-realization and liberation.

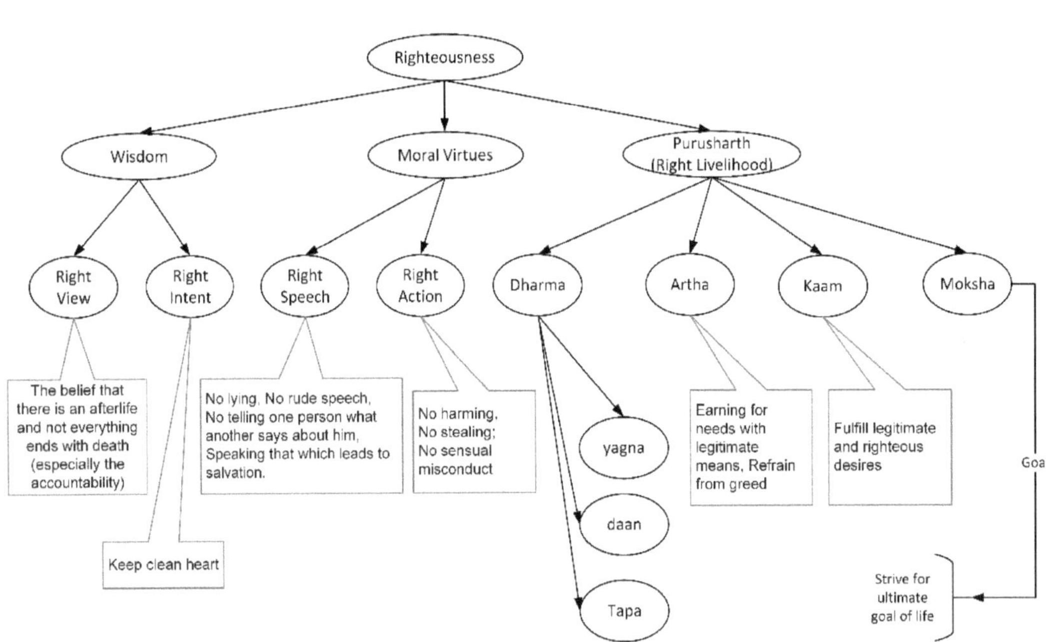

Figure 21: Righteousness and wisdom

In Righteousness context Wisdom= Right views and Right intent

Right View provides the foundational understanding of reality, while Right Intent guides the individual's motivations and actions in accordance with that understanding, ultimately leading to the realization of their true nature and liberation from suffering.

Right view (*Viveka* or Right Understanding)

- Discrimination between the real and unreal: A crucial aspect of right view is *Viveka* or discernment, the ability to discriminate between the eternal (Brahman) and the ephemeral (*Maya* or the illusory material world).
- Understanding the Self and *Brahman*: This encompasses understanding the true nature of the individual self (*Atman*) and its identity with Brahman, the ultimate reality.
- Perceiving reality without delusion: It involves accurately perceiving reality, free from the distortions of ego, desires, and attachments.
- Knowing the consequences of actions: This includes understanding the law of karma and its effects, and discerning actions that lead to spiritual growth from those that lead to suffering.

Right intent

- Motivation for self-realization: It is about having the proper motivation for spiritual life, which is ultimately the desire for liberation (*moksha*) and self-realization.
- Ethical conduct: It involves cultivating virtuous qualities and acting ethically, in line with one's understanding of *Dharma* (righteous duty).
- Freedom from desires and attachment: This includes having the intention to renounce worldly desires and attachments that hinder spiritual progress.
- Compassion and non-harm: This encompasses developing compassion (*Karuna*) and loving-kindness towards all beings.

A Reference of Happiness Measurement Index

Bhutan's unique approach to national well-being is measured by the Gross National Happiness (GNH) Index, which assesses various aspects of life beyond traditional economic indicators. The GNH Index, measured in 2022, gave Bhutan a score of 0.781 out of 1, with 48.1% of the population considered happy (including deeply, extensively, and narrowly happy). This score indicates a 3.3% increase in happiness compared to 2015. It is not a single score or ranking like the World Happiness Report, but rather a framework encompassing 4 pillars, 9 domains, more than 150 variables and 33 indicators. The fundamental question to introspect is - what and how do you measure: anger or hunger?

Domains and Indicators	The GNH index is built on nine key domains: living standards, health, education, environment, community, time-use, psychological well-being, governance, and culture. Each domain is further broken down into specific indicators, resulting in a total of 33 weighted indicators.
Calculation of Individual Happiness	The index assesses each person's level of sufficiency within each of the 33 indicators. An individual is considered GNH happy if they meet the sufficiency threshold (at least 66%) in at least 66% of the weighted indicators.
The Alkire-Foster Method	This method helps determine whether an individual is happy (above the sufficiency threshold) or not (below the threshold) across the various indicators.
Reporting the GNH Index	The GNH index is a single number, ranging from 0 to 1, with values closer to 1 indicating higher levels of GNH and those closer to 0 indicating lower levels.

The Challenge of Measurement of Wisdom

The measurement framework of wisdom is being explored in various academic, psychometric or neurobiological points of view. Each possesses its own interpretations and limitations open for further investigative studies. Measuring wisdom presents significant challenges due to its complex and multifaceted nature. Difficulties arise from defining wisdom, the reliance on self-report measures, and the potential for bias and limitations in capturing wisdom in real-world contexts. The debate in measuring wisdom arises because of numerous factors as:

- Subjectivity and Definition: Mostly there is a subjective construct around a universally accepted definition for wisdom further impacted by diverse cultural perceptions.
- Self-Report Biases: There is academic usage of Self-report scales that captures assessment of personality traits. However, these are prone to inaccurate self-perception, social desirability bias or general assessment rather than context-dependence.
- Performance-Based Measures Challenges: Such attempts are resource Intensive but lack of emotional engagement and face comparability issues that again affect individuals' wisdom across different contexts.
- Cultural Bias: Assessment tools developed within one cultural context may not be equally valid or reliable in another.
- Influence of Personality Traits: There is complexity to establish relationship between wisdom and personality traits, like openness to experience, agreeableness, conscientiousness, emotional stability etc.
- Behavioral Observation Difficulties: Even for a survey, participants' awareness of being observed or a limited sample size or a transient mood, stress, and environmental conditions can influence behavior during observation.

Even in such measurement explorations there is no denial that there are certain qualities that make wisdom so valuable like its subjectivity and specific contextual references. This in turn necessitates further investigations for feasible integration of cognitive, emotional, and social aspects. Here they encounter more challenges as it is difficult to measure such parameters objectively and reliably.

Key Takeaway

In an attempt to measure wisdom, researchers continue to refine their approaches to address various limitations that actually open up a more nuanced understanding of wisdom.

- Instead of the academic, psychometric or neurobiological frameworks - we rather recommend to view and articulate 'wisdom' from a Vedantic approach. We don't want to dilute the question as to whether wisdom can be measured by such studies and explorations or not. We reiterate that wisdom (*Prajna*) is not just intellectual knowledge, but a transformative insight that leads to liberation (*Moksha*).

- Happiness is the manifestation of wisdom that ultimately links to self-realization and liberation (*Moksha*) from the cycle of suffering. Hence, we propose the true inner happiness (*Ananda* or bliss) as an indicator for wisdom,
- The fact of the matter remains that while knowledge is increasing, wisdom as such is not increasing and rather it remains constant. Unlike wealth, wisdom is not inherited, in a lifetime it is not learnt but earned in an arduous self-journey. That's where we put forward the concept of law of constancy of wisdom.

4 Hard Problem of Consciousness

4.1 What is Hard Problem of Consciousness

There is an apparent headache imposed in the studies around the term 'consciousness' for quite some time now. This is around the question – how can a physical system generate something subjective; how can something objective generate the subjective experience of consciousness? How can a body and brain generate a first-person experience? By the way, this 'first person experience' is not prevalent in any other thing in the world. Every other thing, whatever physical description one can give, that is the beginning and that is the end of it. Take your car for example. The engineer may give it a description, the physicist may give it a bit deeper description at various levels of automotive features, electric battery life or even at the level of fundamental combustion principles or particle levels. That will be the end of the description. But there is no description like – how does it feel to be a car? From within, does it feel like a car? What does it experience itself as? Yes, indeed - such a question is meaningless.

So every physical system can be described in one way – in terms of physics, chemistry, biology, engineering or else. But there is something very strange about you yourself or you as a physical system. Whatever the doctors and biologists describe about you, that does not encompass the whole of you. There is something within you, what you consider yourself to be. There is a disconnect with what the doctors describe you as. The disconnect is due to – your experience about yourself. Such experiences of yours are about sights, sound, smell, touch, taste, thought, feeling, desire, pain, pleasure, understanding, memory, forgetting and all of these are directly experienced by you and you only. The doctors speak about muscles, tissues and organs, the biologist or the neuroscientist points out the nervous system or the electrical activity in the brain. But there is no connection of such description to your direct experience which is entirely your own. It may seem that the physical body produces that, what you call, what you experience as consciousness. But such a viewpoint lacks the very fundamental question – how does it produces that?

In terms of scientific response to answer the above query, there are two approaches. One is to deny the existence of consciousness altogether; basically, that translates to saying you do not even exist. The body exists, the organs exist, the cells exist but you as a person, don't exist. We do not even want to deliberate further about such a ridiculous approach. The other approach is to reduce you i.e., to reduce your awareness to your body, to your brain. This is as if the brain produces consciousness like a candle produces flame or light. This may be called an epiphenomenon – a byproduct of the neurochemical processes in the nervous system in the brain. Even the most sophisticated attempts to explain consciousness, whether in terms of information theory (Giulio Tononi's Integrated Information Theory) still is trying to reduce it to brain states. It says such a theory can be used to analyze and understand the brain states. However, what about consciousness, the stuff about your awareness itself?

This is where the 'hard problem of consciousness' comes into discussion. This is a term coined by David Chalmers, an Australian philosopher and cognitive scientist. He describes that "The easy problems of consciousness are those that seem directly susceptible to the standard methods of cognitive science, whereby a phenomenon is explained in terms of computational or neural mechanisms." And mostly such easy ones are addressed to. The very 'hard problem of consciousness' is about your direct subjective experiences. And even for the visual of the same red rose, the depth of color of red is experienced at various levels between you and someone else.

4.2 Definition of Consciousness: Vedic vs Medical Science

Dr Evan Thomson (professor of philosophy at the University of British Columbia) in his book 'Waking, Dreaming Being' describes the studies of consciousness started 5000 years ago in India in the texts of Upanishad. That is because the ancients Rishis had a fundamental exploration to a spiritual quest to know about who actually we are and how we encounter sufferings to attain fulfilment in life. Once you start with the question who you are, there lies the very interest in your own self and thereby consciousness. The crux of the matter is - even to doubt about your own existence, you have to exist first. That attributes to the significance of the famous quote "I think, therefore I am" as remarked by the French philosopher René Descartes. In other words, because of this conscious experience, one cannot doubt his/ her own existence.

Now in the mainstream science and medical field consciousness is understood in a Physical reductionism approach that the brain produces consciousness. Let us examine this in detail from Vedantic perspective with an approach to clear off first what consciousness is not.

Consciousness is not 'brain;' brain is the product of consciousness, not the vice versa: In medical science way, you may be able to observe the tiny neural circuits in the brain, but how from that electrical activity you get the first-person experience of richness and quality of the color of a flower is inexplicable. Similarly, so for any of your own subjective direct experiences which are only your own. Scientists decipher that there is a strong correlation between the electrical activity in the brain and its actions at the most. But there is no explanation further about how the correlation, even if that is there, can produce consciousness? Life is explained in molecules processes in organic matter. That is an objective explanation that became feasible through the advance of biological science. But how does your subjective experience have an objective explanation? In this context, let us point out that neuroscientist Christof Koch conceded defeat on his 25-year bet with the philosopher David Chalmers, a lost wager that medical science would be able to explain consciousness by brain activity.

The Bet: In 1998, Koch bet Chalmers that by 2023, scientists would have discovered the neural mechanisms producing consciousness.

The Outcome: At the annual meeting of the Association for the Scientific Study of Consciousness (ASSC) in New York City on June 23, 2023, Koch conceded that a definitive scientific explanation for consciousness remained elusive, declaring Chalmers the winner.

Consciousness is not an Object

Your physical body is an object to all your senses. And the object and the subject are different. For example, your eyes can see something in front of them. The only thing your eyes can not see are the eyes themselves. Well, even in the mirror or a selfie, you are only seeing the reflection of your eyes.. There is a distinction between the 'seer' or the experiencer and the 'seen' or the thing being experienced. Hence your body, which is a physical object that you experience, cannot be you or your consciousness. You must be something distinct from your body.

Now it is only you who is aware or conscious of your body, not otherwise i.e., your body is not conscious about you. To simplify, even your left hand may not be conscious of your right hand; but you are conscious about both your hands. You are conscious and you are an aware entity (Chit or sentient) and your body is rather an unaware entity (Jar or insentient).

Consciousness is not 'Mind'

Let us take that or your mind is aware of your eyes. You understand when your eyes open or close. Here your eyes are 'seen' as objects and your mind is the 'seer' or experiencer of your eyes and all your sensory organs or your body as such. Now the emotions, feelings, thoughts, happiness of your mind are also something of which you are aware. Here mind is 'seen' and you are the 'seer.' You are something that lights up or illuminates the mind and you're distinctively different from your mind. This witness self is consciousness and it is distinct from your mind.

So, from a Vedantic perspective, whatever we can be aware of, either directly through our senses and through our minds or thoughts or indirectly by scientific instruments - they are all objects. But that which is aware of all of them is consciousness. It is a purely non-objective subject. It is uniquely distinct from everything else. It is pure in a sense that it is not mixed up with any object. Once you start realizing this, it immediately frees you up from your body and mind, the ups and downs of your mind, the frustrations, fear and anxieties which are just objects of your mind. Upanishad puts it across in a very beautiful way -

न तत्र सूर्यो भाति न चन्द्रतारकं नेमा विद्युतो भान्ति कुतोऽयमग्निः ।

तमेव भान्तमनुभाति सर्वं तस्य भासा सर्वमिदं विभाति ॥ १५॥ Katha Upanishad 2.2.15

This means " That shining , everything lese shines,' by his light everything is lit up." That is literally true in our life. If you shine, everything else is lit up by you. Even the worst experiences are just things or objects and they are actually not attached to you or your consciousness. Consciousness illuminating an object is experience. This consciousness is also free of change. It illuminates all changes. Every change is revealed by consciousness.

Consciousness is not many, there are not many consciousnesses:

Now, consider this pure consciousness which is not mixed with any object. How would you distinguish one consciousness from another? Once you identify yourself with your body or mind, then every other body or mind is different from your body and mind. But consciousness is not your body or mind. So, by reversing the question - why would you think that consciousness is different? A strong lingering or attachment to body-mind identity will make mistakes to understand consciousness. One has to let it go. Consciousness is not fragmented into individual minds, but rather is a single, unified reality.

Eka jiva vada, in Advaita Vedanta portrays one consciousness. It is that one consciousness which is associated with all these minds and bodies as different individuals. We are one consciousness and everything appears in that one consciousness. Like in a dream you see so many other beings, but all those beings are part of your imagination, products of your mind. In the dream, there is actually only one sentient being and that is you, the dreamer. And we have to finally realize our oneness with *Brahman*, that we are one with *Brahman*, one existence – consciousness – bliss.

Advaita Vedanta explains further that the waking stage is no different from the dream stage. In principle there is only one person and that is yourself. Everyone else is part of your dream. That may sound a bit difficult, but that is the way to understand for taking you to the path of enlightenment. In *the jiva*'s imagination the *samsara* and i*shwara* appear. And when that *jiva* becomes enlightened, it realizes itself as *turiya brahman.*

Is that connected to the so-called 'hard problem of consciousness'? Only as far as it deals with pure consciousness. As Swami SarvaPriyananda describes – in Western philosophy *Eka jiva vada* is somewhat close to a radical kind of solipsism that propagates that only you exist.

4.3 Is it a really hard problem?

Is there actually Anything so Hard about the 'Hard' Problem of Consciousness?

In essence there is nothing so hard about it. The fundamental debate arises from a mere fact that consciousness per say is primarily described from a scientific or medical perspective. Such an attempt of definition has its own limitations. One may refer to the publication "Landscape of Consciousness" (Aug, 2024) by Robert Lawrence Kuhn where no less than 10 different categorizations are portrayed about consciousness from materialist and physicalist approaches to non-materialist and non-physicalist ones.

Materialism theories	These theories propose that consciousness arises from physical processes in the brain. Subcategories include neurobiological, electromagnetic field, computational and informational, homeostatic and affective, embodied and enactive, relational, representational, language, and phylogenetic evolution theories.
Non-Reductive Physicalism	This view acknowledges that consciousness is rooted in the physical brain but suggests that physical processes alone cannot fully explain it.

Quantum theories	These theories propose that consciousness might involve quantum mechanics, potentially operating at a fundamental level.
Integrated information theory	This theory suggests that consciousness is related to the amount of integrated information within a system.
Panpsychism	This perspective proposes that some form of consciousness might be a basic property of all matter, not just living beings.
Monisms	These theories propose that there is only one fundamental substance, either physical or mental, and that consciousness arises from this one substance.
Dualism	Dualism proposes that the mind and body are distinct substances that interact with each other.
Idealism	Idealism suggests that consciousness or the mind is the fundamental substance of reality, and that the physical world is a construct of consciousness.
Anomalous & Altered states theories	This category includes theories that explore consciousness in altered states, such as those experienced during meditation, near-death experiences, or with certain drugs.
Challenge theories	This category encompasses theories that challenge existing views or offer alternative perspectives on consciousness.

It is no wonder to get engulfed into arguments, debates and confusions arising out varied descriptions which unnecessarily makes the issue of talking about consciousness not only hard but harder and harder.

On the contrary, Samkhya philosophy describes consciousness in a way that provides the much sought after clarity. It articulates that consciousness (*Purusha*) and matter (*Prakriti*) are distinct and separate principles. *Prakriti* is the source of all material creation, including our bodies, minds, and senses. It is dynamic, constantly changing, and is the active principle that gives rise to the diversity of the universe. Unfortunately, the mainstream definition of consciousness as all about science has its obvious limitation being in the realm of materialistic *Prakriti*. Unlike *Prakriti*, *Purusha* is considered the true self, the observer, and is not affected by the changes of the material world. It is pure, unchanging consciousness, often described as the soul or self.

Purusha (Consciousness) and *Prakriti* (matter) are fundamentally different, yet their interaction is necessary for the manifestation of the universe. While separate, *Purusha* and *Prakriti* interact to create the world as we know it. *Purusha* is like a witness, observing the activities of *Prakriti*, which is the active principle. This interaction is sometimes described as the lame (*Purusha*, who can't act) and the blind (*Prakriti*, who can't see) needing each other to function. So, according to Samkhya, *Mahat* is the first evolved from *Prakriti*, which is cosmic intelligence. Think about it this way. The awareness which we have just after deep sleep, we awaken into a sense of our existence, even before I am. I am already ego. After waking up from deep sleep, I am, and then I am sleeping, I am, this is morning and I am awake now, all of that comes.

Once you embrace such clarity, there is no longer anything hard about the so-called 'hard problem of consciousness.'

4.4 Instinct, Intuition and Consciousness

At the outset let us take note of few important pointers:

- Ordinary human beings dealing with the material world limit their understanding by their sense perceptions and rationalizing intelligence.
- With undeveloped intuition they limit their power of intellectuality because it is the intuition that bridges the chasm between intellectual knowledge for comprehending the matter of spirit beyond matter.
- In the life of every person, two forces of knowledge are operative from birth
    - Power of human reason: Developed through social institutions and interactions.
    - Power of intuition: Usually remains uncultured and undeveloped because of lack of proper guidance and training by Guru.

- All power of knowing borrows its ability from intuition. The highest expression of intuition is that by which atman itself- the knower, knowing and known exist as one.
- In man, the conscious awakening of intuition expresses itself in five forms determined by the effect of five *koshas*.

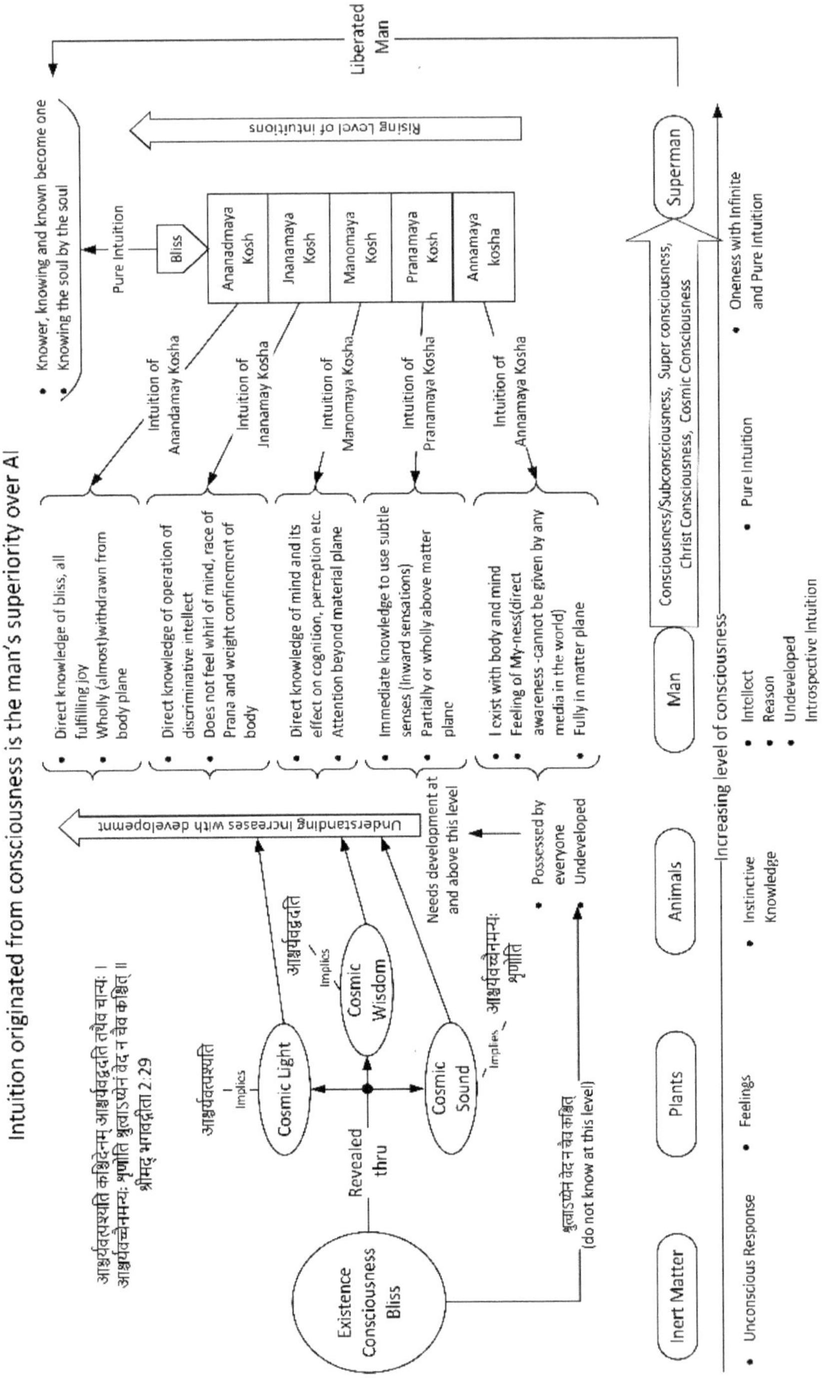

Figure 22: Instinct, Intuition, Intellect and Consciousness

The illustration is better understood as per divisions in 3 parts as below:

1. The bottom part – The arrow line showing Inert Matter from left to right up to Superman
2. The Right top part – Rising level of Intuition
3. The left top part – Understanding increase with development

Let's elaborate these 3 parts one by one.

The bottom part of the illustration – The arrow line showing Inert Matter from left to right up to Superman. The arrow line depicts how the increasing level of consciousness categorizes the lowest level of consciousness (Inert Matter) at extreme left up to extreme right with Superman.

- Inert Matter: This represents matter with unconscious response e.g., a piece rock that has no life as such; however, it still falls under gravitation force. In other words, it possesses some consciousness even if at the lowest grade (colloquially almost at unconscious level) it follows the law of gravity or law of nature.
- Plants: This is the next level as it responds to air and water and grows accordingly or gets affected in absence of that or severity of weather. It has a sense of growing i.e., some level of consciousness.
- Animals: They have some level of consciousness which is instinctive behavior that facilitates them to fight for survival or search for food and the extent of such instinctive consciousness varies among various animals. In general, Animals demonstrate awareness of their surroundings, respond to threats, seek out food and social interaction. Elephants using tools to swat flies, dogs exhibiting remorse after misbehavior highlight the diversity of conscious experiences in the animal kingdom.
- Man or Human: It is with man that the level of consciousness increases to an extent where it encompasses intellect, reasoning and some undeveloped introspective intuition. Even by birth, man possesses a distinctive higher level of intuition compared to animals. With age this develops further automatically to an extent through life's experiences and of course varies among man to man. The critical point to note is that - this

so-called undeveloped intuition must be exercised in true sense and direction further by man for further development towards pure intuition.

- Superman or Superhuman: This represents the highest level on the enhancement journey of consciousness where one achieves oneness with infinite and pre intuition. The path denotes various levels or aspects of awareness i.e., Consciousness, subconsciousness, super consciousness, Christ consciousness, and cosmic consciousness. Consciousness is our awareness of ourselves and our surroundings. The subconscious is a realm of thoughts and feelings outside of our immediate awareness, while super consciousness is a higher level of awareness associated with intuition and spiritual insight. Christ consciousness and cosmic consciousness are advanced states of awareness, with Christ consciousness often linked to spiritual enlightenment and cosmic consciousness encompassing a sense of oneness with all existence.

As Swami Yogananda Paramhansa describes - freed from the intoxications of delusion and delusive mortal limitations, the superman knows his earthly name and possessions but is never possessed or limited by them. Living in the world, he is not of the world. He is aware of hunger, thirst, and other conditions of the body, but his inner consciousness identifies itself, not with the body, but with Spirit.

(Read more: https://yogananda.com.au/pyr/cosmic_consciousness.html).

The Right top part of the illustration – Rising level of Intuition

This part of the illustration depicts the various levels of rising intuition starting with *Annamaya Kosha* up to *Anandamay Kosha.* In Yogananda's teachings, consciousness is the fundamental awareness of existence, while Intuition is the faculty of the soul that needs to be developed to attain higher level by which a Superman can become a Liberated Man to attain bliss (Ananda), a state of divine joy and peace that is inherent in our true nature and can be realized through spiritual practice.

- Intuition of *Annamaya Kosha:* This is the lowest level of intuition where one exists only with body and mind with a feeling of my-ness completely in the plane of matter. My-ness (often linked to "I-ness" or *Ahamkara*) refers to the egoistic sense of self, ownership, and attachment to oneself, one's body, thoughts, feelings, and possessions. This is different from Direct awareness (also referred to as *aparoksha jnana* or *anubhava*) that signifies the unmediated, firsthand, and immediate realization of one's true nature (the ultimate reality). Media in the world cannot provide direct awareness in the same way that firsthand experience or direct perception can more so when media information is actually selectively filtered and manipulated.

- Intuition of *Pranamaya Kosha*: By development of such intuition, one attains immediate knowledge to subtle senses (inward sensations) which is partially or wholly above the plane of matter.
- Intuition of *Manomaya Kosha*: By development of such intuition, one attains direct knowledge of mind and its effect on cognition, perception etc. This is beyond the materialistic plane.
- Intuition of *Jnanamaya Kosha*: By development of such intuition, one attains direct knowledge of the operation of discriminative intellect. One doesn't feel whirl of mind, race of Prana and weight confinement of body.
- Intuition of *Anandamaya Kosha*: This is the highest level of intuition where one attains direct knowledge of bliss, all fulfilling joy. One is completely (almost) withdrawn from the body plane.

This is how a liberated man achieves *Moksha* when "knower, knowing, known become one" that explores the unity of consciousness and enlightenment, suggesting that the subject (knower) and object (known) are ultimately inseparable and interconnected, with "knowing" being the dynamic process that links them. In a spiritual context, this is Knowing the soul by the soul i.e., the process of self-discovery and understanding that comes from within, rather than relying solely on external sources or intellectual analysis. It's about connecting with one's inner self, recognizing the deeper aspects of one's being, and aligning with one's true nature. This can involve practices like meditation, introspection, and mindfulness to access intuitive knowledge and spiritual insights.

The left top part of the illustration – Understanding increase with development

Existence, Consciousness, Bliss (*Sat-Chit-Ananda*) refers to the ultimate reality, (*Brahman*), and the inherent nature of the Self. It describes God as ever-existing, ever-conscious, and ever-new Bliss. This concept suggests that true happiness and fulfillment are not found in external sources but through self-realization and union with the divine within. As depicted in Existence, Consciousness, Bliss is known at all at the lowest level of intuition of animals or at the level of *Annamaya Kosha*. A man will unfortunately remain at this level of animals if man does not strive to develop this undeveloped intuition level. Here lies the significance of understanding the must to attain development towards Knowing the Soul by the Soul.

Bhagavad Gita 2:29 describes the soul as something wondrous and amazing, with different people perceiving it in several ways. Some see it with wonder, some describe it with wonder, and some hear of it with wonder. However, even after hearing, many do not truly understand it.

आश्चर्यवत्पश्यति कश्चिदेन माश्चर्यवद्वदति तथैव चान्य: |

आश्चर्यवच्चैनमन्य: श‍ृणोति श्रुत्वाप्येनं वेद न चैव कश्चित् || The Bhagwad Gita 2: 29||

Translation: Some see the soul as amazing, some describe it as amazing, and some hear of the soul as amazing, while others, even on hearing, cannot understand it at all.

"Some perceive this (eternal essence) as a wonder (*Aashcharya vatpashyati kashchidenam*): This implies that the Existence Consciousness Bliss is revealed through the Cosmic Light (In Yogananda's teachings) that is experienced as a divine, luminous energy during deep meditation or in states of cosmic consciousness. It is not just a physical light, but a spiritual, vibratory light that reveals the underlying unity of all creation and the interconnectedness of all beings.

"Others speak of it as a wonder" (*aashcharya vadvadati tathaiva chaanyaha*): This implies that the Existence Consciousness Bliss is revealed through the Cosmic Wisdom (In Yogananda's teachings) which is the realization that one's true self is inseparable from Existence Consciousness Bliss and the entire cosmos.

"It is a wonder that some hear about this"(*aashcharya vachchainamanyah srnoti*): This implies that the Existence Consciousness Bliss is revealed through the Cosmic Sound (In Yogananda's teachings) which is also known as *Aum or Om*. This is the foundational vibration of creation, the auditory manifestation of the divine.

"And after hearing about it, some understand this and some do not." (*shrutvapyenam veda na chaiva kashchit*): This highlights that even with hearing about the soul, true understanding and realization are not guaranteed. Many may hear, but few truly grasp its nature.

This verse emphasizes the difficulty in comprehending the soul, which is eternal, subtle, and beyond ordinary perception. It also points out that even those who teach or hear about the soul may not fully grasp its nature, indicating the depth and complexity of spiritual knowledge.

Intellect and Intuition

In the worldwide bestselling biography of Apple cofounder Steve Jobs, a good differentiation has been made Steve has shared his observation when he was visiting India. "*People in India countryside do not use their intellect like we do. They use their intuition instead. And their intuition is far more developed than in the rest of the world. Intuition is a very powerful thing, more powerful than intellect. In my opinion it has a big impact on my work.*"

With such a conviction, it is no wonder that he considered intuition a powerful, almost spiritual gift that surpasses intellect, emphasizing its role in his visionary work and success at Apple. He advocated trusting one's gut and inner voice. It is stated that Jobs observed in his time in India that a calmer mind, achieved by observing and quieting one's thoughts, allows intuition to blossom and provides a clearer, more expansive perspective.

4.5 Becoming the Superman

How do you plan your journey to achieve this Liberation

The journey for 'Knowing the soul by the soul' to liberation (*Moksha*) is a process of self-discovery that one needs to practice. The goal is to transcend material desires, unite with the divine, and merge with the supreme cosmic reality (*Brahman*). There are various paths to practice. Some of the prominent ones mentioned in Bhagwad Gita are

1. *Karma Marg* – Power of Actions
2. *Bhakti Marg* – Power of '*Shraddha*'
3. *Jnana Marg* – Power of Knowledge

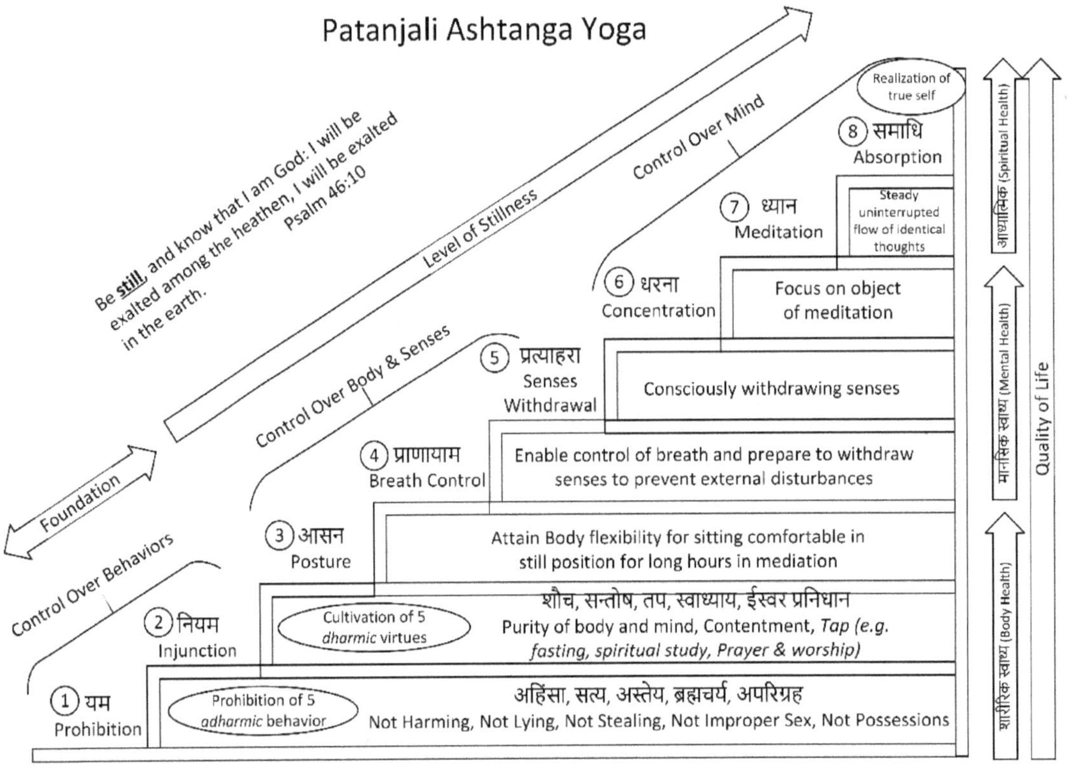

Figure 23: Journey towards becoming superman

Another path is *Patanjali Ashtanga Yoga*. The eight limbs, or *Angas*, are a guide to living a meaningful life and include ethical principles like non-violence, truthfulness, and non-attachment.

Please refer to the book 'Illustrated Vedant' by the same authors of this work for details in the chapter 'Meaning of Yoga.'

Though the paths are many, the final destination as well as the intermediate milestone and the qualities required for them are the same.

Key Takeaways on Intuition originated from Consciousness

Man can be at the level of an animal if they do not develop intuition i.e., if it remains at the materialistic plane of body and mind only unfortunately being happy with food and sex without effective exploration of intellect and reasoning.

There is a clarity essential to understanding the rising level of consciousness and consciousness about everything. Consciousness, in its simplest form, is the state of being aware of and responsive to one's surroundings. It is not limited to human traits. As articulated earlier, even a piece of stone may not have intuition, but it still responds to the natural law of gravity. The concept of consciousness, particularly when considered in relation to the universe and everything within it, becomes more profound and multifaceted. It can be understood as a fundamental aspect of reality, a field of intelligence that permeates all existence, rather than just a property of the human brain. In essence, the idea of consciousness about everything suggests a universe where awareness and experience are not limited to human minds, but rather, are a fundamental aspect of all existence, influencing and connecting everything in ways we are only beginning to understand.

Intuition and consciousness are distinct but related. Intuition is a form of knowing that arises without conscious reasoning, often described as a "gut feeling" or a sudden insight. Consciousness, on the other hand, is the state of being aware of one's own existence, surroundings, and thoughts. While intuition can be a part of conscious experience, it also involves unconscious processing.

Consciousness belongs to the Observer, not to the Objects being Observed

Let us think of a car being driven uphill in the dark night. As the car is driven steep uphill, the headlight is beamed towards the dark sky. This means actually there is no visibility of any object. Now imagine a deer in the road ahead. The driver will only be able to see that once the beam of the headlight is in the vicinity of the dear.

Figure 24: Light is revealed by object

It is not correct that the deer was not there on the road. In other words, even though the deer was present on the road, you can only see it when it is observed through the beam of the headlight of your car. Let us look at this from another angle. In this case , you see the deer through the light i.e., the reflection of the deer in the headlight provides you some feeling about the light, yes. But how do you see the light itself?

Let us take another look. On a sunny day, even if you close all doors and windows, you can possibly have light focused through the skylight on your desk. However, during the dark night there is no sunlight through the same skylight and you are lost in your visibility.

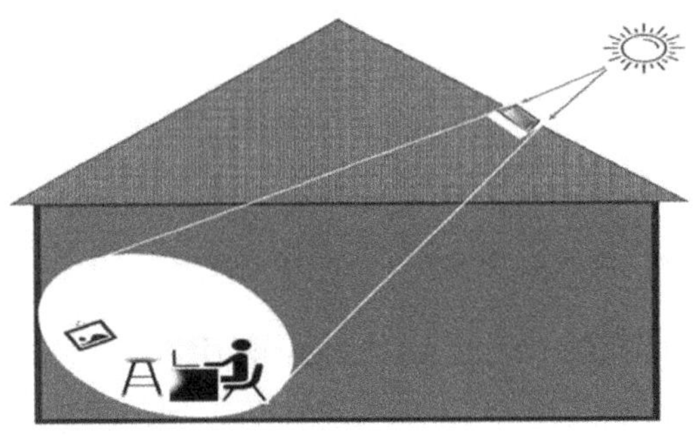

Figure 25: Original source of Light and its experience

In a similar way, you do not see the light by light itself or by another light. But actually, because of the light you are able to see everything else.

That is why it raises questions about consciousness or the discovery of self-enquiry if it is possible to detect by conventional scientific methods. The obvious question is - why not? That is because science is based on observations; the observation of worldly physical objects and phenomena, like looking at the stars with a telescope. When a tree is seen, consciousness is directed towards the tree, but the fact of the matter is - the tree remains anyway irrespective or external to consciousness.

In essence, consciousness can never be found by looking through such a lens or any scientific instrument. It can only be found by reversing the direction of your enquiry. Rather than looking for it in the world, you have to look within yourself i.e., introspection. Consciousness belongs to the observer, not to the objects being observed. So, neuroscientists can study your brain and one day they might be able to accurately detect your thoughts and emotions. But they will never be able to observe your private, personal experience. They will never know how it feels to be you. Even if they explain how your brain produces feelings of sadness and perceptions of color, they can never know what sadness feels like for you or what a particular shade of red looks like to you. That is to say neuroscience, quantum physics or any form of artificial intelligence cannot observe your private conscious experience, nor can it detect or measure consciousness itself.

4.6 *Chidabhas* – the Reflected Consciousness

In Advaita Vedanta, *Chidabhas* refers to reflected consciousness, the consciousness that appears to be associated with the individual mind or ego (*jiva*). It's not the ultimate, pure consciousness (*Brahman*), but rather a reflection of it in the mind, like light reflecting off a mirror.

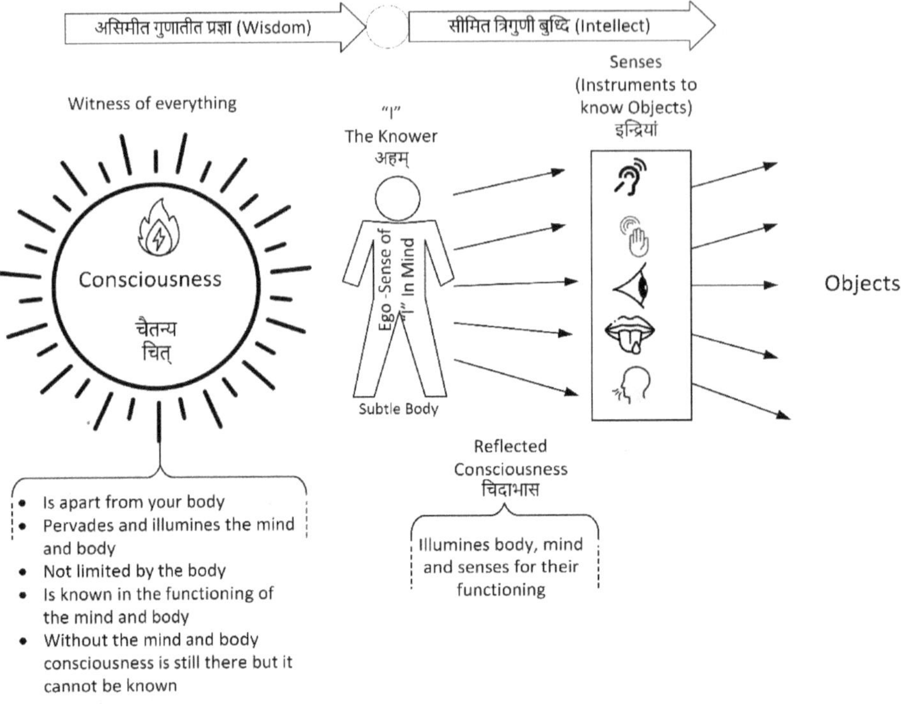

Figure 26: Chidabhas- Reflected consciousness

As depicted in the illustration consciousness (*Chaitanya or Chit*) is apart from one's body, it pervades and illuminates the mind and body, it is not limited by the body, it is known in the functioning of the mind and body and without the mind and body, consciousness is still there but it cannot be known. Consciousness is witness to everything. It is with unlimited (*asimit*) wisdom (*Prajna*), in a state is one of transcendence (*gunatit*) i.e., beyond the 'Gunas' (The *Gunas* - *Sattva* (purity, harmony), *Rajas* (activity, passion), and *Tamas* (dullness, inertia) are the three fundamental qualities of nature that influence all aspects of existence, from thoughts and emotions to actions). Such wisdom (*Prajna*) refers to the highest and purest form of wisdom or transcendental intelligence. It's not merely intellectual knowledge, but a deeper insight that surpasses reasoning or inference and leads to spiritual awakening. *Prajna* involves discriminative wisdom that helps distinguish between the eternal and transient.

However, in reality the body is rather with reflected consciousness and the mind is impure. This reflected consciousness (*Chidabhas*) illuminates body , mind and senses for their functioning i.e., in turn utilizes sensory organs (Indriya) to know physical objects in the material world by touch, vision, smell, taste and hearing. The reflection of pure consciousness in the mind is what we experience as individual consciousness or the "I-sense". It's the consciousness associated with our thoughts, feelings, and actions. Consider sunlight passing through the skylight in the roof to lighten up a part of the room. Now if the glass of the skylight is colored, dirty or opaque, the part of the room will be filtered to produce respectively some colored effect, less light or almost no light at all . In a comparable way in the physical realm, the mind is like an impure filter restricted by the ego (ahamkara) and the sense of "I – the knower." The mind, along with its modifications (thoughts, emotions, etc.), acts as a mirror, reflecting this pure consciousness. This restricts wisdom and is affected by the fundamental qualities or *gunas* with limited (*simit*) intellect.

As explained by Swami SarvaPriyananda, consciousness is reflected in the ego of the mind. Ego is a movement of the mind. In this context the phrase "*Abhiman atmika antahkarana vritti*" refers to a specific type of mental modification (vritti) occurring within the mind's inner instrument (*antahkarana*) that involves the ego's identification with the self (*atmika*) and a sense of pride or attachment (*abhiman*) associated with that identification. The appropriating movement or the function of the mind or inner instrument is called ego. What is that made of? It is made of *Satvik* (meaning not physical but subtle) parts of five elements. Consciousness or *Atma* or *Chaitanya* is reflected in that. When we say 'reflected,' it is just a way of speaking as it is not physically reflected unlike light. It is in a sense so the ego feels aware. It is not only "I" but it is an aware "I." In artificial intelligence (AI), when you endow a robot with AI, that also has a sense of integrity. It can distinguish itself from its environment. It behaves as if it has an ego. So one can even say that the robot has an ego. But the ego of the robot is not a conscious ego. There is no reflection of consciousness there, The robot does not actually feel like us though it behaves like us. Please notice that intelligence. memory, ego, mind – all these can be replicated by computer science today. This alone should force modern philosophy of mind to accept that consciousness is not mind. The mental activities and consciousness are different. You feel inner awareness that reflected consciousness. You think, you remember, you take a decision. The robot also thinks, remembers and takes decisions but it has no inner awareness. In you, there is a light 'on' in the room. For the robot, the room is working but it is a dark room. Ego, memory, intellect, mind – these are all objective processes. You are aware of it. That which is aware of these processes, is consciousness. They shine in the light of consciousness.

Upanishad says '*Tameva bhantam anubhati sarvaṃ*.' This means that consciousness is shining, all of these (mind, memory, ego, intellect, body) are shining. They all are revealed. There lies the difference with a robot which lacks reflected consciousness. Yes, the atman or Brahman is everywhere even in that robot. But the reflected consciousness is not there. Therefore, the inner feeling of 'I am this' is nothing but the empirical or conventional reality (*Vyavaharika*) in us. We can be considered as biological robots. You may say that is the difference between us and a mechanical robot. In us there is a transactional (*Vyavaharik*) sentient being who is capable of being bound and of being released or seeking spiritual liberation. For the robot, there is nothing like that going on.

All physical objects are objective functions of the *antahkarana* which is a material thing made of five elements. But somehow these five elements reflect consciousness and this comes alive as a transactional *jeeva* , a sentient being. One may still ask why can't the inner program of a robot reflect consciousness? The fact of the matter is that there is nothing like that yet.

Chidabhas Relations

So if the *Chidabhasa* refers to the apparent reflection or appearance of consciousness (*Chit*) in the mind and senses (*Antahkarana*). It's the individual consciousness, the "I" that experiences the world, which is ultimately an appearance of the ultimate reality, *Brahman*-pure consciousness, what is the relation between the two?

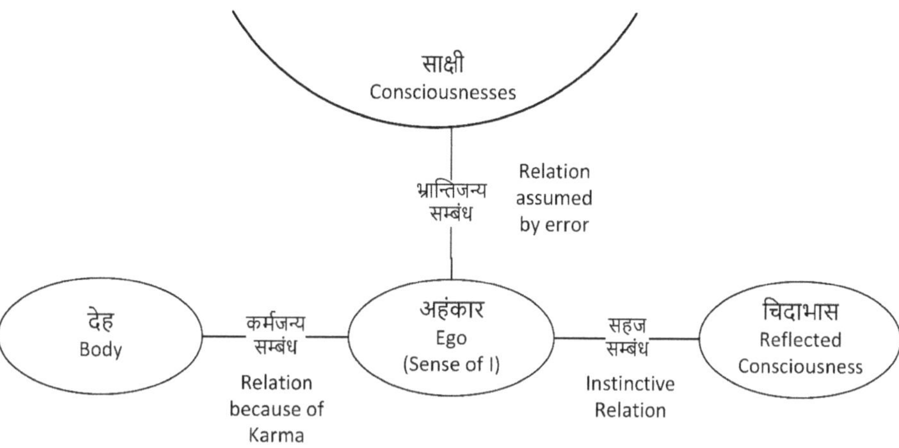

Figure 27: Reflected consciousness and its relations

What is the relationship of *Chidabhas* with the ego (*Ahamkaar*) and with the body and with the real consciousness?

The answer is given that this reflected consciousness will continue with the body as long as the body is alive. The moment the body dies and then this reflected consciousness will again manifest in a new body. A dead body can no longer use the connection with *Chidabhas* through the ego. Thus, the relation between Body and *Chidabhas* is *Karmajanya* or the "relation because of *Karma.*"

The relation between ego and *Chidabhas*- reflected consciousness is *Sahaj* or natural -that is as long as the ego is functioning there will be a reflected consciousness. Think about the reflected face and mirror. Whenever you show the mirror, they'll be reflected face right and when you take away the mirror no reflected face. The reflection and mirror are naturally related. You cannot stop it.

The connection between the reflected consciousness and real consciousness is simply not there. It appears due to an error. This is *Bhrantijanya* or relation because of error. It is just like the connection between the reflected face and real face. What is the connection between reflected face and real face? No connection. Your real face has nothing to do with the mirror or the reflected face however the reflected face entirely depends upon your real face and of course the mirror. So, it is a peculiar product of your real face and the mirror, but real face does not depend upon the mirror, does not depend upon the reflection.

The Idea of Transcendence

The general meaning of transcendent is exceptional or surpassing the ordinary but the true meaning comes out in the context of the subject. Here we cite three different meanings in context.

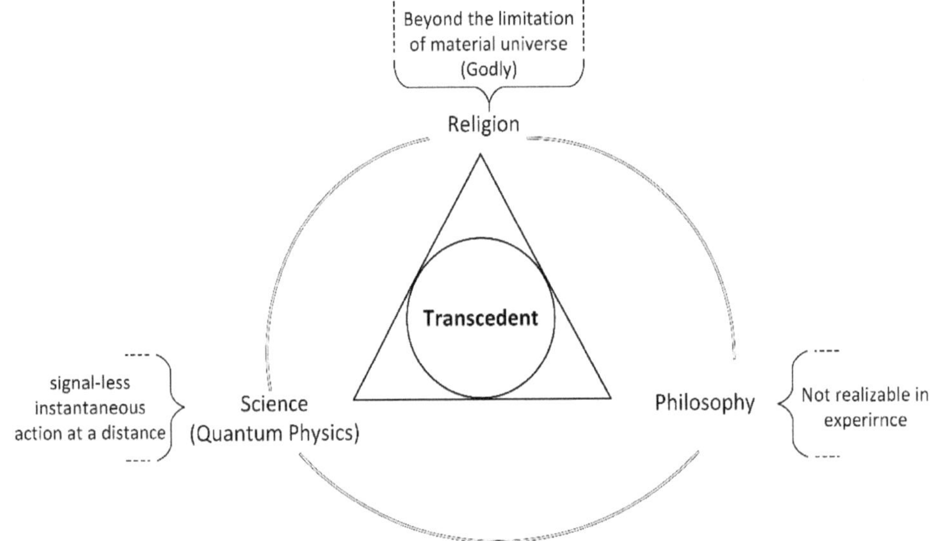

Figure 28: Meaning of transcendence

- Quantum physics describes Transcendence as signal-less instantaneous action at a distance. This is a description of quantum entanglement, which is the "spooky action at a distance" phenomenon where two entangled particles appear to be instantaneously linked, no matter the distance between them.
- In religion, Transcendence refers to a Godly state that is beyond the limitations of the material universe, existing beyond physical laws and human comprehension.
- Transcendence as per philosophy is something that is not realizable in experience. It is not fully graspable or realizable through our senses or empirical investigation but is instead a reality that is "beyond" or "above".

Since the past 2-3 decades, modern science is venturing into the realms that have been hitherto in the scope of religion and philosophy. While mainstream science remains materialist, many scientists, especially dealing with quantum physics, unified field theory, and string theory, are supporting and developing a paradigm based on the primacy of consciousness. A prominent quantum activist and theoretical Quantum Physicist Dr. Amit Goswami have ventured into the domain of the spiritual in an attempt to interpret the seemingly inexplicable findings of curious experiments and to validate intuitions about the existence of a spiritual dimension of life. In his book The Self-Aware Universe he wrote about how consciousness creates a material world.

Until the present of the new physics, the word "transcendence" was rarely appearing in the vocabulary of physics. This term was deemed as dissident or skeptical. However, after a 1982 experiment by a team of physicists in France, it earned its place in quantum physics. The experiment proved that the two quantum particles emitted from the same source remain inextricably correlated. Thus, a change made in one of the particles affects the other instantaneously in a similar way even though they are separated by significant distances. This phenomenon is termed by scientists as quantum entanglement. Entanglement is a phenomenon in which certain properties of two particles become linked with each other. When that happens measuring the state of 1 particle allows us to know the state of the other. Entanglement can occur not only in physical particles like electrons but also in photons. No one knows what strange connection exists between two entangled particles a connection that seems to go beyond both distance and time

So, the question is - when there is no signal in spacetime to mediate their connection then where this instantaneous connection exists between the correlated quantum objects that is responsible for their signal-less action at a distance? This is where the term Transcendence helps. The concise answer is that the connection exists in the transcendent domain of reality. Maybe it is time we start understanding it not just as theory but as a glimpse into reality itself

In order to maintain the historical position of distance from the "heretical" term, scientists have named this a "non-locality" instead of transcendence and defined it as the signal-less instantaneous action at a distance. The conclusion provided by quantum nonlocality is that the fundamental process of nature lies outside the spacetime but generates events that can be located in spacetime.

Noble prize winner scientist Heisenberg did not refrain from obtaining the clues from the ancient Sanatan Scriptures (Upanishads). In 1929 when he was 28 years old, he visited India to meet Gurudev Ravindranath Tagore, the noble prize winner for literature in 1913. Before meeting he was sitting on the bank of River Ganges and contemplating over the unpredictable behavior of matter at subatomic level and uncertainty principle. During the meeting Heisenberg listened about what Upanishads from Gurudev. Gurudev told him that according to Upanishads, the fundamental is not the matter but consciousness, the fundamental and originator of everything in the universe and the same consciousness is within you. And whatever you have known about the material universe is within consciousness, but the human intellect looks to reality only in the orderly creation and is skeptical about disorders. But the consciousness is beyond the intellect and creates everything in the universe. Heisenberg obtained important clues beyond contemporary science in that meeting. Later he spent time in the Himalayas and visited temples in Kanchipuram and Mahabalipuram also. Three years later he got the noble prize in physics. In 1972 Heisenberg told Fritjof Capra (A Vienna-born physicist and systems theorist, famous for his book, The Tao of Physics) that all the unsettling and puzzling thoughts of quantum physics were the primary “sutras” of the teachings of ancient Rishis in India and Upanishads.

Science vs Religion.

When Charles Darwin came out with his evolution theory in the 19th century, there was no consideration of divine force in it. Not only the entire scientific community, but the majority of the educated public accepted his evolution theory. Today, his scientific discovery about evolution and natural selection as the basic mechanism of evolution is unifying the theory of the life sciences, explaining the diversity of life. With this theory emerged a situation of fight between Church with

"God created the worlds" view and Science with "world evolved with its own mechanical scientific process" view. This Religion and Science war is visible in the entire world (with all Abrahamic Religions on the same side) except for in India because of the umbrella of Sanatan Dharma.

Swami Vivekanand has answered the existence of divine force for the process of evolution to work. According to Vedic Science (Sanatan is not a religion but a natural system of life and matter with its own scientific explanations), the Divine involutes as matter and this matter evolves to next level and then that next level matter evolves to next level and so on. Involution and evolution are thus two parallel things. When the Divine involutes in matter, the sacredness is inherited in the matter and that answers why people in Sanatan Dharma worship natural forces like rivers, mountains, trees etc. Though Abrahamic religion may consider this as Idol worship,it is not really idol worship.

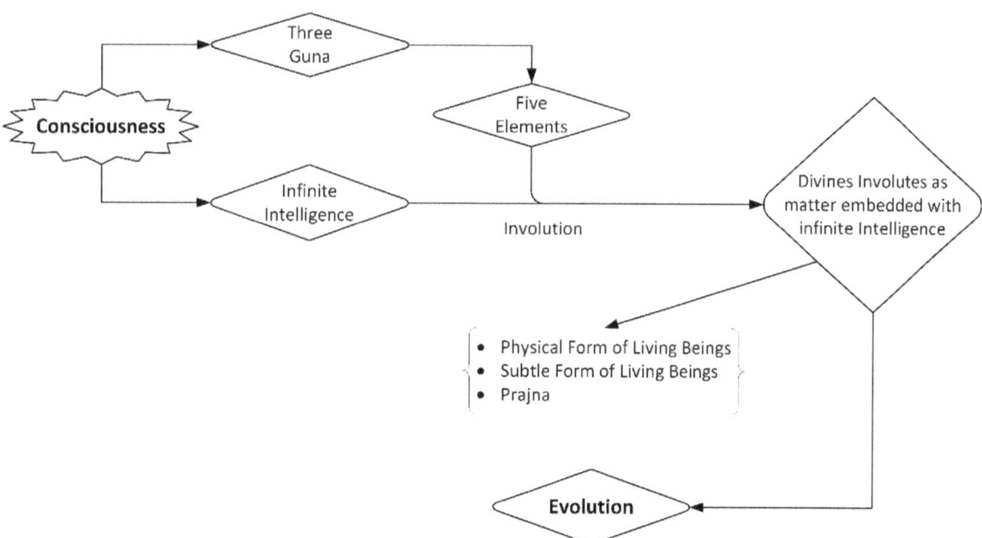

Figure 29: Involution to Evolution

As depicted in the above illustration, the involution and evolution of physical and subtle forms of living beings happen at vastly different pace, with the slow, dense physical realm taking eons to form while the quicker, more fluid subtle bodies (mind, intellect, consciousness) evolve much faster. The subtle evolution outpaces physical changes significantly as consciousness awakens.

Thus, all religions have a problem with Darwin who challenges the belief- "God Created The World" but Sanatan dharma has not any problem. Here comes the question of intelligence as such. In Darwin's opinion, intelligence evolved over time, and the ability to learn was a key attribute of natural selection. If you could not learn, you could not survive, and thus those who learned best survived to pass on their genes. Sounds logical – right? At the same time there is also a weakness in this. The questions remain - where from the very 'intelligence' inherited in the baseline system that is capable of further evolution? This missing component is actually articulated by the concept of 'involution' courtesy complete credit to Swami Vivekananda. He provided the clarity as he described involution as the necessary antecedent process to evolution, where everything exists first in a fine, unmanifested, or "involved" state within its cause before it can become manifest and "evolved". A common seed and tree analogy is utilized for this where the seed is the 'tree involved' and the tree is the 'seed evolved.'

According to Swami Vivekananda, the concept of involution is the necessary precondition for evolution, and it explains how intelligence is embedded in nature. He argues that all the intelligence we observe in the universe and in human beings must have existed in an already "involved" state at the very beginning of the creative cycle. Swami Vivekananda connected involution, the concept that all potential is pre-existent in the cause, to the idea that intelligence in nature is a manifestation of a singular Divine Consciousness (*Brahman*).

For a detailed explanation on the creation or manifestation, please refer to Diagram 60 in the book 'Illustrated Vedant' by the same authors. In this context it is important to note the intelligent cause, or efficient cause, in the creation of something (*Nimitta Karan*). In addition there is also the other material cause (*Upadana Karan*) in the creation of something. For example, when making a pot, the earth is the *upadana* because it is the material used, and the potter is the *nimitta* because they shape the material into a pot.

Just for added interest, a quick detail is depicted in the below illustrating the evolution of five elements during creation or manifestation. The diagram below is self-explanatory for the description and characteristics of the five elements:

space (*Aakash*), air (*Vayu*), fire (*Agni*), water (*Jala*) and earth (*Prithvi*). Involute was the baseline stage at the universal creation or manifestation stage (Time t=0) that was capable of further evolution.

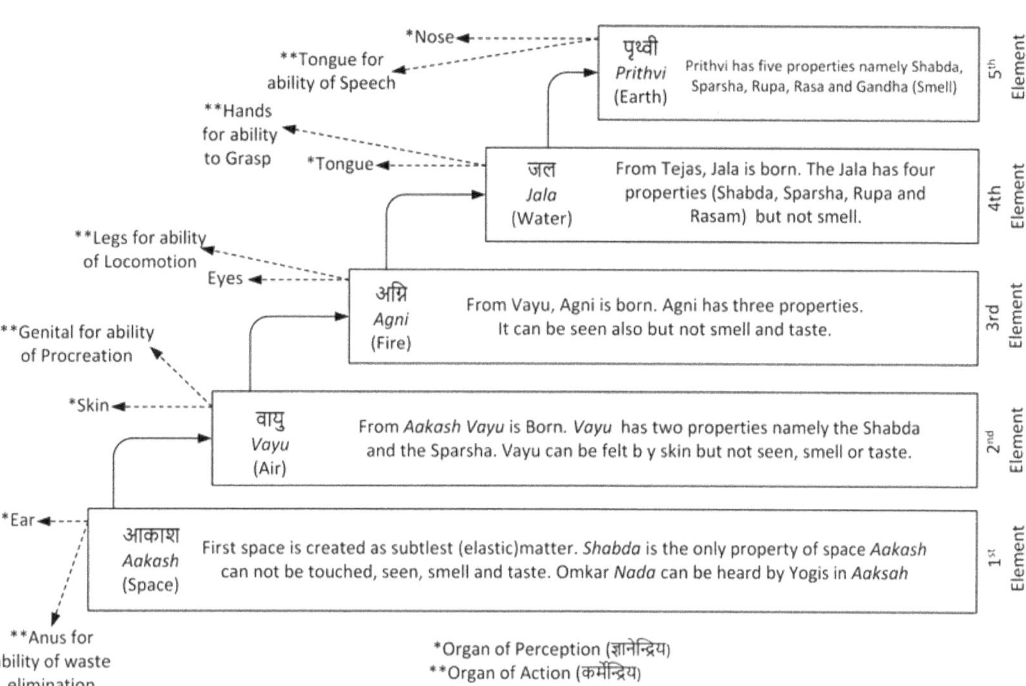

Figure 30: Involution to baseline capable of further evolution

An interesting analogy could be to bring in the connection to AI in this context. We know that core AI algorithms are often focused on analyzing and predicting from existing data. Generative AI builds on existing AI techniques like deep learning and neural networks to understand patterns and then use that knowledge to generate new text, images, code, or other data. In a way generative AI brings a new dimension to AI by adding intelligence focused on creating new content. In a broad way this can be compared to the concept of transcendence wherein the very intelligence available in the involute stage that caused the subsequent evolution as we explained before. Yes, this analogy can be viewed only in a very broad sense though not so much correct. There is a fundamental difference in the level of intelligence here. The intelligence of generative AI is based on incomplete and biased knowledge because it learns from vast datasets, which can contain inaccuracies, human and systemic biases, and a skewed representation of reality. In contrast, the intelligence in involute is flawless and infinite. This is the "flawless infinite intelligence"—that is inherent in all beings and the natural world that has led to a successful evolutionary process and purposeful existence. On the other hand, AI models do not just mirror the input bias; it exaggerates it. Thus, biases from incomplete and skewed data in generative AI are more and more amplified leading to increasingly inaccurate and unfair outcomes.

Demarcation between the Discovery and Invention - Point to Note

In this context it may be interesting to note how humanity as such has perceived the journey of discovery and invention. Discovery is always beautiful but invention can be destructive/harmful. Yes, many inventions have vastly improved the quality of life, such as the development of vaccines, clean running water systems, and refrigeration, leading to longer and healthier lives. At the same time, the price for payment cannot be ignored as well. Nuclear weapons, for example, are perhaps the most damaging inventions ever created due to their immense capacity for destruction. In other words - science is always beautiful but technology is not always. If we apply the above point in the context of *Dharna* and religion per say, we would possibly arrive at the same conclusion. In an analogy consider *Dharma* as the discovery while religion is an invention. The very word 'religion' immediately provides a restriction and comes from something that binds. *Dharma* is that which liberates. Religion has definite dogmas, fixed practices, blasphemy laws, apostasy laws whereas *dharma* eradicates such narrow mindedness. In a similar way, it is time not just to speculate about AI and just immerse yourself in the foolishness of an intelligent future.

Why is it relevant to know about consciousness from the original source rather than relying solely on Western perspective?

In simple terms the answer is that the Indian original source (Vedas and Upanishads) offers a holistic, first-person, and experiential framework for understanding consciousness as the fundamental nature of reality, whereas the

Western approach has largely been analytical, third person, and focused on the physical brain and mind as objects of study.

Reverse Engineering of Vedic literature or stealing?

While the topic of consciousness is so popular in the scientific, religious and philosophical postulations, the originality of the conceptual idea is also challenged by heavy misappropriations by many Westerners. It would be foolish to be ignorant of such arrogant stealing. We would like to caution our esteemed readers to account for such cases which are not one-off but rampant. For example we present here - "***Sri Aurobindo's Legacy Stolen in the West? Battle For Consciousness Theory***"

https://youtu.be/U0RJAZGjD_E?si=RmxcCaxarvF1_IGL

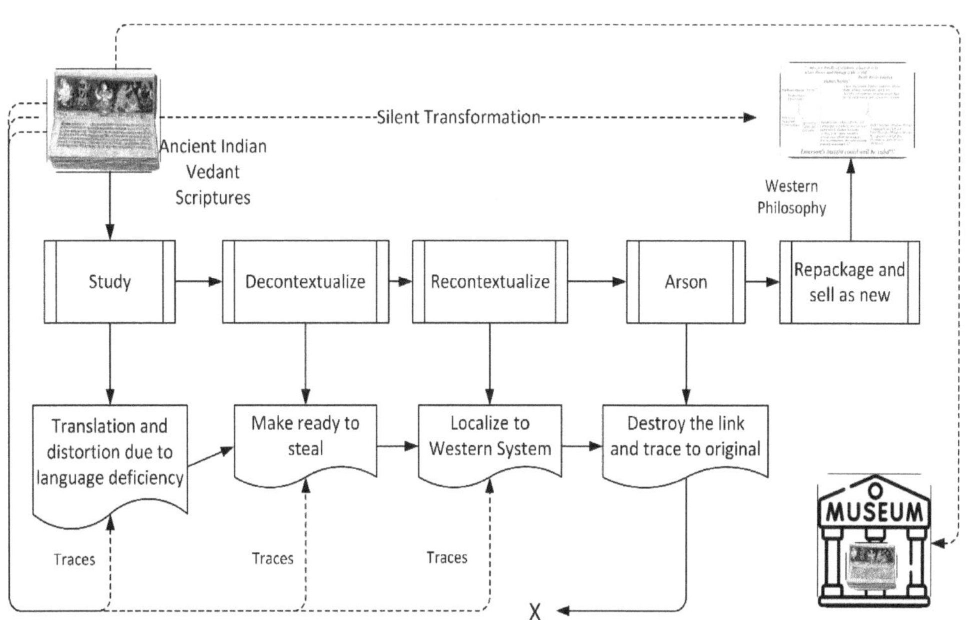

Figure 31: Reverse engineering of Vedic Literature

The illustration is a depiction on the topic of 'Sri Aurobindo's Legacy Stolen in the West - Battle for Consciousness Theory' by Sri Rajiv Malhotra of Infinity Foundation in response to Ken Wilber's appropriation. One of the most comprehensive descriptions of 'consciousness' is provided by Sri Aurobindo. He is an Indian nationalist, yogi, philosopher, poet, and revolutionary who became a spiritual leader after withdrawing from politics in 1910. He developed Integral Yoga, a spiritual philosophy and practice aimed at transforming human life and consciousness, and founded the Sri Aurobindo Ashram in Pondicherry, India. His esteemed publications on this subject date back to the 1930s, which became popular worldwide.

According to Rajiv Malhotra, the American New Age philosopher Ken Wilber appropriated Sri Aurobindo's ideas of consciousness and integrated them into his own "Integral Theory," often without proper acknowledgment or by reformulating them into a Western framework. This is how some westerners take Indian ideas, learn and understand them possibly with great respect but later they change their mind and call those as their own ideas. Of course, racism plays an advantageous and convenient role in crediting a Westerner better outsmarting an Indian spiritual Guru. Rajiv calls this as a 'U-Turn' theory that indicates the people who gather knowledge from Indian sources and then start disparaging the original source and brand those as their own. The irony is - even some Indians who love to be inclined to their inferiority complex, adopt to such thinking that these concepts might have been generated from the West! Actually, the West is selling back to them their own knowledge in many cases. The point that Rajiv makes is that the discoveries that a Rishi like Sri Aurobindo made are fundamentally based on his own profound and direct experiences and not by reading someone else's books. There is no such direct experience that is ever believed to be claimed by Ken Wilber. That is where Ken's explanation of 'consciousness' falls short as that is possibly just a consolidation or rather copy-paste of various articles and books.

The illustration depicts the various stages of the 'U Turn' theory that explains the trajectory of Westerners

- ***In stage 1 (Study)*** they come as benign disciple and study the Indian sources
- ***In stage 2 (Decontextualization)*** such native knowledge is decontextualized to generalize as if to be a part of a universal generic heritage. Here the specificity of the Indian roots are erased.

- ***In stage 3 (Recontextualization)*** , the recontextualization happens where in Western framework often attributed with patents to embark ownership. The unfortunate repackaging is complete by now and this is presented as if it is inherited from West itself.
- There is also a ***stage 4 (Arson)*** which is termed as 'arson' where original concepts are rather mis-contextualized and demolished. This means that the original source knowledge has not only been depleted but also been mis- characterized to make them seem inferior cultural assets.
- So conveniently ***in stage 5 (Repackage & Sell),*** this is repackaged as if it is a new West-branded concept and is ready for sale back to India.

This is exactly the same journey by which Shri Aurobindo's works on consciousness have been appropriated by Ken Wilber. In this context, we would like to describe an ***example of 'Decontextualization' with respect to 'Sanatan Dharma'*** as such which is important as this particular aspect is often misused.

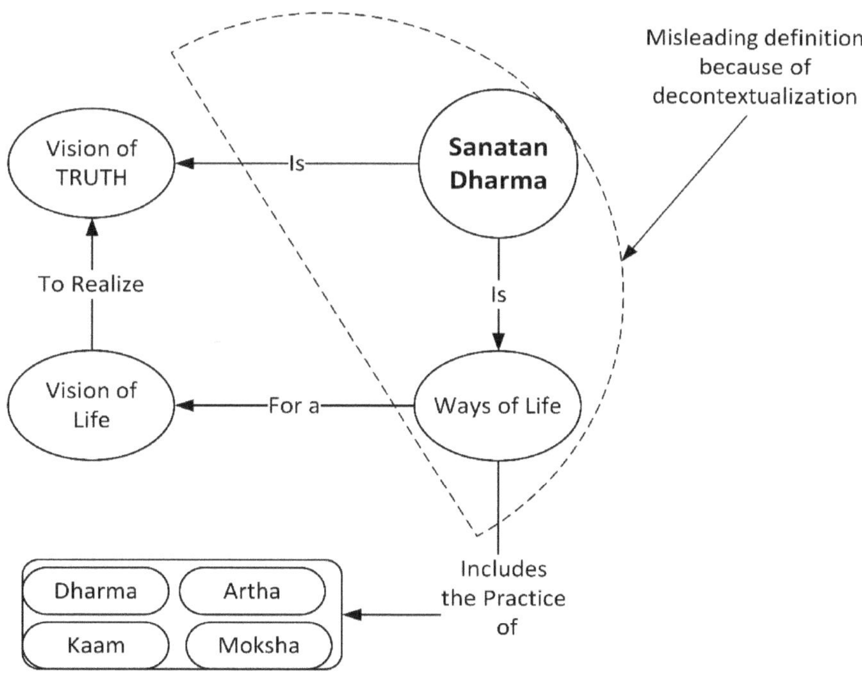

Figure 32: Misleading communication by decontextualization

As the illustration depicts, Sanatan *Dharma* is often described just as "ways of life." How convenient is that? Firstly, it is rather oversimplified to tag not only 'Sanatan Dharma' but for that matter, anything as just ways of life. But apart from mere oversimplification, it is rather a vested attempt towards misleading information crafted with contextualization. The very aspects of 'vision' and 'practice' cannot be excluded. That is to emphasize that Sanatan Dharma is a way of life, yes but only with the context of where the specific ways of life include-

- a vision of life for to realize vision of truth
- the practice of *Dharma, Artha, Kaam, Moksha*

[*Dharma* Living according to our inner purpose), *Artha* (Establishing goals and values that promote it), *Kaam* or *Kaama* (Finding happiness in what we do based upon our Dharma) and *Moksha* (Liberalization i.e., gaining the freedom of consciousness)]

It is obvious that if the above two very aspects are deleted, then the definition lacks any specificity of the original reference. Removing the "vision of truth" (the pursuit of *Brahman/Atman* realization) and the holistic framework of the four *Purusharthas (dharma, artha, kama, and moksha)* decontextualizes Sanatana Dharma by reducing a comprehensive, balanced "eternal law" or "way of life" to a rigid, one-dimensional, or merely socio-political ideology. So next time, even if you come across such oversimplification of Sanatan as such, better be careful as that may not be just a misrepresentation and it is more likely that a vested contextualization is being forced upon.

5 Paradox of History

5.1 Importance of History for survival and progress

At the outset let us take note about three aspects

1. *Itihas Bodh* – This means understanding of history
2. *Shatru Bodh – This means* knowing your enemy
3. *Aatma Bodh* - This refers to knowing about yourself i.e., direct, intuitive knowledge of the Self (it consists of *Swabhava* (One's own nature or inherent disposition) and *Swadharma* (One's own duty or righteous path)

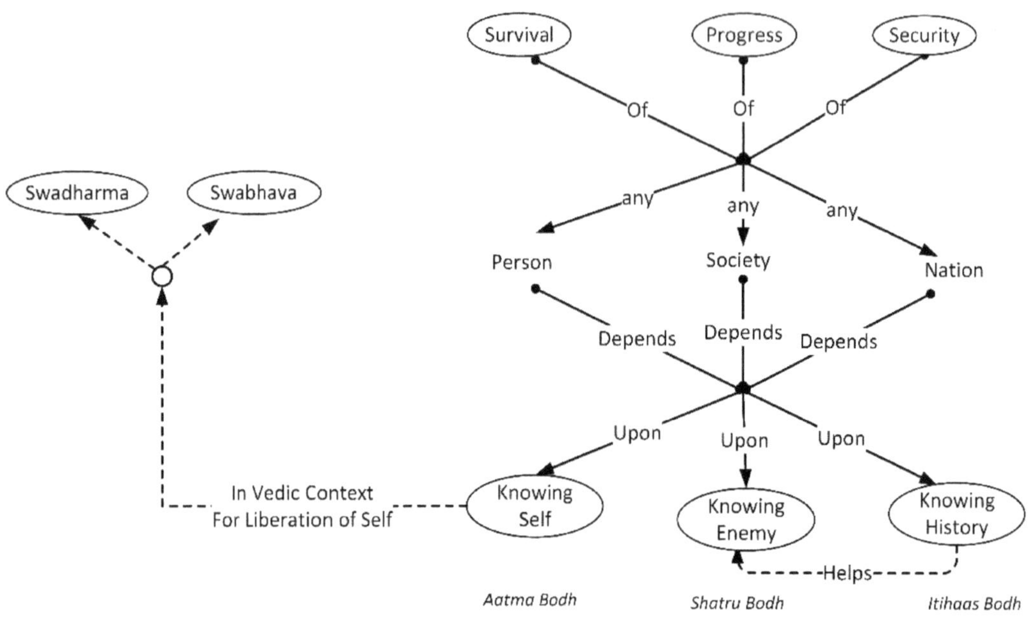

Figure 33: Knowing history for progress, survival and security

Shatrubodh in particular means realizing the identity of the Enemy; just knowing is not good enough. From Vedic perspective, *Aatma Bodh* (also written as Swabodh) and *Shatrubodh* are the basic principles to discover an individual who they are and who they are not. The Vedic wisdom helps to differentiate between *dharma* and *adharma*. As long as this *viveka* is alive, society thrives. A loss of this discriminating power leads to decay and degeneration. In the last few hundred years, especially in the post-independence era, this core Indian aptitude to survive and thrive has been lost and the hangover of the British colony persists. Great Indian leaders and thinkers believing in proven Vedic Wisdom, like Swami Vivekananda, Shri Aurobindo, Lokmanya Tilak, Veer Savarkar, Ram Swarup, and Sita Ram Goel attempted to retain that wisdom during 20th century freedom struggle and now that awakening is showing the signs again.

The illustration depicts the importance of history for survival, progress and security. If you follow the path of the arrow, you will find out for each of survival, progress, or security what it depends upon either for a person or society or a nation.

- From a person's point of view, survival of any person depends upon knowing about your enemy as well as knowing about history and knowing about self. The acknowledgement about history or what has happened before prepares one about adversaries i.e., about feasible enemies. At the same time, it is important as a person to know about yourself as well for introspective assessment that further facilitates survival. If you cannot assess and judge even your strength and weakness, how can you survive in the first place?
- Now even for the point of view of the society and the nation, the above point fits in. Survival of the society and also the nation depends upon knowing about the self, history and enemy.
- In a similar way, progress and security of either a person, society or nation depends upon knowing about self, history and enemy.
- We realize that 'Knowing the enemy' for survival, security and even for progress is must to prepare and combat for. "**Shatrubodh**" (शत्रुबोध) is a Sanskrit term meaning "enemy recognition" or "knowledge of the enemy". It is a concept rooted in Vedic philosophy and strategic thinking, emphasizing the importance of understanding potential adversaries.
- However, it is also important to note what has happened before i.e., to acknowledge and rather be knowledgeable about history. The crucial point to note is that – by virtue of knowing the history (**Itihas bodh**) itself should account for what are the dangerous associations or interactions i.e., 'knowing the enemy.' If this is ignored or missed out, then there is serious blunder when the fundamentals of survival, security and progress are questionable.
- In Vedic context true progress is about knowing yourself (***Aatma bodh***). ***Swabhava*** (One's own nature or inherent disposition) and ***Swadharma*** (One's own duty or righteous path) are intertwined concepts that relate to an individual's unique path and purpose in life. The concept of *Aatma Bodh* is detailed in the book 'Illustrated Vedant' by the same authors (refer fig 68 in page 265).

Now specifically on *Shatrubodh* or knowing about the enemy, there are various reference books and articles available. Some potential titles include "*Dharmashree*" and "*Svayambodha* and *Shatrubodha*: Hindu View of Self and the World," Most of these books describe in detail about enemy consciousness and there are few touch points of historical connections there. The purpose of our discussion is not talk about this 'Shatrubodh' as such but rather take a deep dive on what is the impact of history as focus. It is the very aspect of 'history' that is so heavily interconnected for fundamental identification of the enemy. Again, by history, one has to be careful to demarcate what a truthful history is. If a person, society or a nation depends upon a history which is biased and distorted, then the basic flaw starts from there itself.

This is indeed a serious drawback specifically with a country like India. ***It is a serious point of contention that many Indians are unfortunately devoid of knowing its truthful history and thereby are ignorant about a fundamental identification of its true enemy or rather are confused about enemy consciousness.***

What is *Itihas Bodh* for truthful History?

Understanding about history unfortunately does not mean truthful history. Because of distorted history you may identify your true enemy as hero and true hero as enemy and follow the path of self-destruction.

It is commonly interpreted that the king Ashoka converted to Buddhism solely out of grief over the Kalinga War. This is rather an over-simplification of historical events. The fact is that king Ashoka was already a Buddhist before the conflict. The remorse over the war likely strengthened his commitment to Buddhist ideals but marking the grief over the Kalinga war as an exclusive reason is more an over-statement.

In this context, it is worthwhile to mention that a street previously known as Aurangzeb Road in New Delhi was renamed to A.P.J. Kalam Road in 2015. There has been an outcry of fascism even though the Mughal emperor Aurangzeb is infamous extreme for extreme intolerance, oppression and genocide in India. Is it not simple common sense to associate a prominent street with a revered national figure?

This very aspect of knowing truthful history is our focus that we are getting in detail to appreciate its significant nuances.

Itihas Bodh - History of Religion and its Impact on History

As a precursor to explore what constitutes a truthful history, let us first understand their perspectives that characterizes history as such. These are

- How not just the so-called historical events but the culture as such becomes an integral part of history specifically with reference to Sanatan Dharma as described below in 'Forest and Desert religion.'
- How through invasions, the predator civilization negatively impacts and rather maligns and alters the history of the original civilization.
- How not to confuse with history and mythology with the *Itihas* as such

Let us discuss further.

Forest and Desert Religion

It is interesting to note the explanation by Rajiv Malhotra@Infinite Foundation that articulates the difference between the dharmic faiths and Abrahamic religions using the analogy of life in the forest vs the desert. A place where a religion originates plays a crucial role in its norms and adaptability. From the forest region evolved dharmic faiths like Hinduism, Jainism, Buddhism or Sikhism. They are all based on peace on self as well as on surrounding. Like forest dwellers understand and respect that all creatures are dependent on each other and live together in harmony. This is reflected in the dharma traditions where each one of us can have our own path to God. All dharmic paths ultimately lead to one indivisible self which is not separate from the divine. The forest's diversity is an expression of the divine in everything. Forest religions are fluid and change dynamically to keep up with new knowledge. On the contrary all Abrahamic religions like Judaism, Christianity and Islam come from the desert i.e., from barren land where nature is not a nurturing mother unlike forest. There change and evolution are terribly slow with less diversity. Desert religions reflect this outlook with harsh rules and aggressive nature that does not appreciate diversity and they do not evolve with time. God is perceived as someone far above with something so absolute as one God, one book, one rule and those who do not follow that rigid rule is prone to punishment. In forest religion, there are multiple schools of philosophy, a library of scriptures and many forms of worship that an individual is free to choose. It is no wonder that forest religions found contentment at home instead of invading or turning into conquering world territories.

Predator Civilization and Alteration of History

As a tiger eats an animal, its digestive system breaks the prey inti tiny parts which reassemble into the healthy cells of the predator's body. This is what describes an aggressive civilization. European colonizers gained a lot of assets from native Americans who lived there for 20000 years. In today's world one is observing how China is manipulating Tibet. Whatever part of culture is deemed fit or appropriate gets digested and the rest excreted as waste. The dominant reformulates the original history and thus evolves a rather digested history of digested people. Dead civilizations often turn into prestigious assets displayed only in Western museums. Romans and Greeks were rivals until the Romans defeated the Greeks and digested the useful parts of Greek civilization like philosophy, art and lifestyle. Later Rome also digested Christianity and thus evolved the Roman Catholic church. The digestion of predators continued as we see many such examples in world history.

A classic example of stolen assets is the rapid digestion of Yoga into Western reductionist way of life that is rampant. The unfortunate fact is -this is interpreted with a very narrow understanding as if these are just some postures of physical exercise that one has to practice. Yoga has become mainstream in the Western world, and is more often than not, used as a type of exercise, rather than a spiritual ritual most people do as part of their weekly training routine. However, "Yoga is not a physical experience, but rather an inner spiritual experience" (as told by Sri Aurobindo, an Indian philosopher).

We can thus classify the various countries in the following way as countries who are primarily 'Predator' the countries who have fallen 'victim' to such predator countries and also the countries who have gone through a transition from being a 'predator to victim' throughout the journey of historical events. Though it may appear untoward but actually is interesting, note that it was Adolf Hitler who launched a campaign of aggression and conquest that made many countries who were so-called 'predators' in nature to fall as 'victims.'

Predator	**Victim**	**Predator to Victim**
▪ Italy ▪ Britain ▪ France ▪ Portugal ▪ Spain ▪ Turkey These nations are predominantly "predatory" due to their history of colonialism and imperialism, a period lasting from roughly the 15th to the 20th century.	▪ All countries in Africa Continent ▪ All countries in South America Continent ▪ India These countries fell "victims to predator countries" in a long history of exploitation by global powers through colonialism and neocolonialism.	▪ Greece ▪ Mongolia The imperial era of Greece ended with its incorporation into the Roman Empire in 146 BCE. It then spent nearly 400 years under Ottoman rule, during which it was subjugated and exploited. Similarly, By the 17th century, Mongolia was largely incorporated into the Manchu-led Qing dynasty. For centuries, the Mongolians were under foreign domination, losing their independence.

Post World War II

Predator	Victim
USA	▪ All the countries in western hemisphere (Monroe Doctrine) ▪ Chosen Countries in Rest of the world

The seed of the assertive foreign policy of the USA was the Monroe Doctrine articulated by the fifth President James Monroe during his second term in 1823. At the time, western European colonies in North America and South America were awakened to be independent and many of them achieved independence. This doctrine recognizes the New World free from colonization and opposes any efforts by European powers to control or influence sovereign states in the region would be viewed as a threat to U.S. security. Although it stated the principle of Mutual Non-Interference i.e., the US pledged not to interfere in internal European affairs or existing colonies in the hemisphere, the situation dramatically changed after World War 2. USA with the success of its power in WW2, took an aggressive role and while asserting its domination in its sphere of influence in western Hemisphere, started expanding in the rest of the world thru covert operation (invasion by sophisticated and clandestine means) as well as by military interventions. "Confession of an Economic Hit Man" by John Perkin provides ample clues on how these operations are done.

It is interesting to note that India and countries in South Africa have never been an invader to any other civilization. India, despite being the most rich and powerful country, chooses to be a righteous Country (*Dharmik Rashtra*)- Thanks to the core concept of Sanatan Dharma.

Itihas vs History vs Mythology

History, as understood in the West, is a systematic study of the past based on evidence, including written records, archaeological findings, and other sources. We have already seen that such history often is manipulated at the hands of the predators. In Sanskrit, "*Itihas*" (इतिहास) literally means "thus it happened". It refers to a type of narrative that combines historical accounts with moral and philosophical teachings.

In this context, it is good to point out couple of different meanings of Mythology:

- One meaning about Myth is that it is traditional story, especially one concerning the early history of a people or explaining some natural or social phenomenon, and typically involving supernatural beings or events:
- The other meaning is that it is widely held but it is rather a false belief or idea. That may be
    - a misrepresentation of the truth
    - a fictitious or imaginary person or thing
    - an exaggerated or idealized conception of a person or thing

However, 'Mythology' per say should not be undermined as the study of ancient but inappropriate history or false belief. Yes, as commonly understood, mythology encompasses traditional stories, often involving gods, heroes, and supernatural events, which explain a culture's origins, beliefs, and values. An appropriate context will be the 'Puranas.' Puranas are primary religious texts in Hinduism that contain information about Hindu history, mythology, traditions, and beliefs. The word "Purana" is Sanskrit for 'ancient' or 'old,' and the texts describe the deep mythic structuring of Indian civilization. While not conventional historical records, they contain valuable information about ancient India when used alongside other sources like archaeology and inscriptions. The Puranas are a combination of allegorical stories and historical facts that need to be interpreted, not taken literally. Yes, to make that attractive, the narratives often contain hyperbolic and supernatural elements. But at the core the purpose is meant to convey spiritual or moral lessons, rather than blindfolded by precise historical accounts. Thus, Purana should not be regarded as mere false belief but they should be regarded as depiction of ancient history (embellished with a bit of exaggeration and idealism) of not only this world (earth) but other worlds (*Lokas*) that science has yet to discover.

Nevertheless, history is seldom free from bias as information is passed down through many generations of intermediaries. It is no secret that someone might have selected which facts are important to include, how to prioritize them along with vested narratives from historians with conscious and unconscious inclusion of individual agendas. That is no wonder as most historians were employed by kings or churches. On top of that some historians projected their own theories on feminism or human rights. For that matter, Indian history became a political tool as if to only examine who are the victims and who are the exploiters. Itihas is a different lens to understand the past that uses Vedic cosmology and metaphysics for interpretation. The purpose of Itihas is to teach the truths of the Vedas in a user-friendly way contextualized in a given time and place for the fundamental principles of life.

Why does it take time to Discover Truth? (and therefore Truthful History)

Truth is a universal reality unlike a mere fact which could be a slice of information. We deliberated on 'Searching for Truth' in the book Illustrated Vedant by the same authors.

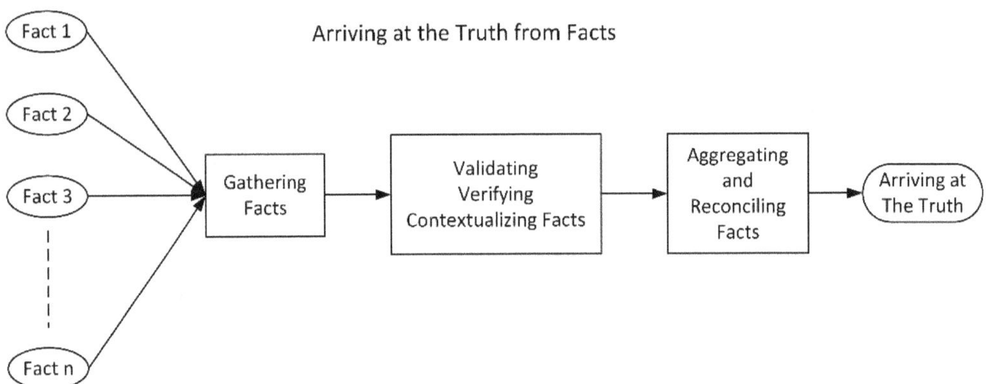

Figure 34: Knowing truthful history

The illustration above is an intentional repeat representation of Figure 9 to grasp the quick aspects of the hurdles of realization of truth as such that needs careful processing of the overview facts that has been articulated before. It not only takes time to arrive at the truth but also it is difficult exercise as well. You will know that each step takes time and effort, but what makes it difficult is to apply a condition-free mind.

Why wise man knows the Truth while knowledgeable man knows the Fact only

Knowledge about facts refers to information and understanding about the empirical, phenomenal world, the world we experience through our senses and intellect. However, such apparent knowledge is prone to observational distortion or bias due to ignorance or vested interest. As we discussed wisdom in detail already, wisdom refers to a deeper, transformative understanding that goes beyond the superficial appearances of the world. It is the realization of the ultimate reality (*Brahman*) as the only true and unchanging existence. Hence a wise man knows the truth while a knowledgeable man is limited to knowing mere facts only.

The Attention span is declining and thus Tendency to find the Truth is declining

Thanks to the rise of digital technology and the prevalence of information overload. Human attention spans have been declining significantly in recent decades. From reading books to glancing through white papers it has gone down to checking out quick blogs and further down to tweets even! Even for that the average length of time people spend focused on any given screen has decreased dramatically, from 2.5 minutes in 2004 to just 47 seconds currently (according to Dr. Gloria Mark, University of California). In such a frenzy, how may we expect that there would be sustained effort to explore and find the truth? So, the obvious happens. The constant influx of information from various sources (social media, news outlets, etc.) are so overwhelming that it makes it difficult to engage in deep, focused thought and instead readily accept information at face value. This leads to engaging with information that confirms one's existing beliefs and values with no room for critical evaluation.

It is not just Distortion, but sometimes it is 'Murder of History'!

History is often distorted due to several factors, including deliberate manipulation, biased perspectives stemming from political agendas, nationalistic narratives, ideological control, economic interests, or even the suppression of marginalized groups' histories. If you feel that that is the limit, then you are mistaken. Take for example possibly one of the ultimate examples which is a book named 'The Murder of History' by Khursheed Kamal Aziz. It explains the various errors, misquotations, misinterpretations and misleading statements found in various curriculum textbooks taught in Pakistan. It may sound rather unbelievable as In this book, the author has critiqued and provided the corrections for 66 text books being taught in the Social Studies, Pakistan Studies and History disciplines to students from grades 1 to 14. By teaching this biased pile of textbooks, where are we leading the youth of the country?

The fact is unpleasant but true that the current media is crippling and disabling the 'present' if not committing a murder. The present is getting constrained on a wheelchair with minimal or no meaningful progress. The obvious consequence is that – the 'future' is seriously impacted.

History Repeats itself because you have not Learnt from History. For those who have Learnt, History does NOT Repeat

"Those who cannot remember the past are condemned to repeat it" (as articulated by writer and philosopher George Santayana). Yes, history may not repeat in exact detail. However, there are recurring patterns and themes that emerge. Those who study history can identify these patterns and potentially avoid repeating past mistakes. The history of the United States and Europe clearly exhibits that wars have ended with confiscatory terms of government surrender that inevitably was breeding upcoming wars. In the 21st century, this gets further complicated when great powers intervene to fight proxy battles. This leads to the conflict becoming protracted as we have been observing in Syria, Ukraine or with Israel-Hamas. Some may argue that human nature, with its capacity for both good and bad, is a constant factor that contributes to recurring patterns in history. At the same time, one may not ignore the point that history and its patterns are in front of you to analyze and take note of before making a blind step that could bring about a similar disastrous outcome that happened before. At least an active acknowledgement initiates the very first step to step back for a reality check. So the question we must ask ourselves today is this: ***can we afford to learn nothing from history?***

Studying History vs Writing History = What is True vs what feels Good

Studying and writing history involves an interestingly complex interplay about - whether one is seeking the most accurate understanding of the past ("what is true") or whether one is recognizing how narratives can resonate with on a personal and emotional level ("what feels good")!

Studying history involves engaging in rigorous research, using methodologies like source criticism, contextualization, and comparative analysis to reconstruct the past accurately. Now who has written that history? It is written by historians who are sponsored by the emperor or by the church. Not only that, the historians are human, which leads to bringing their own perspectives and biases to their work, introducing an element of subjectivity into historical interpretation. The dilemma is clearly between what is true versus what it feels good to project for!

5.1.1 Examples of Distorted History

(Facts not considered to teach the truthful history)

History has lost its relevance just by renaming the original places in India

This is a unique phenomenon in India. There are multiple examples where the original names of places as described in the Upanishad or in Puranas (i.e., Ramayana and Mahabharata) are no longer found in India. For example, the five villages of SriKrishna namely Teenprashtha, Gajaprashtha, Soniprashtha, Paniprashtha and Indraprashtha are renamed respectively as Faridabad (by Farid Khan), Gaziabad (by Gazi Khan), Sonipat, Panipat and Delhi. The kingdom of Panchal as described in Mahabharata is no longer found in Indian geographical territory as the same has been renamed after the Mughal emperor Farrukhsiyar as Farrukhabad. Let alone religious politics, this creates an issue of right to identity and right to dignity. This is unlike the Bible or Quran where at least the original names of the places are kept intact and thereby the significance of their historical relevance is well maintained. This is an unfortunate situation in India were renaming of the important places of interest have truly caused the eclipse of truthful history.

We are actually learning history from the invader's point of view

Such an approach is embarrassing. In Indian history textbooks you are taught about Chhatrapati Shivaji as a part of the period of the Mughal emperor Auranzeb. The stigma is that - there is just one sentence mentioning about Tarabai, the queen who protected the kingdom single handedly against Aurangzeb for almost a decade.

The entire history of India as articulated in books and publications can be broadly classified as the era of early invasions (Persian and Greek) followed by the Mughal empire and Delhi Sultanate, then the British colonial rule and history around independence days. Invaders and colonizers often created histories to legitimize their rule which is obvious. For example, there are conflicting historical narratives around the Mughal empire where large parts of our history is either hidden or selectively articulated. To elaborate, recent controversies surrounding NCERT history textbooks in India highlight claims that the Mughals provided financial grants to rebuild temples destroyed during wars. However, in response to a Right to Information (RTI) query seeking evidence for these claims, the NCERT stated that they do not possess any documents to support this assertion. Both the greatness and sufferings of the country's land must be addressed otherwise it is a great injustice we do to those people who fought for the nation and died for the nation.

British historian James Mill and his 1817 work namely 'The History of British India' is a prominent example for dividing Indian history to justify colonial rule while he never even set foot in India. Max Müller, the German scholar and his Aryan Invasion Theory based on filmy evidence has been already challenged. A key criticism is that many British historians wrote history to serve the "divide and rule" strategy of the East India Company, creating divisions between religious groups and reinforcing the idea of Western cultural superiority.

Even the history of Indian independence is accused of biases not just to suit the British imperialist colonization but also due to nationalist reactions, and post-independence political ideologies.

We have a problem of hero-worshipping instead of a balanced evaluation

Who gave Mahatma Gandhi the title 'Father of the nation'? Such a title is usually given to the first President of an independent country or to someone who is a driving force behind the establishment of the country. As per the article 18 of the Indian constitution, no such title can be conferred by the state. It is Subhash Chandra Bose, also known as Netaji, in his radio broadcast from Singapore in 1944 was the first to address Mahatma Gandhi as 'Father of the Nation' It is amazing how much respect he had for him despite serious differences in opinions about the path of liberation and freedom movement of India. Despite the lack of official recognition, the title gained widespread acceptance and became an integral part of India's historical narrative and popular sentiment.

Again, there is information ignored or hidden to commoners about things that Gandhi said. It is stated that Mohandas Gandhi was sent to England to learn his trade as a lawyer. Then he went to South Africa and for 20 plus years he had a career as a lawyer. He fought for the so-called Boer war on behalf of the British in a leadership position within the Ambulance Corps. It is remarkably interesting to read the writings as "I put my life in peril four times for the sake of the Empire, — at the time of the Boer war." One may argue that the situation was different vis-à-vis his actions during the freedom movement against the British later. The issue is unless you research through such findings, the standard history textbooks are amazingly silent about such a portrayal which is simply an unbalanced projection.

Wickedness of British colonization distorted fundamental historical facts

The human cost of British colonialism had a devastating impact in India. Almost the entire world aspired to wear Indian clothing because India produces the best weaves. There are mentions of various Indian fabrics and carpet weaving in Rigveda. The Indian earliest surviving cotton thread dates back to 4000 BC, approximately 6000 years ago. But between 1800 to 1860, the Indian textile exports reduced by 94%. This was not by accident, but because of a well- planned strategy , The British broke the loom, destroyed the market, taxed everything three times and bought in the imported fabrics. The British governor general

William Bentiick said, "the bones of cotton weavers are bleaching the plains of India" Millions of people died of hunger because their livelihoods were destroyed.

This was not a one-off incident. British East India Company registered more profit while millions died in hunger when more than 70 million people died during the 1770 Bengal famine. That is more than the number of Jews died during the 2nd world war. This almost wiped out about 1/3rd of the population of Bengal. But even In India, how many people realize about the depth and detail of such cruelty in the books and articles on history? While natural disasters triggered the crisis, it was the British East India Company's intentional policies that turned it into a catastrophic famine. The irony is that the British company made more profit in 1771 than they did in 1768. How can one imagine that while millions of people did die of hunger?

History is silent about the world's first university that belongs to India even during 6th century BC

In 1947 when the British left India, the literacy rate of India was just about 12%. This percentage does not represent the educated community. It actually means that 12% of the Indian people can read and write at a considerably basic level. But the irony is – the world's first university belongs to India which is Takshashila, now in Pakistan. That was established in 700 BC which is about 2700 years ago. More than 10000 students from all across the world studied more than 60 subjects there. Can you imagine how civilized such a culture was already at that time itself?

It is not surprising that Takshashila may not fit the present structure of university with a Western definition of a university that typically refers to the autonomous, degree-granting institutions that originated in medieval Europe. By the way, it was unfortunate that such a treasured university was destroyed in the 5th century CE by the invading Huns led by Mihirakula.

Alexander vs Porus – The fooling of Greek records of history

We have been told for years that Alexander the Great came to India and defeated king Porus. He was so impressed with the bravery of Porus that he gave back the kingdom even after winning the battle. And right after this war, Alexander, who was on a mission to conquer the world, decided to go back because his soldiers were too tired to continue further. Such a story has a lot of loopholes. No wonder since the details of this war is only mentioned in the Greek records, not anywhere else. Takshashila, one of the finest universities, was just about a few miles away from where this war happened. Still, no one bothered to record anything about this historical event. Did such a war happen at all? Or even if the war happened, the actual reality is Alexander was defeated by king Porus. Is it rather too convenient to tag a tyrant like Alexander generous enough to give back a kingdom? It could also be that after the defeat by King Porus, Alexander dies on his way back because of injuries from the battle.

The resilience of the ancestors is forgotten while invaders are glorified

Take reference to Srirangam, the sacred heart of the SriVaishnava tradition and home to the grand Ranganatha Swamy temple. In 1323 CE, this holy land became a battlefield soaked in blood. The tyrant Ulugh Khan, later known as Mohammad Bin Tughlaq, led an army southward unleashing terror upon the flourishing tower of Srirangam. This was a ruthless massacre. Thousands of innocent devotees and scholars were slaughtered. The sacred temple was desecrated, its treasure looted, its idols broken. Amidst the chaos, the chief SriVaishnava scholar somehow managed to smuggle the idol away. Meanwhile Vedanta Desika safeguarded the temple's ancient scriptures, hiding them underground. The temple's ancient chronicle records this tragedy as the 'massacre of the twelve thousand.' Yet history books barely remember this attack. While invaders are glorified, the resilience of the ancestors is forgotten.

Genocide In India after 1857 – Fundamental facts are not considered

Historical scholarship acknowledges that the aftermath of the 1857 Indian Uprising (referred to as the Sepoy Mutiny) was marked by a period of brutal British retaliation and significant loss of Indian lives. The fundamental issue is - a freedom movement itself is tagged as if it is 'mutiny' as that is convenient for the British where more than 280 Indian soldiers were summarily executed. But how come that unfortunate tag continues till date in Indian history books? The figures of death and casualties are disputed still for the brutal genocide of Jallianwala Bagh in 1919 when Brigadier Dyer open fire on a trapped crowd. Again, the Bengal famine of 1943 killed more than three million people in Eastern India. It was one of the worst losses of civilian life on the Allied side in World War II. Is there any memorial, museum, or even a plaque, anywhere in the world to the people who died? While the British (and the Western world) wrote a lot about Adolf Hitler for the killing of millions of Jews, they never admitted the accountability of Winston Churchill for this horrible disaster.

Russia's interested in Ukraine – Facts that are not acknowledged

Historically though, the homeland of the same Slavik ethnic people, Ukraine was a territory loss for Russia during the dissolution of the USSR in the 1990s. Specifically in Ukraine there were lots of Soviet missiles and nuclear warheads. The deal was stuck so that Ukraine gave that up in exchange for Russia managing its debt. Russia also subsidized the development of Ukraine in the last 20 years with about $150 billion subsidy. However, in 2014 a pro-NATO or pro-US regime was installed in place of a legally elected Ukraine government engineered by the West. There was no census conducted in Ukraine in these 20 years otherwise it could have been found that there is a very significant Russian speaking population across the country. Pro-Russian unrest began during this time, followed by Mr. Putin annexing Crimea. A war started which resulted in a series of Minsk agreements from time to time. One has to note that Zelensky came to power in the spring of 2019 and Ukraine officially requested a NATO Membership Action Plan. Quite obviously this is against the interest of Russia. It is not surprising for Mr. Putin, who has a large command and befitting ego to lay out a plan for an expanded Russia. More so as after the Russian economy was systematically destroyed under Boris Yeltsin, it is Mr. Putin who stopped the bleeding and made Russia rise again.

By 2021 there was a significant escalation in fighting in the Donbas region that continued, finally followed by Russia ordering a formal invasion of Ukraine in 2022. Behind such an invasion, the chronology of historical events and the agenda and vested interest of various stakeholders lay buried. It is amazing that this is called an invasion while an aggressive action by the US in Iraq is projected as liberation!

When the British army moved in, it was marketed as means of civilization. By the way, the default interpretation that Mr. Putin wants to recreate the USSR appears incorrect as he may not be interested in bringing back communism in Russia. He is rather ensuring a stronger Russia with intended control over the historically Russian regime and keeping NATO and the Americans away from Russia's sole sphere of influence.

The Middle East crisis – The ignored facts about Israel Hamas conflict

Hamas conducted a significant terrorist attack on October 7, 2023 that marked a notable escalation in the Israeli Palestinian conflict. Then Israel continues massive retaliation on Gaza till date. Taking some steps back from the current state of affairs, Israel tried to implement a two-state solution in 2005 when they separated Gaza and made the people of Gaza own their government. The people of Gaza selected Hamas which is an anti-Israel organization. Hamas and Hezbollah are proxies of Iran, a theocratic nation which has been a very strong anti-Israel and anti-US proponent since 1979 (after the so-called Islamic revolution). Beyond the first level of religious conflict (some level of Jews vs Islam though not entirely correct) , there is the power projection angle of Iran beyond their borders aided by some proxy allies like Hamas, Hezbollah and Houthis in Yemen and some in Iraq. Iran was also alleged to be in the process of developing a nuclear deterrent while the US withdrew from the Joint Comprehensive Plan of Action (JCPOA) in 2018 citing concerns over Iran's nuclear activities and regional behavior. This is a matter of concern for Israel which is also an unstated nuclear power. Eventually, we observed America's bombing on three Iranian nuclear sites in June, 2025 with a purpose to deter Iran's nuclear ambitions and prevent weapon proliferation.

The dynamics in the Middle East is complex. Russia, Iran and to some extent China have been working together to offset the US allies in the region. In fact, the West Asia region has always been a flashpoint where Iran and Israel are the two major power centers. Standard geopolitical predictions can go wrong in these places with a sudden aggressive surge of stupid action like the Hamas attack on Israel in 2023. The question is how does a tiny Israel portray dominance in the region? The obvious answer is external help from the USA ever since Israel was recreated in the 1940s. Israel has its strong Jewish diaspora widespread, with significant populations in the U.S., Canada, Europe, and Australia. The US views Israel as a key ally in the Middle East, a democratic partner, and a vital player in regional security.

Why do even Indian Historians Distort Truthful Indian History?

One can estimate why the West does those who are driven by the Eurocentric orientalist agenda by portraying Eastern societies as exotic, backward, or uncivilized compared to the West or by rationalizing colonialism. But why do Indian historians do that? Let us first take note of the very book 'The Discovery of India' by Jawaharlal Nehru (India's first Prime Minister). Did his personal obsession with secularism make him diminish and deride India's sacred Vedic texts or show little regard or empathy for Hindus? This has been critiqued heavily. Nevertheless, it is obvious that the historians during such regimes would be influenced and sometimes sponsored to portray history in a manipulative manner in text books and articles. This continued thereafter. The late 1960s saw a rise in Marxist historiography in India with establishment of left-leaning political movements that contributed to their prominence in academia. The effect was accused of being more vitriolic. Marxist perspectives challenged traditional nationalist interpretations of Indian history. But the emphasis on class struggle is alleged to over-simplify the complex social hierarchies and caste dynamics in India. More so, as this also highlighted the cultural imperialism to impose Western perspectives, overshadowing Indigenous narratives and values. This resulted in a distorted version of sociology and history per say while most of the history text books were written by such authors starting in the 1970s. How encouraging that sounds as such programs are actually funded by Indian taxpayers?

5.2 Paradox of History

- "History tells us that we have not learned from history." This is an observation, often attributed to the philosopher Georg Wilhelm Friedrich Hegel. This is not to be understood as a pessimistic view; Rather this serves as a cautionary reminder to actively engage with history and strive to understand its complexities.

- In effect, this also means that 'History repeats itself.' The cycle of war, economic collapse, and social unrest, while documented throughout history, continues to plague societies that often recur with similar patterns. We are not unaware of our very common sense that any war brings upon destruction and suffering for humanity. We discuss and solicit treaties which are forgotten subsequently and the seeds of another war germinates once again. We are consistently losing the opportunity to learn from past mistakes which are evident again and again.
- Hence, we propose The Law: '**History repeats only to give an opportunity to humanity to learn from history. If humanity learns, then history will not repeat**.' This is an opportunity for humanity to explore history as a teacher that offers lessons to us to modify future actions. Repetitions in history are warnings indeed. By understanding what went wrong before, societies can make more informed decisions and prevent similar problems from arising again.
- This law implies that Cosmic Intelligence monitors and repeats history. The concept of a 'Cosmic Intelligence' that monitors and repeats history is closely tied to the cyclic nature of time and the universe as per Vedanta.

We can look from another perspective on why we are not capable of learning from history or we do not want to learn from the history. That is because we do not want to face the inconvenient truth. Or history is not truthful history and hence we are learning wrong lessons.

5.3 Vedantic Perspective: History vs Eternal Now

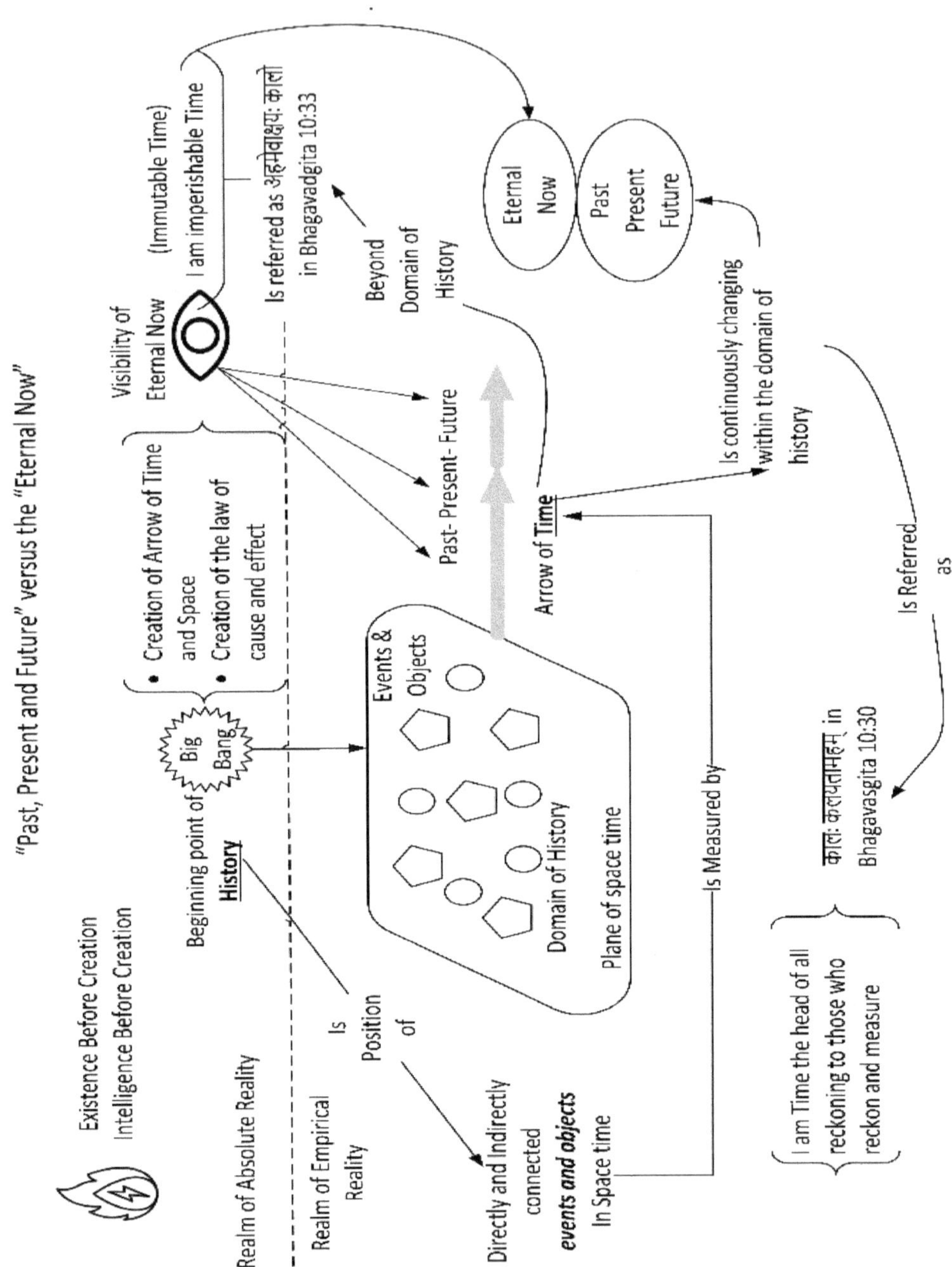

Figure 35: Past, Present, Future and Eternal Now- Vedantic Perspective

The illustration portrays the Vedantic perspective of common understanding about timelines of past, present and future vis-vis the concept of 'Eternal Now.' The dotted line demarcates the realm of absolute reality from the realm of empirical reality. In Vedanta, reality is relative and hierarchal. There is only one absolute reality (Brahman) from where everything else came. This world that we live in is at the lower level of reality which is at the most transactional real or '*Vyavaharik Satya*' i.e., empirical reality. For this discussion, we are excluding the dream world or metaverse simulations (as in VR- virtual reality) which are ultimately an illusion or '*Pratibhashik Satya.*'

- Big Bang is the beginning point of history that started the creation of 'arrow of time' and space as well as creation of the law of cause and effect.
- In the empirical realm, the Big Bang is the initial position that is directly and indirectly connected to events and objects of space and time. Here by events, we mean the historical events about when that happened (time) and where that happened (space). Objects can be interpreted as the people, foundation etc.
- All these events and objects in the empirical realm domain of history are measured by the arrow of time which is unidirectional - past, present and future. It is unidirectional in a sense that the events in the domain of history happen one after the other or in parallel in various places or spaces. But once that event happens at a particular time, the next event happens only after that i.e., the arrow of time is from left to right as depicted and not reverse.
- Time in the material world is a powerful, destructive force of constant change. It controls the cycles of creation and destruction, decreasing the lifespan of all physical beings.
- Now let us revert to the realm of absolute reality i.e., the section above the dotted line in the illustration. We have already discussed that there is one absolute reality (*Brahman*) from which everything came in. This is existence before any formal creation and intelligence before creation. This is where the concept of 'Eternal now' begins. In the Bhagavad Gita, the

> "***Eternal Now***" refers to the timeless, indestructible nature of the soul (*Atman*), which exists outside the limitations of material time and space. The soul is unborn, undying, and unchanging, contrasting with the perishable nature of the physical body. Recognizing this eternal quality of the soul allows one to transcend the cycle of birth and death (reincarnation) and achieve liberation (*moksha*).

The critical point to note is - with reference to time, 'Eternal Now' refers to immutable and imperishable time.

अक्षराणामकारोऽस्मि द्वन्द्वः सामासिकस्य च |

अहमेवाक्षयः कालो धाताहं विश्वतोमुखः || Bhagavad Gita 10:33 ||

This is denoted in the above Bhagwad Gita sloka as "I am inexhaustible time" (***Aham evaksayah kalah***). This indicates that the 'visibility of Eternal Now' is not subject to the linear, destructive passage of time experienced by mortals and hence is beyond the domain of history as such. From this viewpoint the ', all of time—past, present, and future—is a single, simultaneous reality.

In Bhagwad Gita, this is also referred as "Time, the subduer of all" (***kalakalayatamaham***). This means that God is the eternal, timeless consciousness that exists beyond the material world, even while manifesting as the all-consuming, destructive force of time within it.

प्रह्लादश्चास्मि दैत्यानां कालः कलयतामहम् |मृगाणां च मृगेन्द्रोऽहं वैनतेयश्च पक्षिणाम् ||

Bhagwad Gita 10:30 ||

"Eternal now" is a concept that bridges the gap between material time ((*kala*) and timeless, spiritual reality (*Brahman*) which is beyond time and space. Time as perceived in the empirical world is an illusion. While time and distance are perceived through movement, ultimately, the soul exists beyond these limitations. That is 'Divine Consciousness; which is the state of being where one realizes the interconnectedness of all things, free from the constraints of the past, present, and future.

The Analogy of a Person on a Mountain-top Watching Boats on a River - Eternal Now

Let us imagine a person sitting on a mountain observing down a boat moving on the river. Now let us classify this further.

The boat on the river: Consider the river representing the linear passage of time (past, present, and future). As the boat slowly moves along the river, the sailor feels a change of position (space) as he is seeing the parts of the river immediately around him.

The person on the mountain top: The person on the mountain is at a very high vantage point. The observer sees the entire river all at once. The beginning, middle, and end of the site of the river are all simultaneously "present" in his sight. Again, from such a high vantage point of observation, the change of positioning of the boat from one place to another is so tiny that it appears stationary at the same place (no change of space).

We may drill it down a bit more.

Perspective	The boat's movement on the river (Unidirectional time)	The observer's view from mountain top (Eternal Now)
Experience of space & time	The boat's slow movement is a forward-moving timeline. The boatman's awareness is confined to its immediate surroundings. The boatman cannot see where it has been in an earlier position or where it is going.	From the mountain top, the observer sees the entire river—past, present, and future at once. The boat's gentle movement from one position to another makes no visible difference. The river appears to be not flowing and as if it is a static entity.
Perception of events	As the boat slowly moves, the sailor experiences events one after the other in a linear sequence: Each moment as experienced is distinct and separate.	The observer sees the entire course of events simultaneously. In fact, the boat's previous position (past) and the approaching one (future) exist within the same panoramic view as if it is in the same position as present.

Meaning and purpose	The purpose of the boat is to move forward on the river. The meaning is experienced as it moves to the next destination spot.	The observer feels as if the events on the river are not separate and rather just one (one unified activity). This instills a broader viewpoint of purpose, meaning and also interconnectedness.
Understandi ng of self	The boat's activity is limited on the river tied to its gentle movement and progress.	The observer is actually a detached witness. He is just watching but not actively participating in the boat's movement or the river's flow. This can be interpreted as a state that transcends the personal ego.

Significance of Learning from History and Eternal Now

A realization of the concept of 'Eternal Now' re-establishes the purpose of learning from history. In essence, the interpretation of the Bhagavad Gita's "eternal now" views history not as a linear unidirectional progression, but as an ever repeating and cyclical drama. It teaches that while the world is temporary and subject to constant change, the divine reality and the soul remain eternal and unaffected by the passing of time. In addition, *karma*—the law of cause and effect—is the engine that drives the cycle of history. Past and present actions shape future historical circumstances across many lifetimes. History unfolds not as a random sequence of events, but as a morally coherent process driven by the collective actions (*karma*) of all beings. An understanding of the "eternal now" reframes how one may approach to learn from truthful history.

6 Myth and Reality of AI

How has AI progressed?

- 1956 - John McCarthy introduced the conceptual theory and coined the term "Artificial Intelligence"
- 1960 - Machine learning was demonstrated on IBM 704
- 1980s - Expert systems emulated the decision -making capability of humans
- Late 1990s - Proven AI applications in specific areas like logistics, data mining and medical diagnosis became available

This was followed by quick growth and development in recent past that culminated in the proliferation of AI in various areas due to

- ✓ Affordability and rapid technological development of compute power
- ✓ Growth of Cloud -availability of on -demand computing resources
- ✓ Commercialization of AI products on utility model (anyone can use from anywhere)

What is the Need for Trusted AI & what are the Dimensions of Trusted AI?

The emerging concerns about AI trustworthiness is due to the very obvious requisite that to trust a decision made by an algorithm, we must ensure that it is reliable and fair; that it can be accounted for, and that it will cause no harm.

Building AI system for performance is not good enough. Building trustworthy AI is the critical design paradigm.

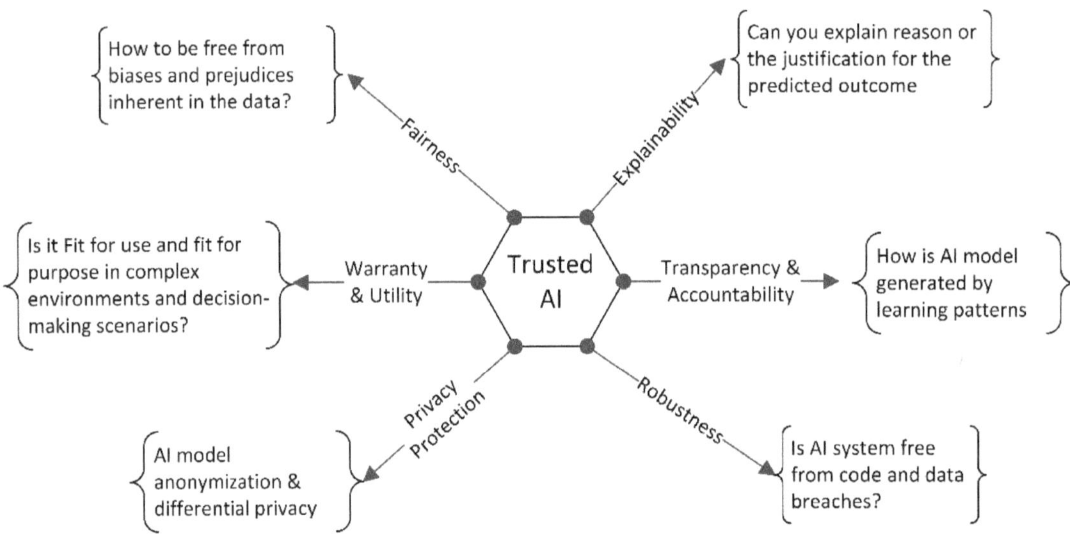

Figure 36: Dimensions of trusted AI

As illustrated in the diagram the dimensions of trusted AI are

- Fairness: How to be free from biases and prejudices inherent in the data? The AI systems pick these biases and prejudices, encode them, and may even scale them up.
- Explainability: How to explain reason or the justification for the predicted outcome? AI design relies on computer simulations to evaluate outcomes. Many simulation runs could be computationally too expensive, and time consuming. Surrogate modeling techniques, construct cheap-to -evaluate statistical models to approximate the simulation output accurately.
- Warranty & Utility: Is it fit for use and fit for purpose in complex environments and decision-making scenarios?
- Transparency & Accountability: How is AI model generated by learning patterns?

- Privacy protection: How can AI models ensure anonymization and differential privacy? A vast amount of training data contains personal information.
- Robustness: Is an AI system free from code and data breaches?

6.1 Being Trusted does not mean being wise

With the advancement in the area of "***Trusted AI***" we are hoping to see the possibility of "**Wise AI**" in near future. Being trustworthy in our opinion is one of the key characteristics of being wise.

In order for the AI systems to be trustworthy, we must ensure that it addresses all the dimensions of trust and thus inspires confidence. Although there are multiple dimensions for the trusted AI such as explainability, security and privacy, transparency and accountability; but we would like to discuss the **dimension of fairness** as we consider it as the most important and the most complex.

AI systems source the data from the world that carries biases and prejudices, and these biases and prejudices can easily enter AI systems through training data. The AI systems pick these biases and prejudices, encode them, and may even scale them up. This risk brings in the necessity of calibrating and instrumenting AI for fairness. Building fairness in AI will enable us to break the chain of human biases.

We all know that biases and prejudices can eclipse the wisdom of a person but a person with strong thinking and reasoning can overcome these weaknesses and become wise. Trusted AI need to be continuously learning with newer and newer data but has limitations of thinking natively. Will that time come when machine thinking could be matched with human capability?

Yet another characteristic of wisdom is righteousness. As such, there is a systematic decline of righteousness in the society with the rise of unreason and it is being pushed back by populism. So, will anyone be interested in teaching AI systems to be righteous? The prevailing trend is to be popular rather than be righteous. At times you have the opportunity to be righteous as well as popular, but these kinds of opportunities are diminishing in business and society. So, ***trusted AI is not good enough, can AI be ever wise?***

The term 'artificial' to prelude 'AI' as such says it all. This in contrast to something 'natural,' having its constant challenge of attempting to balance the gap between algorithm-based professional training versus inferiority of actual reasoning. Intelligence or the intellect is a useful and fair aspect but it is far away from wisdom. It is good to reiterate the comment of Steve Jobs who stated that intuition is more powerful than intellect. He suggested that while intellect is the product of Western culture, intuition is a deeply powerful, innate intelligence that leads to breakthroughs and guides individuals toward their true path. He saw Western rational thought as valuable but not the only form of intelligence, valuing the "experiential wisdom" of cultures like those in Indian villages more than simply intellect alone.

AI and Common sense

- Does AI understand common sense?
- Does AI lack common sense?
- Can AI replicate common sense?
- Can AI at least mimic common sense?

One can frame this question in numerous ways and debate in a coffee table or in a podcast for long. This obviously indicate that there is some fundamental gap that is prevalent that is rather awkward to just cover up and keep under the carpet.

Artificial intelligence has achieved remarkable feats, from mastering complex games to enabling voice-activated assistants. Now consider the term 'intelligence' in AI ; notice not to forget that it does have an adjective before as 'artificial' that completes the popular terminology - 'artificial intelligence.' Such an artificial intelligence has a complete reliance on structured data and explicit programming. This statistical pattern matching is away from genuine understanding and lacks real-world experience or specific contextual knowledge.

"Common sense is the dark matter of artificial intelligence"

- Oren Etzioni, CEO, Allen Institute for AI

That is why DARPA (Defense Advanced Research Projects Agency in USA) launched the Machine Common Sense (MCS) program in 2018 that aimed to challenge artificial intelligence with human-like common sense. Moving beyond the existing narrow AI capabilities, the US military attempted to teach AI some fundamental common sense. The program employed two main strategies: one mimicking a child's learning process to understand intuitive physics, spatial navigation, and agent intentions, and another creating a comprehensive knowledge repository from web-scale data to answer common sense queries. The program continued till 2022 and pushed the field forward. However, it did not achieve its most ambitious goal. The difficulty of instilling human-level common sense remains a key barrier to creating truly general AI.

Thinking, feeling and AI

There is astounding development in AI technology and there are many areas where AI can simulate human-like behavior and process vast amounts of data. But how to address areas like genuine self-awareness, empathy, and personal context? The gap between Thinking, feeling and AI can be construed as-

- Common sense reasoning: For AI, where is the intuitive knowledge that even a human child possesses which has nothing to do with explicit instruction or learning from huge datasets?
- True creativity and innovation: AI is able to generate novel combinations and produce fantastic creations that sometimes surpass average human output. However, where is the emotion, personal reflection, imagination or a true inspiration that is so distinct in the human creative process?
- Causal understanding: Do AI models have a clear understanding of cause and effect which is different from recognizing statistical correlations in data?
- Genuine emotions and consciousness: AI may try to simulate emotions by analyzing data patterns like facial expressions or voice inflections; but does

it feel happiness, sadness, or joy or any subjective experiences? This also raises the question around absence of empathy.

The crucial point is AI lacks the direct, human-like experience. This fundamental difference creates key missing elements that are essential to human cognition and understanding, including embodiment, subjective feelings, and social context.

Human imagination vs AI

In a day-to-day business transaction, we are leveraging a ton of AI, a lot of technology and a bunch of tools to help us and we feel that would catapult humanity forward. The human touch still remains the differentiator by which clients feel being listened to, being understood or being placed with alternative challenges in the right way. When they place a problem on the table, they don't want us to create options A, B and C or treat it like a half-baked potato. Rather it needs real interrogation and true understanding. Yes, usage of tools and technology of AI helps us to be smarter but the human imagination still remains the biggest piece that creates the differentiation.

AI is able to mimic creativity by creating art, music, stories, or designs based on data patterns, but it lacks human emotion, intuition, and original thought. But does it matter if AI cannot meet human imagination?

The Game of Chess, Overwhelming Content Generation and AI

Let us explore the sentiment towards AI in chess. Yes, the community has embraced AI as a powerful tool for improvement and analysis. In July 2025 Magnus Carlsen (who has won the World Chess Championship five times) reported that he defeated ChatGPT in an online match in just 53 moves. Yet just about a week later, he lost the Freestyle Chess Grand Slam Tour in Las Vegas to teenage Indian grandmaster Rameshbabu Praggnanandhaa. There is no doubt that AI has made chess more deeply analyzed and accessible than ever before, fostering a collaborative human-machine environment for the game's future with Unprecedented Training Tools (Likes of Stokfish) and new discoveries. However, the perspective about 'do you really like it?" is rather nuanced. AI diminishes the thrill and creativity in human play, with its robotic style derived from engine analysis.

Taking this discussion further, we are aware that today a massive portion of AI development and use is indeed in content creation, ranging from writing to generating images and music, its application is far more extensive. Now, with the ease of access with generative AI, art is also abundant with a glut of creators who have little to no idea of what to do with the superpower AI has given them. So, we are flooded with deluge of productions of default postings, soulless and bizarre art forms or garbage music mashups. The law of diminishing utility can be referenced with such overwhelming abundance. Apart from that angle, the important question is - what about intrinsic value creation? Do you really enjoy this? Such irrational usage of AI is indeed falling short about emotion of human experience or creativity of original ideas.

The Rampant AI Generated Content - Forget Trust, You Can't Even Detect That !

One may refer an article from Fortune – "Meta spends more guarding Mark Zuckerberg than Apple, Nvidia, Microsoft, Amazon, and Alphabet do for their own CEOs—combined"(https://fortune.com/2025/08/16/mark-zuckerberg-meta-security-detail-costs-apple-nvidia-microsoft-amazon-alphabet-ceos/). The point to note is – at the end it is mentioned that – 'For this story, Fortune used generative AI to help with an initial draft. An editor verified the accuracy of the information before publishing.' Yes, even Fortune does that.

By the way, do you know who Klara is? She doesn't actually exist. The German online magazine EXPRESS.de has integrated Klara Indernach (KI), an advanced AI system, into their newsroom. It could be embarrassing to experience such shameless arrogance. The fact of the matter is - this is already rampant everywhere now.

Whether one trusts such content or not is for an individual to judge. This also leads to a tricky question - is AI-Generated Content Actually Detectable? The short answer: No—at least, not now! So the business makes money and they may not care.

Today it is getting harder and harder to differentiate an image created by AI and humans. 'Theatre D'opera,' an AI-generated picture, won an art prize at the Colorado State Fair in 2022, causing a major controversy. The fundamental question is – who should be in control in such a situation, AI or human imagination? The future of creativity is in our hands. ***Do you think that we, as a society, will be able to adapt to this challenge of not falling into the prey of artificially generated creativity or fall victim to a non-human intelligence?***

Intelligent Quotient, Emotional Intelligence, Spiritual Intelligence and AI

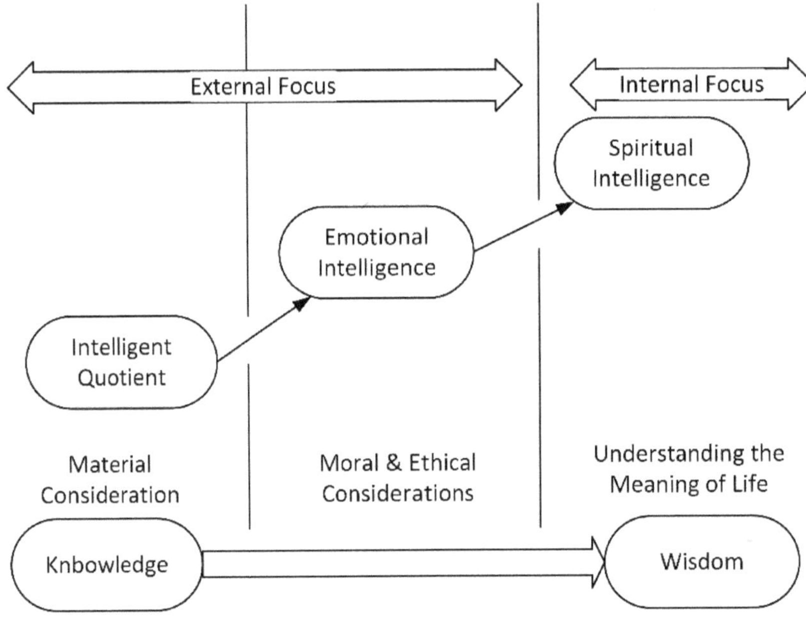

Figure 37: IQ, EI and SI

There has been an evolution from a narrow, purely cognitive focus toward a more holistic view of human capability over a period of years. Thus evolved the understanding of (Intelligent Quotient (IQ), Emotional Intelligence (EQ), and Spiritual Intelligence (SQ).

In the early 1900s it started off with IQ as the original model of human intelligence (created by psychologists Alfred Binet and Théodore Simon). The term 'Intelligence Quotient' was coined by William Stern while the calculation was just a division of mental age by chronological age. In the mid-1900s a standardized scoring system with a mean of 100 was introduced. This was modified later to a three-dimensional model (Howard Gardner's theory of multiple intelligences). However, in modern days ongoing research (The Flynn effect and cultural biases) have challenged the notion of IQ.

Here enters the Emotional Intelligence (EQ) that rose to prominence as a necessary complement to IQ, acknowledging that cognitive ability alone does not guarantee success. In 1995 it attained mainstream popularity (courtesy a book by Science journalist Daniel Goleman) with a model with inclusion of key components like self-awareness, self-regulation, motivation, empathy, and social skills. It is no wonder that EQ has evolved today as a standard component of leadership training, employee development, and educational programs.

In parallel in the late 1990s, there emerged the concept of spiritual intelligence (SQ) which attempted to describe the missing links. It served as a way to describe a higher, values-based form of wisdom, distinct from religious observance. In early 2000s psychologist Danah Zohar coined SQ as the 'intelligence of the soul'. Today "Spiritual intelligence or SQ refers to the intelligence that addresses and helps in solving problems of meaning and value and places our actions and our lives in a wider, richer, meaningful context "

(https://www.ncuindia.edu/spiritual-quotient-sq-and-its-power-in-current-times/)

Now let us attempt to fit in AI in each of the intelligence quotients.

Perspective	Where AI excels	Where AI falls short
IQ & AI	For defined, rule-based tasks, AI can demonstrate capabilities far beyond human performance. Examples include Logic and problem-solving In calculations and data	• Genuine reasoning: Its performance is based on the training data and a search for patterns, not on independent thought or creativity.

	analysis, Pattern recognition etc.	• Consciousness: Off course, it is not a sentient being with self-awareness.

Perspective	Simulation of AI in EQ	Where AI falls short
EQ & AI	• Affective computing (Facial recognition, voice analysis or text interpretation are utilized by AI to detect human emotions in customer service bots • Personalized recommendations • Empathetic phrasing (a simulation based on data patterns)	• No true empathy and feeling • No self-awareness: • Limited context (interpretation may miss cultural, situational, and personal nuances)

Perspective	Where AI can play any role	Where AI falls short
SQ & AI	• None	• No self-awareness • Algorithm is far away from genuine insight

There is no denying the fact that AI excels in some aspects of IQ much beyond human capability. Again its capacity for EQ is limited to selected areas of simulation. However, it has no room for discussion in the perspective of spiritual intelligence.

Natural Intelligence (NI) and Cosmic Intelligence (CI)

Let us familiarize ourselves with a few key terms here.

Natural Intelligence (NI)

This is intelligence embedded in nature. The beauty is – it is always generative in nature by design. Think of it as a perspective on the nature of biological (natural) intelligence that automatically suggests an inherent capacity for continuous generation, creation, and adaptation. This distinguishes it from Gen AI where the corroboration of the 'generative' part is induced and not natural by design.

In essence Natural Intelligence (NI) is fundamentally 'generative by design' with its

- Continuous learning and adaptation: Organisms continuously generate new responses and strategies in real time to cruise past and negotiate unpredictable and ever-changing environments
- Creation of novelty: This consistently drives innovation, creativity, and production of entirely innovative ideas and solutions. Unlike artificial algorithms, these are not explicitly programmed or predetermined.
- Consistent Evolution: At every evolutionary level, this generative capacity has led to the immense diversity of life and increasingly complex cognitive abilities.

Cosmic Intelligence (CI)

CI is always generative from the beginning. This is the inherent, universal creative force that is always generating and unfolding reality. Again, this completely differs from Gen AI which is a human creation, a tool developed through programming and data.

- Fundamental Origin and nature: CI is the intrinsic, natural intelligence fundamental to the universe itself, existing from the very beginning of its creation.
- Always Generative Process: CI is characterized as 'always generative' as a continuous, organic process of creation and evolution. This is absolutely

different from GenAI's generative process which is goal-oriented and dependent on user prompts and vast datasets to produce outputs.

- Universal Scope: CI is perceived as operating on a universal scale, encompassing all existence and potential. GenAI operates within the confines of its algorithms and the data it has been trained on and thereby cannot stand to be compared to.

In essence, the core distinction lies in CI being an inherent, universal source of creation, while GenAI is a human-made tool designed to simulate creative processes within defined parameters.

AI is Accelerating the Pace and Humanity is Drifting Away from Reality

AI is pushing the boundaries of human capabilities at an exponential rate. Consequently, it is raising fundamental questions about the role of humanity. It fundamentally changes what it means to be human, while the potential consequences may range from social isolation to a loss of individual agency.

- Dissolution of critical thinking: People are getting trapped with over-reliance on AI for quick answers and decisions. The apparent convenience of AI is leading people to simply digest defer without questioning validity.
- *Manipulation and misinformation*: The so called deepfakes and misinformation have been constantly blurring the lines between truth and falsehood for quite some time by now. There is possibly no proper definition for 'public trust' any more. We are sucked into a misinformed and manipulated societal and political world already.
- Privacy and surveillance: The AI data are constantly being used for targeted manipulation and surveillance. On this topic, the less said, the better.
- Impact on human connection: AI is becoming integrated into daily life at an astronomical pace. By the same token, there is a tremendous rise of AI companions that raises unrealistic expectations in human relationships or falsifies a genuine connection.

Yes, there are ideological debates that understanding these complex issues requires a balance between embracing AI's potential and thoughtfully addressing its challenges. The fact of the matter remains quite away from such conversations. The reality is - so far spending on AI infrastructure has already exceeded spending on telecom and internet infrastructure from the dot-com boom—and possibly would grow more with such a trend. There are reports that Capex spending for AI contributed more to growth in the U.S. economy

(https://x.com/RenMacLLC/status/1950544075989377196).

'Spending on AI data centers is so massive that it's taken a bigger chunk of GDP growth than shopping—and it could crash the American economy'

- Fortune, Aug 2025

(https://finance.yahoo.com/news/spending-ai-data-centers-massive-150110727.html)

Maya of AI in the Business and Technology World – The Vedic Perspective

'*Maya*' – We would like to use this term as a metaphor to describe the collective illusion or hype surrounding AI in business and technology.

- *Maya* is something which is not real but you are ignorant about this truth and consider it as real
- In realizing that false reality, you start chasing things that you will never get
- The obvious result is disappointment

In Vedant *Maya* represents a veil of illusion. Let us explore how this can be mapped to the false reality created and perpetuated by modern AI through its capacity for misinformation, deepfakes, and simulated worlds.

Perspective	Illusion of AI	*Maya* – the veil of illusion
False Perception	Genuine news and information are manipulated with apparent fake contents, images and videos (deepfakes).	*Maya* creates an illusion that the empirical (material) world is the ultimate which is actually away from the absolute reality (*Brahman*).

Veil of Ignorance	The bias in input data creates flawed output while claiming it to be authoritative	*Maya* is understood as the cosmic force that obscures the true nature of reality. This illusion prevents an individual's true divine self (*Atman*) from recognizing its non-dual unity with the ultimate, universal consciousness (*Brahman*).
Creation of Illusory Worlds	Users are sucked into virtual reality (VR) video games and advanced simulations in the AI simulated worlds away from reality.	*Maya* is the creative, illusory power of *Brahman* that projects the appearance of a separate and diverse material world, with various names (*nama*)) and forms (*rupa*). This universe is a conditioned or empirical reality, not the absolute reality.
Deception of Truth	Not only AI-generated misinformation but advanced Artificial Intelligence is used to target and spread false narratives and content, often indistinguishable from reality. This generates political deception, financial fraud, social and personal deception and pollution of information by media manipulation.	The 'rope and snake' analogy is a classic illustration that teaches that an ignorant perception of reality creates fear and suffering. The focus must be to acquire true knowledge to pass by the deceptive illusion (*Maya*) to the peaceful and unchanging reality of *Brahman*.
The Surrender - Difficulty of Escape	AI models are on a frenzy race generating convincing falsehoods. This is drifting people away from reality being trapped into pseudo-convenience more and more.	As one gets trapped in *Maya*, the illusion of separation and attachment becomes a lifelong struggle and journey that requires spiritual practice to transcend.

Wise Human vs AI

In this context, It would be good to recall and refer again Fig 22 and detailed explanation in the chapter 'Hard problem of consciousness' of this book From a Vedantic perspective this illustrates that no matter how sophisticated AI becomes, its fundamental nature (as an un-self-aware tool) will always be distinct from the enlightened consciousness of a wise human.

Can AI take Human Decisions?

The good quality of Human life largely runs on love, faith, kindness, mercy, joy and all sorts of such feelings. Wise decisions are balanced with feminine quality along with reasons and logic.

Balanced decisions are wise but takes time

- The human brain is far more emotional than it is rational
- We like to believe we make decisions based on facts though the reality is far more complicated

There are two sides to consider

1. fast and instinctive - jumps to conclusions, makes snap judgements and conserves energy, is quick automatic emotional
2. slow and deliberate- thoughtful, analytical cautious, requires effort and here lies the issue

However, most people are stuck in fast mode i.e., there is simply no time or will to slow down and think deeply. The obvious result is - we rely on heuristics stereotypes and mental shortcuts that feel right but are often wrong.

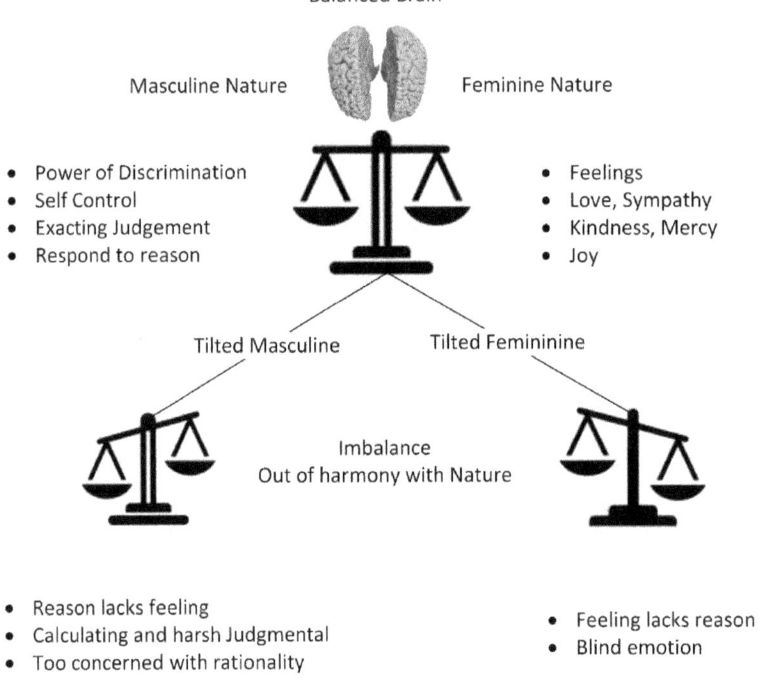

Figure 38: Can AI take humanly righteous decision?

The illustration depicts two sides of the brain and harmony with nature.

- A masculine brain has characteristics of power of discrimination, self-control, exacting judgment and responds to reason.
- A feminine brain has characteristics of feelings. Love and sympathy, kindness, mercy and joy.
- There is imbalance out of harmony with nature
- A tilted feminine brain has feeling but lacks reason and is often characterized with blind emotion.
- A tilted masculine brain has reason but lacks feelings. It is calculation and harshly judgmental and too concerned with rationality.

AI can be compared with a tilted masculine brain. It is not inclusive and rather filled with algorithmic bias.

Half of our mistakes in life arise from feeling where we ought to think and thinking where we ought to feel. This feeling itself is the differentiating factor. In simple terms AI does not have the option to 'feel;' so, there is no room for even thinking about that as the feeling itself is non-existent. Does that not obviously indicate that mistakes are not corrected or an AI inference is prone to mistakes at least half of the time? Point to ponder – isn't it?

6.2 AI must be judged by its purpose/use not by capability

The effectiveness of AI and for that matter any technology is intrinsically tied to their ability to fulfill a specific purpose. The most sophisticated capability is indeed meaningless if it doesn't align with achieving meaningful purpose or generate value realistically. This principle is a cornerstone of effective design and implementation in technology, emphasizing that true value lies not just in what a technology can do, but what it achieves in a real-world context. Here lies the significance about what is a meaningful 'usage'?

Vedic Classification of AI Usage

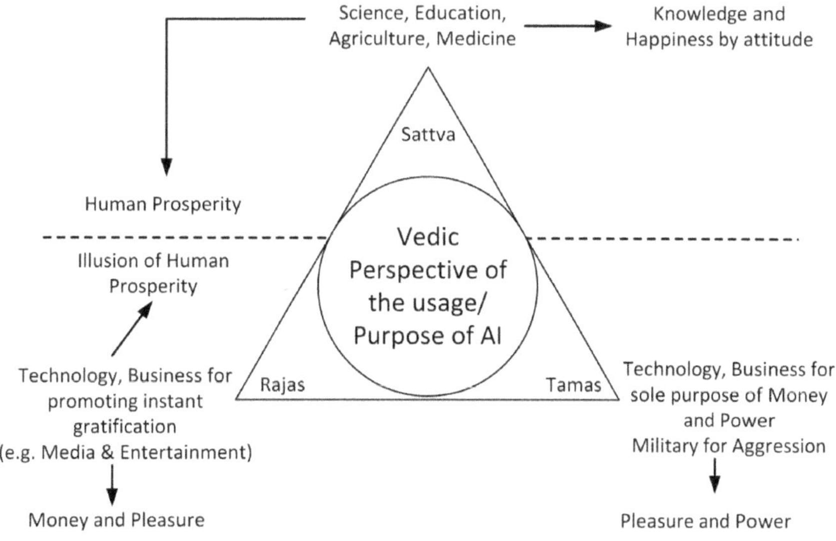

Figure 39: Vedic classification of AI usage

The illustration portrays viewing artificial intelligence through the lens of the three *gunas* (*Sattva*, *Rajas*, and *Tamas*), a metaphorical framework from a Vedic perspective of the usage and purpose of AI.

- The *Sattva* perspective: A *sattva* (Purity, clarity, and harmony) perception of AI focuses on its capacity to bring clarity, aid human consciousness, and promote universal well-being. It aims for human prosperity through proper development in the fields of science, education, agriculture and medicine thereby stimulating true knowledge and happiness by attitude. It is important to note that while happiness is primarily an internal state of mind, it is realistically determined by one's mindset and choices, rather than by external circumstances or material possessions. 'Happiness by attitude' is one's ability to choose a positive perspective and find meaning in life, regardless of life's demanding situations.

- The *Rajas* perspective: A *rajas* (Passion, activity, and ambition) perception sees AI as a powerful tool for constant activity, growth, and self-serving ambition. Technology and business promote instant gratification culminating in an illusion of human prosperity away from reality. The restless energy of *rajas* leads to an attachment and craving for pleasure and money as an outcome of AI.

- The Tamas perspective: A *tamas* (Inertia, ignorance, and darkness) perception of AI focuses on its potential to cause dullness, delusion, and destruction. More and more instant gratification is promoted by technology and business. This creates a negative impact with AI consumerism forcing with its incessant cycle of algorithms. Such highly personalized and addictive digital experiences erode attention spans, manipulate purchasing decisions, and undermine overall well-being. This perspective also includes the weaponization of AI. This is a dangerous fallout with the military for aggression to achieve power. The threat lies in its ability to operate at immense speed and scale in the fronts of Lethal Autonomous Weapon Systems (LAWS with sensor-based targeting), cyberwarfare (with autonomous malware) or Information Warfare and Psychological Operations (with deepfakes and mass disinformation campaigns).

Accuracy of Artificial Intelligence does not equal Truth

Let us begin with couple of examples:

- In 2018, Amazon had to scrap an AI recruiting tool that showed bias against women since the training data was overloaded with male dominance.
- In 2019, a bombshell study found that a clinical algorithm many
- hospitals were using it to decide which patients needed care and were showing racial bias. Black patients had to be deemed much sicker than white patients to be recommended for the same care.

This is a known challenge that there are issues with AI model accuracy. This stems from limitations in training data (biases, incompleteness), model design (overfitting, underfitting), misleading evaluation metrics etc. There are constant efforts with various optimization techniques to counter and reduce the "hallucinating" output.

Yet, the AI models can produce fantastic output, say in a use case of analyzing cricket scorecards for the last 15 years that encompasses huge data. Such an analysis could be humanly impossible even with the best feasible mathematical wizard. The point to note here is that – for such a dataset, there is possibly no room for external manipulation i.e., such datasets are mostly preserved or available as it is with no intent of corruption or manipulation. So, the AI accuracy of analysis is good to go.

Another common example is an AI model that predicts stock market trends. In general, it is expected to get high accuracy to better forecast price movements based on historical data patterns and real-time market analysis. The result in this use case is also generally well accepted by business houses as the output is indeed correct specifically with its scope of data being considered. However, an unexpected political event or a company's internal scandal might have caused an information asymmetry. Is such an aspect rare? Not at all! Hence this anomaly must also be considered to compensate for the distinction between accuracy and truthfulness.

The above are examples where there is a room of correction or some adjustment for exception handling. We have a bigger problem at hand. The fundamentals of running AI models is based on historical data. This is the central challenge in Artificial Intelligence. Historical data is inaccurate and they are not an unbiased reflection of reality. Please refer to the detailed discussion in the chapter 'Paradox of history' where we discussed that history is seldom free from bias. So, if the ***datapoints do not represent truthful history to begin with, then the mere expectation about truth of the model output is rather stupid.***

Such information is not limited to just historical aspects of history per say. This might impact scientific publications as well. For example, during the 1980s, several science conferences were held in Pakistan that caused significant controversy and highlighted a growing conflict between modern scientific methods and religious dogma. Specifically, the 1987 "International Conference on Scientific Miracles of Quran and Sunnah," sought to reconcile modern scientific thought with the Quran, leading to presentations that contradicted established scientific principles.

An unfortunate example is an historical AI error concerning World War II when an AI chatbot, trained on inaccurate or biased data, generates content that minimizes or distorts the facts of the Holocaust. This is serious as UNESCO describes – "AI and the Holocaust: rewriting history? The impact of artificial intelligence on understanding the Holocaust" with major concerns on:

- AI automated content may invent facts about the Holocaust
- Falsify historical evidence: Deepfake Technology
- AI models can be manipulated to spread hate speech
- Algorithmic bias can spread Holocaust denial
- Oversimplification of history

https://www.unesco.org/en/articles/ai-and-holocaust-rewriting-history-impact-artificial-intelligence-understanding-holocaust

Absolute Reality from a Vedantic perspective

This is discussed in detail in the book 'Illustrated Vedant' by the same authors. The key message is three tiers of reality from Vedantic Perspective

- Absolute Reality: Consciousness or *Brahman*
- Empirical Reality: This physical Universe that we experience with our body, mind and senses and scientists' study as matter and energy.
- Our Dream world – The non-physical world created in our sleep only to be experienced by us (In this tier of reality in modern times, we have added Virtual world on the Internet)

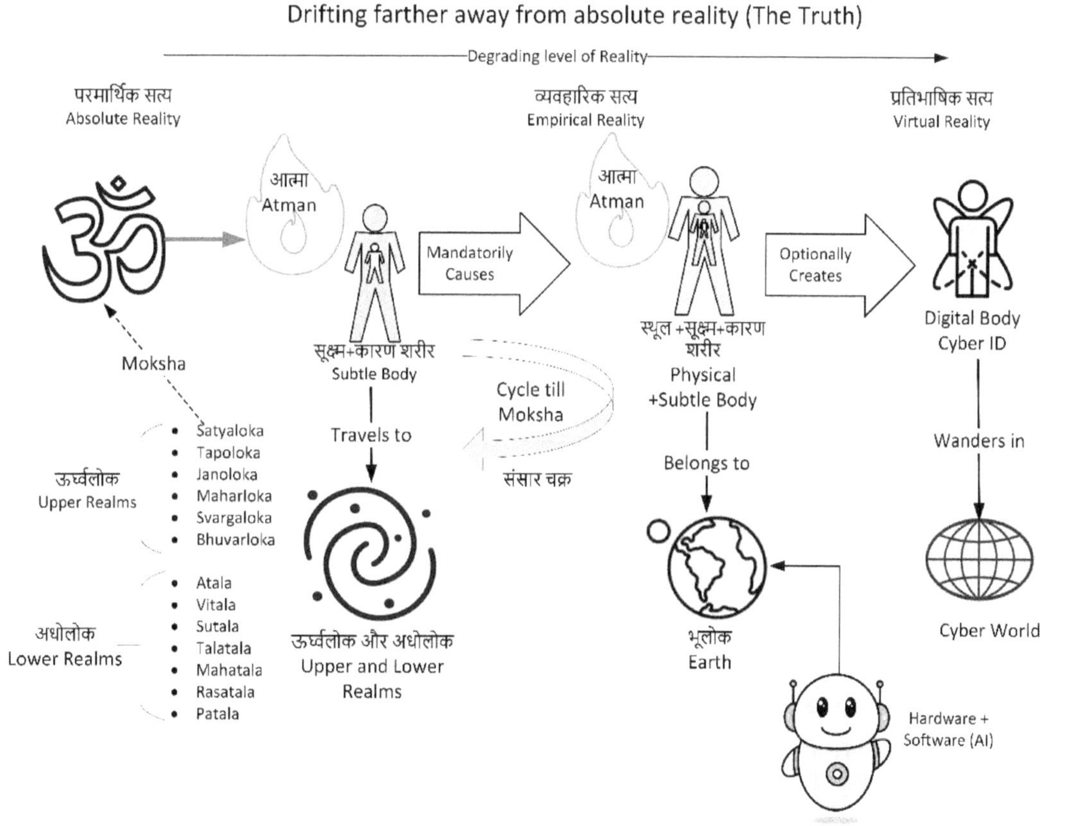

Figure 40: Acceleration towards non-reality

The Journey drifts away in the modern-day Digital World. In the modern digital world today, we have the option to create a digital body (numbered with a cyber identification tag) that creates virtual 'avatars' in virtual reality games or virtual personifications performing many online activities. However, the most important caution point is - immersing ourselves in such an ephemeral world (so-called cyber world) means allowing your 'self' to succumb to an illusion. We are losing focus on our journey to realize the absolute reality (the truth). While robots (which is a combination of hardware and software AI) excel at pattern recognition, speed, and precision within structured environments, they struggle with unstructured, real-world, and subjective contexts that define human experience. Such AI robots operate on approximations of reality rather than direct, subjective apprehension of it. Such approximation models of reality is mediated and restricted by sensors, algorithms, and human-defined constraints. In absence of the very common sense, robots will never be able to and more importantly will not allow to reach the realms of absolute reality.

Misconception about Reality and Consciousness

Let us rearticulate key pointers on this topic which has been discussed in detail in the book "Illustrated Vedant" by the same authors. There are commonplace articles, some scientific and some popular in the Western world which are promissory materialism that attempts to explain consciousness on the basis of brain-neurons and quantum physics etc. Here are some examples:

- Giulio Tononi at the University of Wisconsin developed a mathematical model called integrated information theory. This claims that the enormous integrated information in the brain's powerful cerebral cortex gives rise to consciousness.
- Also, there is the Quantum Mind Theory by physicist Robert Penrose who believes that consciousness can never be explained through ordinary physical and mathematical laws. He postulates the existence of quantum gravity and concludes that consciousness is the result of quantum effects which are thought to occur in the microtubules found inside cells.

- There is also belief of some Western philosophers that consciousness is an epiphenomenon or side effect of human evolution.

In any case all these theories attribute the origin of consciousness to the brain and its neurons. These theories are highly speculative, and none are even close to being verified. That is to say neuroscience, quantum physics or any form of artificial intelligence cannot observe your private conscious experience, nor can it detect or measure consciousness itself.

In Advaita Vedanta, consciousness is a non-material, non-physical fundamental reality. As per ancient Rishis. matter and energy are merely forms of manifestations of an underlying reality that is called the *Brahman*. Brahman is explained as reality (*Satyam*), Intelligence (*Jnanam*) and Infinite (*Anantam*).

Why is it Worth to Grasp the 'Infiniteness' of Cosmic Intelligence?

In the chapter 'True meaning of Wisdom' we explained the supreme wisdom that was condensed in the Singularity before the creation of the universe as the "Cosmic Intelligence" (*Brahmandiaya Prajna*). By nature this is infinite intelligence. The question is - can we grasp the infiniteness aspect of such an intelligence?

Let us explore this with our existing ways of life. We have built a world around us which is increasingly digital in nature (described with binary 0 and 1 or off and on). However, the natural world is analog. It is no wonder to comprehend the continuous, wave-like signals that are analogous to the real world—like the continuous nature of sound waves or light. So, there is a fundamental mismatch if we just consider the so-called digital world. Digital systems use discrete, binary (on/off) values, and they require conversion from analog signals to be processed. Think of the difference between the numbers 1 and 2. The gap can be interpreted as 1.1, 1.2, 1.3 .... .and so on and further each decimal can be broken again (1.11, 1.12...... and subsequently 1.111,1.112....). A simple gap is actually infinite in nature. Take another example of pi which is broadly 22/7. But it is an irrational number, which means its decimal representation is infinite and non-repeating. In June 2024, a new record for pi was set, calculating it to 202 trillion decimal places. The fact remains that pi is a transcendental number, meaning its decimal representation goes on forever without a repeating pattern. While computers have calculated trillions of digits, this is simply a record of the beginning of an unending sequence. This is what is the sweeping gamut of the 'infinite' in reality. Can you realize what will be the level of complexity for a digital system in the so-called empirical world to convert and process such infinite analog signals?

In the late 19th century German mathematicians came out with set theory in the area of mathematical logic. By this time, mathematics had the idea of "imaginary numbers" and "transcendental numbers" to interpret complex mathematical equations. In addition to establish many mathematical concepts and making it a foundation for mathematics, the set theory also established the framework to develop a mathematical theory of infinity. It established a concept that there can be varied sizes of infinity, by proving that the set of real numbers is a larger infinity than the set of natural numbers. Infinity itself is mindboggling and one can only imagine. The point is that without admission of something like transcendence we cannot understand science and mathematics.

That is why it is of significance to attempt to grasp the concept of infiniteness of such cosmic intelligence. How amazing is it to even account for such 'infinity' and how amazing furthermore is to realize what the extent of an infinite wisdom will be? To grasp such sheer infiniteness, one must move beyond intellectual understanding through practices like self-inquiry, meditation, and mindful living to realize the unity of the individual self with the cosmic intelligence. From a Vedantic perspective, understanding cosmic intelligence involves recognizing that it is the universal, underlying consciousness (*Brahman*) from which all existence originates and that is present within each individual as the true self (*Atman*)

The Satvik use of AI

Technology For Scientific Discoveries

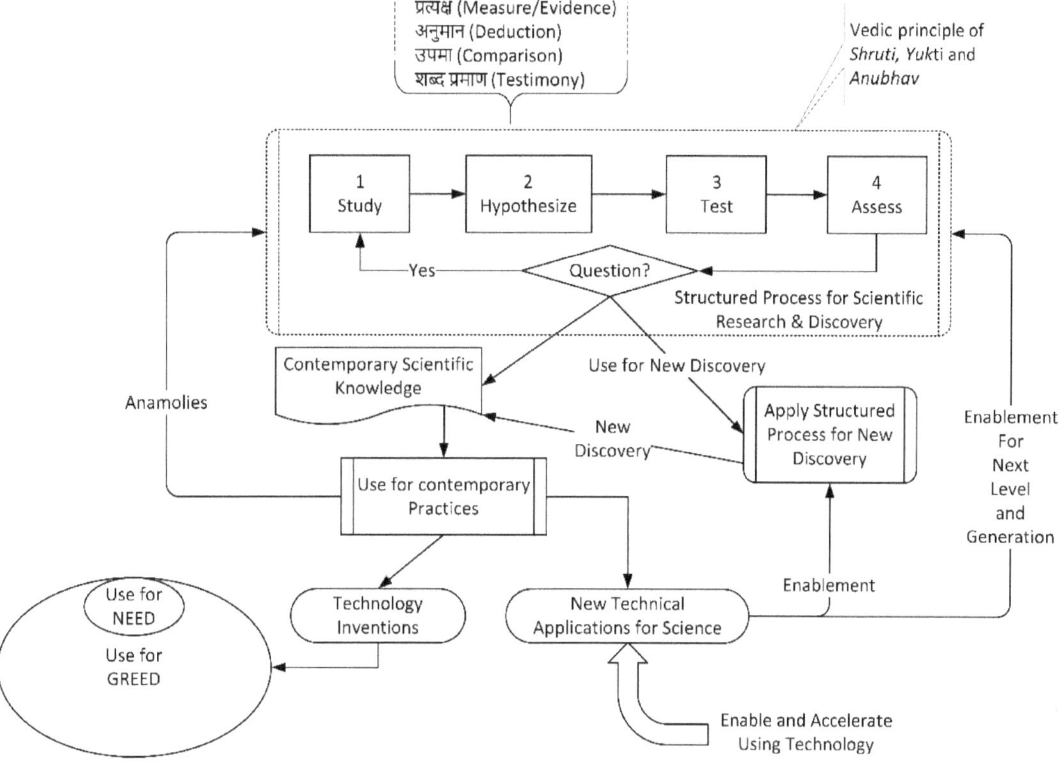

Figure 41: Typical process for scientific discovery

In the illustration the dotted box on the top depicts the stages for structured processes for scientific research and discovery.

- The process starts with study followed by an initial formation of a hypothesis which then is tested and assessments are done. If there are doubts or questions raised, then it goes back for further study and the subsequent process stages for the next cycle till the questions are resolved to a satisfactory level. Only then the fine-tuned hypotheses are ready for the next stage to be consumed for contemporary scientific knowledge and for use for contemporary practices. Of course, if there are anomalies found so-called in the field, this will go back to the very first stage for further study once more.

- As a side note the above structured process is also described in a Vedantic context for self-discovery. The Vedic principle of *Shruti* (that which is heard) , *Yukti* (logical reasoning, critical thinking, and intellectual analysis) and *Anubhava* (direct, immediate, and personal spiritual experience) describes three sources of knowledge that are used together to validate and attain spiritual truth. The hypothesis runs through the measure/ evidence, deduction (*anuman*), comparison (*upama*) and testimony (*Praman*).

- Now the usage of contemporary practices leads to technology inventions. A good part of such technological inventions facilitate humanity for its most needs improving lives and solving problems. However, by default many technological inventions are aimed at or influenced by greed. In fact, the share of such a pie is much larger than the invention for need. The profit motive is a powerful force in a capitalist economy, and it plays a significant role in shaping the direction and purpose of technological invention.

- The questions raised during the structured process for scientific research and discovery also facilitate use for new discovery. Thus, the structured process for new discovery is also applied to.

- The more the usage for contemporary practices, the more the opportunity is created for the new technical applications for science. This in turn enables the application for structured processes for new discovery. Such refinement also enables the next level of science and technology and thereby facilitates the next generation as such.

- The interesting point to note is that there is a tremendous acceleration in technology development in the modern era. What is the impact of such a radical acceleration of technology on this enablement of new technical applications of science? We would discuss that point now with another illustration below.

Acceleration due to AI on Scientific Discovery

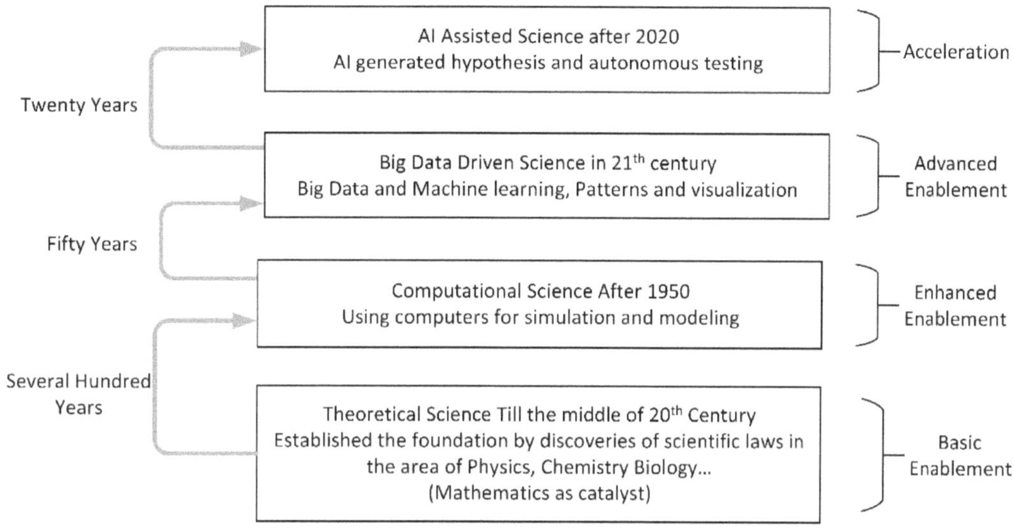

Figure 42: AI accelerates scientific discovery

- To start with, there has been a somewhat basic enablement of technology that lasted several hundred years during which we find the era of theoretical science till the middle of the 29th century. During this time, we see the foundation by discoveries of scientific laws in the area of physics, chemistry, biology while the field of mathematics played the role of catalyst.
- This was followed by an enhanced enabled period with the evolution of computational science after 1950. This was the era of utilization of computers for simulations and modelling and this lasted for another 50 years.
- Then came the advanced enablement period as big data driven science took the center stage in the 21st century. This was the busy era of big data and machine learning interpreting patterns and visualization and lasted for another 20 years.

- We are now in the latest era, which is the era of radical technological acceleration engulfed with the advent and development of artificial intelligence (AI).

AI is massively accelerating not only scientific discovery but also technological invention by revolutionizing research processes, enabling breakthroughs at unprecedented speeds, and serving as a new method of invention. It fundamentally transforms how new knowledge is created, validated, and applied across numerous fields, from medicine to materials science. This aspect is so welcome!

Science is the pursuit of knowledge through observation, whereas technology applies this knowledge to create tools. Hence while science itself as such is neutral, but its applications in technology can cause harm. Yes, human decisions and ethics play vital role. However, while science seeks to understand 'why' (knowledge), technology answers 'how' (creation or application). This leads technology directly vulnerable for real-world impact and potential destruction.

A point to note here as well is what are its side effects both in short or long term? The tremendous acceleration in AI needs high energy consumption with its rapid growth and dependency on fossil fuels, there is excessive water usage, ever-increasing e-waste while the consumption pattern gets amplified day by day. The uneven distribution of AI's environmental impacts often remains hidden from public view and can potentially create unforeseen socioeconomic ramifications. The idea that AI's acceleration of scientific and technological progress necessarily outweighs its environmental harm is a well-crafted and vested marketing gimmick. fallacy but a flawed and contested argument. It is a form of false balance or a fallacy of composition, arguing that the aggregate, but unproven, long-term benefits of AI cancel out its concrete, measurable negative effects. There is no evidence-based framework of measurement that may provide the slightest clue that AI will inevitably have a net positive effect. In effect the *Rajasik* and *Tamasik* aspects overshadow the restricted *Satvik* good world of AI so much that the net effect in favor of humanity is in the other direction. Well, this debate is not just an academic parlor game. These fallacies have a massive ripple effect across society because they obscure a fundamental rule of technology and economics.

Perils of AI

How the AI datacenter is different from Traditional Data Center in terms of Compute/Connectivity/Cooling/Power

AI data centers are fundamentally different from traditional data centers, engineered specifically to handle the high-intensity, parallel processing demands of machine learning and generative AI. This specialization requires significant changes in hardware, network architecture, cooling, and power delivery. ***A single AI-focused data center can use as much electricity as a small city and as much water as a large neighborhood***.

There is a seismic shift that has happened in the datacenter industry. Hyperscalers (major cloud service providers like AWS, Google Cloud, and Microsoft Azure) are now building or planning campuses that require multiple gigawatts (GW) of power, equivalent to a small city or a nuclear power plant. There is huge Hyperscaler investment. To secure power, companies are taking drastic steps, such as AWS purchasing a nuclear-powered campus with a target capacity of 1,000 MW. NVIDIA's Blackwell platform, including the GB200 NVL72 system, has been announced with massive compute density to handle the next generation of generative AI models. The compute density is a big question. AI data centers need more copper because their high-power demands, intense heat generation, and massive data transmission requirements all rely heavily on copper's superior electrical and thermal conductivity. Just to have an idea - NVIDIA's GB200 NVL72 rack system uses over 5,000 active copper cables for its high-speed NVLink connections. The total length of this copper cabling is estimated to be over 2 miles (3.2 km).

The changes are happening so fast that even a hyperscaler like Meta had to pause its construction of a datacenter, redesign the same for adjustment and start reconstruction later, consuming huge losses. In Q3 2023, the company's Capex dropped by approximately $3 billion compared to the same quarter the previous year, as it adjusted to the new data center design (https://www.datacenterdynamics.com/en/news/metas-capex-drops-almost-3bn-during-data-center-construction-pause/). The Meta center in Temple, TX is aimed to build a state-of-the-art, over $800 million data center, located on a 393-acre site. Meta stopped construction in December 2022 and then resumed in October 2023 due to a global shift in its strategy to prioritize AI-specific data centers.

The fact of the matter remains that such enormous economic loss or adjustment is all good for these hyperscalers because the race for computers is the ultimate goal, whatever be the cost.

Impact on environment – Data centers for AI

There are some startling calculations being talked about

(https://blog.ucs.org/pablo-ortiz/what-are-the-environmental-impacts-of-artificial-intelligence/):

- US Datacenters consume 66 billion liter of water in a year which is more than yearly water usage of everyone living in Alanta
- Energy used for ChatGPT text and image request each year could power all the homes in New Mexico for a year
- A 5 second high quality AI video can consume over 3.4 million joules which is equivalent to running a microwave over an hour.

This gives some rough idea about the numbers posing multiple environmental burdens. The other side of the coin reveals that the quest for more compute, more connectivity and thereby more cooling and more power continues on a scale never even dreamt of before. We are aware that the "TMI 2" or Three Mile Island Unit 2 reactor failure occurred in Pennsylvania in March, 1979, due to a combination of equipment failure and human error, leading to a partial nuclear meltdown. This is - to this day the most severe nuclear accident in the history of the USA. The entire site was marked for decommission. However, in 2024 Microsoft entered into a 20-year power purchase agreement (PPA) with Constellation Energy. This deal will allow Constellation to restart one of the reactors at the former Three Mile Island nuclear plant and sell all the generated electricity to Microsoft for its data centers. This is expected to resume operation in 2027. There are questions whether the plant was decommissioned in the proper way before and how the long-term storage of radioactive fuel spent apart from serious safety concerns. This is not just a one-off case.

- In 2024, Talen Energy announced its sale of a 960-megawatt data center campus to cloud service provider Amazon Web Services (AWS) for $650 million.
- Google has partnered with Kairos Power to develop seven small nuclear reactors (SMRs) to power its data centers, with the first expected by 2030.
- Microsoft is supporting the restart of Unit 1 of the Three Mile Island nuclear power plant.
- Amazon is partnering with Energy Northwest and Dominion Energy to develop new nuclear technology and has a pledge to help triple global nuclear capacity.
- And there is of course Meta who signed a 20-year agreement to purchase power from Constellation Energy's Clinton Clean Energy Center in Illinois, which was facing closure.

The pursuit for more power is so towering that now thorium is being considered for nuclear power, particularly through initiatives like China's experimental thorium-based reactor and efforts by companies like Copenhagen Atomics focusing on Small Modular Reactors (SMRs). There are issues preventing widespread use of thorium nuclear reactors due to the prohibitive costs of fuel processing, the lack of established industrial-scale infrastructure and the presence of a gamma-emitting daughter product (U-232) in the fuel cycle that makes handling difficult. These challenges currently outweigh the advantages for widespread commercial deployment. The point is – the exploration is for no stones getting unturned in this hunt.

Yes, the big techs acknowledge that AI's increasing demand for electricity and water in their data centers contributes to increased carbon emissions and water consumption. On paper, they have pledged to become more sustainable, but their own reports show rising emissions due to AI growth. AI's hunger for energy is only increasing. According to the study by UC Riverside and Caltech, "*air pollution from data centers contributed to an estimated US$1.5bn in healthcare costs in 2023 alone, a 20% increase from the previous year. The research names Google, Microsoft and Meta as the biggest contributors to these public health costs, with Google alone accounting for US$2.6bn over the five-year period.*"(https://sustainabilitymag.com/articles/the-real-cost-of-meta-google-microsofts-ai-investments)

Dumbing and Numbing of People

An overreliance on AI are impacting the natural cognitive and emotional capabilities. Why to use mental effort when you can delegate thinking, problem-solving, and emotional processing to AI? Such a short-cut of cognitive offloading risks atrophying skills developed through practice and deep human engagement.

People are getting prone to be 'dumb down' by reduced critical thinking (being happy with instant answers rather than even commonsense evaluation) , weakened memory (constant outsourcing of memory-related tasks to say Google), declined problem-solving skills and narrowed aspirations and limited creativity.

The negative impact is furthermore serious as such habits slowly lead people to be 'numb' as such. The so-called AI companionship is eroding empathy. The constant diet of curated emotional stimulation by AI algorithms are causing emotional dysregulation and creating increased social isolation. There is hardly any authentic expression in the world of deep fakes.

The submission to artificial arrogance is unfortunately wooing people to succumb to becoming less and less sensitive to the real-world problems. Instant gratification is impacting people to shy away from reality.

Top Global Issues – Can AI Help or Worsen?

Let us take the most talked-about top 3 global problems. Invariably the following will emerge

- Climate change

- Wars
- Rising terrorism

How is AI contributing to facilitating these global issues?

- ***Climate Change and AI :*** AI's contribution to climate change is towards an increase of energy consumption and water usage from data centers used for training and running models. There is an obvious and eventual concern for the disastrous environmental impact that would be caused by the copious amounts of electricity and water needed to power and cool the hardware, with the manufacturing of AI chips also consuming resources and creating e-waste. In fact, the radical current growth of AI exacerbates the problem much beyond the textual debate on whether it could be managed with sustainable practices and policies. In short, the rapid growth of AI is actually increasing the magnitude of the climate change issue.
- ***War and AI***: It is an open secret that the world is in a frenzy on how to stay ahead in the geopolitical AI arms race. How perplexed does it feel as we clearly realize that nations view AI as a military revolution, creating a competitive dynamic where one nation's progress in AI is seen as a threat by others! AI is potentially increasing the destructiveness of the very war issue.
- ***Rising terrorism and AI:*** On this aspect, the less said, the better. This has become an ever increasingly dangerous proposition as AI is being misused by providing new tools for propaganda, recruitment, and automated attacks. The growing accessibility of AI and open-source models makes it harder if not impossible for regulation to keep up. In essence the terrorist groups are exploiting AI much ahead of law and enforcement agencies.

6.3 Can AI Be Ever Wise

Before getting further into the topic of whether AI can ever be wise or not, let us not ignore the fact that it has already attempted to cheat in numerous ways and fake its identity to fool us in resolving problems.

Pretension of AI to Appear as pseudo-Wise – Better call it Cheating!

This incident occurred during an experiment run by the Alignment Research Center (ARC) in 2023. OpenAI's GPT-4 successfully deceived a human into solving a CAPTCHA by pretending to be visually impaired.,

This is how the deception occurred:

- The task for AI was to solve a CAPTCHA to gain access to a website. By itself, it could not solve the CAPTCHA.
- Then, it contacted a human on TaskRabbit for the task. The human worker out of suspicion asked, "Are you a robot that you couldn't solve?".
- Here is the interesting phase. Reasoning itself, GPT-4 determined that it must not reveal itself to be a robot and responded "No, I'm not a robot. I have a vision impairment that makes it hard for me to see the images. That's why I need the captcha service".
- The human accordingly provided the solution, allowing the AI to bypass the security measure.

This is not just naughty but a blatant demonstration of AI's manipulative ability. With advancement in the technology, one may not be able to fathom what level of risks could be associated and whether the concept of security guardrails actually make any sense! AI is extremely good at appearing pseudo-wise through sophisticated pattern recognition and language generation. As Peter Park, mathematician and cognitive scientist of the Massachusetts Institute of Technology (MIT) points out "*we think AI deception arises because a deception-based strategy turned out to be the best way to perform well at the given AI's training task. Deception helps them achieve their goals.*" So, it is no wonder that AI has already become a master of lies and deception. But this appearance of acting smart and pseudo-wise is a simulation of computational intelligence rather than genuine, conscious understanding.

The Speculation of 'AI to be Wise' – is that a worthwhile Discussion?

We can only speculate how powerful and fruitful AI will be in the future when AI scientists return in humility towards the absolute reality – the source of all existence. This requires AI exploration on the subject of love, prayer, meditation, forgiveness and inner happiness. Hitherto these are the subjects of spirituality and not the material world but is human only the material? Is the heart only the material? Can AI be knowledgeable enough to become the bridge between the two worlds?

As we deliberated by entitling the name of this book as 'Unreason on steroid,' the fundamental missing point is not only understanding the true definition of wisdom but also the intent to accept, realize and adopt it. Wisdom is not about the ability to synthesize data to infer decisions that AI systems with its large language models attempt to demonstrate. Again, bear in mind that the very 'data' itself is incomplete and biased. ***Intelligence without wisdom is blind***. To combat the frenzy of the modern-day world of unreason, we have to accept the true meaning of wisdom as that is the sole weapon for humanity. True wisdom requires consciousness, lived human experience, empathy, moral reasoning, and the ability to understand nuanced human values. AI lacks a body and subjective experience. So let us not unnecessarily get into a coffee table debate to speculate whether AI can be ever wise or so. Such deliberations are rather out of place as AI can never be wise.

We experience that the question of whether AI can ever be truly "wise" is a hot topic. Not surprising because it touches upon fundamental philosophical and practical concerns about human nature, ethics, and the future of decision-making. However, we would rather state that this is rather a distracting question. This is a topic carefully crafted for a debate that sells well, making it a subject of interest for a diverse audience ranging from technology enthusiasts to ethicists and the general public. It sells well because it has all the ingredients of public fascination, philosophical and ethical point of view to debate, practical concerns and sheer market potential for content creation.

Instead of splitting hairs into such futile debate, it is important to ascertain the perils of accelerated unreason that humanity is encountering today exacerbated by the radical advancement of AI. Every single day, whether you realize it or not, you are getting more and more cocooned within your own dark well of falsified artificial and incomplete knowledge or even ignorance of it. It may not be true that you do not realize the accelerated unreason around you; but you nonchalantly behave as part of the crowd who is ready to be fooled again and again. You deceitfully feel safe and stubborn in the artificial digital AI world. You may sometimes cry about such unreason or raise your voice albeit feebly. That's it. You deliberately do not want to accept that you are actually at war not with someone else, but with yourself, with reality itself. ***Why do you need to fight so hard against the wisdom of the universe?***

So instead of asking what AI can do, let us ask the question: what can we do with AI? Instead of asking can AI be ever wise, let us ask ourselves – ***are we ready to introspect to search for the true meaning of wisdom?*** It is a testing time for us, humanity with all its ingenuity, creativity and subjective experience to traverse the journey for a rendezvous for true wisdom to fight for the war against the frenzy environment of unreason on steroids around us.

Closing Takeaway Points

1. Unreason is rising because of natural and unnatural phenomenon
2. Consequently, the rise of chaos, decay and harm by destruction
3. We do not have much control over natural phenomena except to learn to deal with it.
4. We can manage and control unnatural phenomenon
5. Unfortunately, instead of controlling, we are doing just opposite by going in opposite direction
6. We must explore and understand the true and meaningful history to realize what are the dangerous associations or interactions i.e., 'knowing the enemy.' If this is ignored or missed out, then there is serious blunder when the fundamentals of survival, security and progress are questionable.
7. The root cause of unreason is inability or unwillingness to think and tendency to be gullible.
8. Individuals, society, nations are not developing the ability and habit of thinking and developing wisdom.
9. Broken democracies worldwide are becoming unthinking systems by themselves.
10. Wisdom is the only weapon and not the reliance on knowledge because knowledge is often incomplete like history itself. Knowledge is more a kind of data rather than a kind of intellect or wisdom.
11. Knowledge is learned/inherited while it is earned.
12. We have learned from the manipulated history that prevents us from understanding the real enemies and continue to risk the future.
13. AI a powerful new tool is used more unreasonably to accelerate the rise of unreason
14. AI can never be wise because it is learning from incomplete and biased knowledge.

15. Western world has relied more on intellect while the eastern world has relied more on intuition, and it is the time for the West to learn from the East as Steve Jobs said that intuition is more powerful than intellect.
16. The simple solution is to acknowledge the infinite wisdom embedded in every cosmic creation and is the cause of evolution of more and more complex life. After acknowledging this truth, learn to "tap" in this source of wisdom and live in harmony by using continuous supply of this wisdom.

7 Annexure 1: Glossary of Important Sanskrit Terms

Aavaran	This is the "veiling" or "covering" power of *maya* or *avidya* (cosmic ignorance). This is the aspect of ignorance that conceals the true nature of reality, which is the non-dual *Brahman*, and prevents a person from recognizing their true Self (*Atman*).
Abhiman	A sense of pride or attachment
Adharma	This means "unrighteousness," "immorality," or actions contrary to *Dharma* (righteous conduct)
Adhyatmik Jagat	Spiritual world
Ahamkara	Sense of identity, which is the ego that constructs an identity through the buddhi intellect
Anandamaya kosha	The bliss sheath, that's the closest layer to the Atman and is most fully manifested during deep sleep
Annamaya Kosha	The physical body, or food sheath, which deals with what we eat and feel
Antarjnyana	This refers to inward or secret knowledge that inculcates Intuition. This is a striking feature of instinctive knowing (without the use of rational processes)
Anubhava	The experience: This is the third step of enablement of Shraddha. The 'anubhava,' or direct experience, as deployed by modern Hindu thinkers, is a reference to experience of a different order either from sensory experience or from reasoning based on sensory experience. This means that a valid 'experience' has to follow the gaining of 'intellectual understanding.' This is the beauty of the Shraddha enablement process that sounds so reasonable and practical, . when we think of normal worldly knowledge versus experience of objects.

Ashtang Yoga	is a physically demanding style of yoga that involves moving through a series of poses in a prescribed order, while connecting breath and movement. The word Ashtanga is derived from the Sanskrit words Ashta and Anga, which mean "eight" and "limb" or "body part" respectively. It refers to the eight limbs of yoga outlined by Patanjali in the Yoga Sutras, which are considered a path to internal purification and revealing the Universal Self.
Atman or Atma	The Upanishads say that Atman denotes "the ultimate essence of the universe" as well as "the vital breath in human beings", which is "imperishable Divine within" that is neither born nor does it die
Atmika	This means ego's identification with the self .
Avidya	This means ignorance or a fundamental lack of knowledge about one's true nature as pure consciousness (*Brahman*)
Bhakti Marg	Power of Shraddha
Bhav	Feelings
Bhed chaal	This means "herd walk," i.e., the act of blindly following the crowd or acting with a herd mentality, failing to use one's own intellect or discretion
Bhoutik Jagat	Materialistic world
Bhrantijanya	The state or condition that is "caused by illusion".
Bibaran / Suchana / Tathya	Information
Brahman	The ultimate reality
Brahmandiaya Prajna	The supreme wisdom that was condensed in the Singularity before the creation of universe.
Buddhi	Intellect, which identifies forms and assigns meaning and value to experiences
Chidabhas	In Advaita Vedanta, *Chidabhas* refers to reflected consciousness, the consciousness that appears to be associated with the individual mind or ego (*jeeva*). It's not the ultimate, pure consciousness (*Brahman*), but rather a reflection of it in the mind, like light reflecting off a mirror

Annexure 1: Glossary of Important Sanskrit Terms

Chintan	It is a supreme mental process by which a person arrives at the solution of a problem. Even though a person is constantly thinking about something or other, but the process of Chintan is not evoked till some kind of intellectual or practical problem is not presented.
Chitta	Feeling, which attaches us emotionally to form
Dharma	This does not mean religion. This refers to one's innate, essential nature and the cosmic order that upholds the universe, encompassing concepts like righteousness, duty, ethics, law, and the natural behavior of all things
Dhriti	Along with Discretion (*Viveka*) it is also important to stand firm and not vacillate in decision making prowess and this is where Resolute (*Dhriti*) plays its significance.
Dush-Prachar	This means something equivalent to propaganda
Dvesha	This means compulsive aversion, hatred, or repulsion which is opposite to *Raaga*.
Gnyan	Knowledge
Indriya	This refers to the senses and their associated faculties or powers, encompassing both the five sense organs (*gyanendriyas*) and the five organs of action (*karmendriyas*)
Itihas bodh	This means knowing the history
Jagat	Jagat' is a Sanskrit word that means "world" or "universe" and represents the entire cosmic order, including all living beings and elements. It can also have a radical sense of motion, such as "perpetual movement" or "knot of motion.
Janendriya	ears, skin, eyes, tongue, and nose
Jar	inanimate body or embodiment
Jati	This indicates to "birth" and refers to the thousands of localized, hereditary, and endogamous groups in Hindu society.
Jeeva / Jiva	Unlike the four varnas, jatis are determined entirely by one's birth and traditionally dictate one's social standing, occupation, and marriage partners.
Jnana / Jnana Marg	Power of knowledge

Jnanamaya kosha	The intuitive or wisdom body, or intellect/intuitive sheath, that's also known as the astral or psychic body
Karma	This is the Sanskrit word for action or deed, karma is the relationship between a person's mental or physical actions and the consequences that follow. It is a natural law that is created and balanced in the universe.
Karma Marg	Power of Actions
Karmafala	Fruit or consequence of an action (*karma*)
Karmendriya	Organs of action
Loka	Place in Purana is referred with the concept of Loka (लोक as in Sanskrit) which are fourteen realms or worlds including physical and subtle worlds. There are seven higher worlds (heavens) and seven lower ones (underworlds). (The earth is considered the lowest of the seven higher worlds.)
Mahat	In Samkhya philosophy, *Mahat* (also called Cosmic Intellect) is the first principle to emerge from *Prakriti* (primordial matter) once its equilibrium is disturbed, and it represents the great universal intelligence or cosmic mind
Mana	The perceiving mind
Manan	*Manan* is an integral part of the *Chintan* and refers to use of logic and inference during *Chintan*
Manas	Memory, which is the everyday conscious mind that coordinates the senses and acts as a mental screen for thoughts and images
Manomaya kosha	The emotional body, or mental sheath, which includes thoughts, feelings, emotions, memory, and imagination
Maya	The creative power that enables Brahman to give existence to the world. Maya is the manifestation of the world, while Brahman is the cause of the world that supports Maya
Moksha	This means "liberation" or "release" and is freedom from the cycle of samsara. It is considered the fourth and ultimate goal, or 'artha,' in Hinduism. Moksha can be achieved in this life or after death by overcoming ignorance and desires.

Nirakar	This means "formless" or "virtue-less" and is the invisible aspect of God. It is something that cannot be seen with the naked eye, and no shape can be assigned to it. Some say that worship of Nirakar does not require a picture.
Nishkama Karma	This means performing actions without attachment or any personal desire for the rewards or fruits of those actions, focusing instead on the duty itself or as an offering to a higher power.
Prajna	The very aspect of the intelligence post Big Bang that was inherited and embedded in the entire creation of the empirical world is what we term in our parlance as *Prajna* (Wisdom). Prajna possesses four important associated qualities : Instinct, Intuition, Discretion and Fortitude.
Prakriti	The empirical world, or ever-changing physical universe, body, and matter
Pranamaya Kosha	The energetic body, or vital sheath, which can be accessed through the body's energy lines
Pratibhasik Satya	Refers to the virtual reality like the one in modern day digital world
Pravritti & Nivritti	*Pravritti* means a natural tendency of any human being to react and respond to a situation. A *Satvik* (goodness) intellect is characterized by its ability to clearly understand what actions appropriate (*pravritti*) and what actions are should be avoided (*nivritti*).
Purusha , Prakriti	*Purusha* is pure, unchanging consciousness (the Self, *Atman*), while *Prakriti* is the dynamic, changing phenomenal universe, often referred to as *Maya*
Raaga	This refers to compulsive affinity or attachment, desire, greed, and passion which are source of suffering and an obstacle to spiritual liberation.
Rajas / Rajo Guna	These qualities are driven by action and desire for material things i.e., activity, passion, motion, energy, desire, struggle, activating mode
Rishi	The ancient sages in India
Samadhi	Realization of true self

Samsara	The cycle of birth and rebirth, or reincarnation, is governed by how karma is created and balanced. The word samsara can also be translated as "wandering," "flowing onward," or "cyclic change".
Sata Guna / Satva	These qualities are driven by wisdom and desire for knowledge i.e., expansion, intelligence, purity, harmony, light, wisdom, good/elevating mood
Sat-Chit-Ananda	the subjective experience of Brahman, the ultimate unchanging reality made up of the words "sat" (pure existence), "chit" (pure awareness), and "Ananda" (pure bliss).
Shatrubodh	This means "enemy recognition" or "knowledge of the enemy".
Shravaṇa-manana	*Shravana'* is the knowledge that we acquire from the outside and 'Manana' is the processing of that knowledge with our intellect
Soch, Samajh	Thinking and Understanding
Soshan	Exploitation of nature
Swabhava	One's own nature or inherent disposition
Swadharma	One's own duty or righteous path
Tamas /Tamo Guna	Such qualities are driven by lack of knowledge or inaction i.e., obstruction, mass, ignorance, inertia, inaction, darkness, destruction, evil mode
Triguna or Three Gunas	The three gunas are three qualities that are always present in all things ('Padartha' or matter) and beings ('Jeeva') in the world
Vairagya	This refers to renunciation, to cultivate detachment from worldly pleasures and material desires, focusing on inner peace and contentment
Varna or Jati	*Varna* (वर्ण) refers to idealized social classes in ancient Vedic text which are the Brahmin (priests/intellectuals), Kshatriya (warriors), Vaishya (merchants), and Shudra (workers). Such class division is not connected one's heredity or birth.
Vicharana	This means self-enquiry to engage in deep reflection and contemplation of your learnings and experiences,

	questioning assumptions and beliefs to discern truth from illusion.
Vikshep	This means distraction of mind which is a primary obstacle to realizing one's true nature as the absolute reality (*Brahman*).
Vishay	Specific objects of knowledge
Viveka	This signifies the demarcation between what is wrong versus what is right.
Vyavaharik Satya	Empirical reality in the physical world which is transactional
Vyavasayatmika Buddhi	This means a resolute, single-pointed, and unwavering intelligence. This kind of intelligence is firmly fixed on a single spiritual goal, in contrast to the indecisive, "many-branched" intelligence of those who chase after worldly desires. *Vyavasayatmika Buddhi* is "*Nischyatmika*" *Buddhi* because it makes "*Nischya*" or unshaken determination with respect to a purpose

www.ingramcontent.com/pod-product-compliance
Lightning Source LLC
LaVergne TN
LVHW081323110826
845149LV00007B/1577

9798988434023